Blood, Fire & Gold

The story of
ELIZABETH I &
CATHERINE
DE MEDICI

ESTELLE PARANQUE

hachette
BOOKS

NEW YORK

Hachette Books
Hachette Book Group
1290 Avenue of the Americas
New York, NY 10104
HachetteBooks.com
Twitter.com/HachetteBooks
Instagram.com/HachetteBooks

First US Edition: December 2022
Originally published in June 2022 by Ebury Press in the United Kingdom

Published by Hachette Books, an imprint of Perseus Books, LLC, a subsidiary of
Hachette Book Group, Inc. The Hachette Books name and logo is a
trademark of the Hachette Book Group.

The Hachette Speakers Bureau provides a wide range of authors for speaking events.
To find out more, go to www.hachettespeakersbureau.com or call (866) 376-6591.

The publisher is not responsible for websites (or their content)
that are not owned by the publisher.

Library of Congress Control Number: 2022945370

ISBNs: 9780306830518 (hardcover); 9780306830532 (ebook)

Printed in Canada

MRQ-T

10 9 8 7 6 5 4 3 2 1

To the one who makes everything better and brighter,
Nick St. John Gill

Contents

Prologue

The Art of Making Peace

The day was April 27, 1564, and the English ambassador at the French court and advisor to Elizabeth I of England, Sir Nicholas Throckmorton, had recently earned his freedom. He had also been invited for dinner by Artus de Cossé-Brissac (known as de Gonnord), one of Catherine de Medici's and Charles IX's closest privy councillors. Advisor to one queen, Throckmorton had been drawn into the lair of another: Catherine was the French queen mother, and mainland Europe's most influential woman.

Wearing his usual gold and black attire, conjuring an air of wealth and dignity, de Gonnord welcomed his guest, for whom he had prepared a replenishing meal. Throckmorton was grateful—after all, he had just spent months in a gloomy cell in a French castle, miles away from the capital, fighting for his release and negotiating on behalf of Elizabeth with the French queen mother, who had only recently stopped acting as regent for her son Charles IX of France. By now, the two women had been at each other's throats for months, and their advisors had been caught in the crossfire.

"If only your mistress, Elizabeth, the queen of England, and Catherine de Medici, the queen mother of France, could get along well," said de Gonnord over dinner. "The authority of the pope could then be extinguished in both countries."

After a moment of reflection, the English ambassador conceded that "the diminution of the pope's authority would greatly please his mistress, the queen."[1] The dinner continued with discussions of more trivial matters; the two men spoke of anything other than Throckmorton's difficult experience as a prisoner of the French crown.

But Monsieur de Gonnord had been right. If only these two queens could forge an alliance—if only these two queens could forge an invincible friendship—what, then, could they not achieve? Together, they could rule all of sixteenth-century Europe.

But fate had decided otherwise. And Throckmorton, along with other representatives of both courts, had lost months of their lives that could never be reclaimed.

*

It all began on the night of August 10, 1563. Sir Nicholas Throckmorton was arrested for traveling without a valid safe-conduct, a diplomatic permit that would allow him to move freely through the country. This was an insult to the English court, for ambassadors were usually allowed free passage, and the message from France was clear: your men are here at our pleasure, and will play by our rules.

Under escort, he was transferred to the Castle of Saint-Germain-en-Laye, thirteen miles from Paris, where he was guarded around the clock by rude Bretons. While there, thanks to one of his secretaries who had not been arrested and managed to bribe some of the guards, he arranged for his correspondence to remain undisrupted, perfectly aware that his letters would nevertheless be scrutinized by French officials. But he had no choice but to find a way to resolve this diplomatic incident via correspondence.

Three weeks later, his counterpart and colleague—another English ambassador, Sir Thomas Smith—was also arrested at his habitual residence in Poissy, though he was sent to the Castle of Melun, southeast of Paris, for his imprisonment. Smith had a far better experience than his colleague, spending only two rather uncomfortable nights in a cell before being brought back to the capital.

On September 13, Catherine de Medici and her son Charles IX of France allowed Smith to return to his residence in Poissy, but the arrest was a clear message to the English ambassador: in this country, he was and always would be at the French queen mother's mercy.

On his deliverance day, Smith sent a letter to Throckmorton lamenting his treatment. He said he had become sick from riding from Corbeil in an extremely cold wind on the previous Thursday and complained, "I am still ignorant of all things as I was the first day of my imprisonment. My books and papers still locked from me, English matters kept from me."[2]

But for the French rulers, this wasn't just a simple show of strength. For Charles and Catherine, it was a clear retaliation—a warning to Elizabeth I, who had re-imprisoned four French noblemen at the Tower of London, having promised repeatedly to release them.

And Catherine had other things on her mind too. Her son, Charles, was now of age, and was therefore able to rule the country without a regency, but was he ready? Catherine didn't think so, and she certainly wasn't ready to renounce the crown herself. After all, she had been successfully acting as regent for the last three years and it was a position that had suited her thirst for power. The bond she had with her son was about to be tested, but she remained resolute, confident that the king would do what was best for the country.

On August 12, the young king entered Rouen and, three days later, the princes of blood and the whole court followed, joining Charles at the Palais de Justice. In the splendid hall built by Louis XII and the Cardinal of Amboise, Charles sat under a canopy on a throne made of gold and azure, the splendor reminding everyone that he was now king of France in his own right.

The Chancellor de L'Hôpital, one of the most influential privy councillors at court, was also in attendance, wearing a long "black velvet robe, with his white beard, looking serious and imposing." As expected, he sat at the feet of the king.

When all were gathered, Charles declared that he was now of age and apt to rule the country himself, before hastily adding, "my mother, the queen, will also be in charge of the realm." Catherine then stood and bowed in front of her son: she may have been apprehensive at the shift in power, but she knew she could rely on his love.

Charles grabbed her by the arms and lifted her into an embrace. He kissed her on the cheeks and insisted affectionately before everyone "that she was still the one ruling the country."[3]

This display consolidated Catherine's authority at court and, once proceedings were complete, the Englishman Smith was brought in and received by the French rulers. He immediately inquired about Throckmorton's safe-conduct, which had been granted by the French ambassador at the English court, Paul de Foix.

"I have changed my mind," said Catherine, her face unmoved. "I never thought that the safe-conduct was for Throckmorton, who has done so much evil in this country in the last two years by conniving with the Protestants of this country and striving to undermine my authority."[4] Smith tried to respond but Catherine dismissed him abruptly, cutting him off mid-sentence and sending him away before he could say another word, though he would continue to demand Throckmorton's release on behalf of the queen of England.

During the next audience with the king and queen and their privy council that took place days later, Smith asserted that the queen of England was surprised that her dear ambassador had been made a prisoner of the French crown. Were these two kingdoms not allies? Catherine repeated what she had already told Smith four days earlier: that Throckmorton, who had already been a problematic ambassador in the past, "ought not to have come without a safe-conduct."[5] She added that as long as the English were keeping the hostages at the Tower of London, she would keep him in a cell in France. After all, if these great nations were to be allies, then both parties needed to show their good intent.

It was clear to all who observed them that in these diplomatic shows of strength, Elizabeth and Catherine were using their subjects to go at each other's throats, playing with the lives of men they had at their disposal. They both had something extremely important to prove: their legitimacy and ability to rule in a male-dominated world.

★

This queens' war had begun five years before this diplomatic incident.

In 1559 at the Peace of Cateau-Cambrésis, Elizabeth had inherited her predecessor Mary's humiliation at losing Calais, the last English stronghold in France. It was a vital piece of symbolism, its loss perceived by the English as an unbearable slight. Elizabeth was not ready to renounce Calais as easily as Mary. The peace treaty specified that France would restore Calais within eight years. If they failed to do so, they would have to pay England 500,000 crowns as compensation for the city.

In 1559, as a way of ensuring that the French monarchs would keep their end of the bargain, Elizabeth ordered the capture of several French noblemen: Frederic de Foix; Louis de Sainte Maure, Marquis de Nesles, Count de Laval; Gaston de Foix, Marquis de Trans; and Antoine du Prat, Seigneur de Nantouillet, Provost of Paris. They were rounded up and sent to the Tower of London, where they would reside indefinitely.

By the time the first war of religion erupted in France in 1562, French ambassadors Gilles de Noailles and Michel de Seurre had negotiated the release of the first three men. However, Antoine du Prat remained imprisoned, and he was later joined by three other French noblemen: Esprit de Harville, Seigneur de Palaiseau, Knight of the King's Order and Colonel of the Legions of Normandy; Monsieur du Moy; and Monsieur de la Ferté. Elizabeth wanted to keep a tight rein on the Frenchmen she allowed in her kingdom: her country, her rules.

During this first war of religion, Elizabeth exacerbated the tensions, choosing to side against the French rulers and with the Huguenots, sending an army of 6,000 soldiers, munitions, and gunpowder to Le Havre (also called Newhaven by the English at the time). Not only did the English lose the resulting battle, but they were also betrayed by the Huguenot leader, Louis de Bourbon, Prince of Condé, who signed a peace treaty with Catherine and Charles. Elizabeth was out in the cold.

As a result of this French victory, the four imprisoned French noblemen believed they were now free, and so they attempted to escape. They didn't get far. After being caught about twenty miles away, they were re-imprisoned at the Tower of London and this time were handled like criminals, forced to pay excessive amounts for everything, including to redeem their garments and possessions.

Calais and Newhaven were now right at the center of Elizabeth's and Catherine's political battle for European dominance—but only one of these two powerful women would be victorious in this particular fight.

During Throckmorton's imprisonment at the Castle of Saint-Germain-en-Laye, Captain La Salle, who was acting as his custodian, suggested to the prisoner that he contact Anne de Montmorency, Constable of France and powerful advisor to Catherine and Charles. Throckmorton agreed, and after Montmorency received the deposed English ambassador's letters begging for an audience, he also agreed, inviting him for dinner on October 1, 1563.

Things looked promising, but although the dinner was pleasant, none of Throckmorton's requests was accepted; namely, he would not be granted an audience with the French rulers and he would not be allowed to communicate with Elizabeth—at least officially—so all his correspondence with the English crown continued to be seen as a crime in itself, even though, as he protested, it was his very job.

His only chance to rectify this diplomatic incident, therefore, would be through his correspondence with Smith. As two competing ambassadors, each pushing to be topmost in Elizabeth's affections, they had considered each other to be rivals for quite some time, but they now had to find a way to work together for both their sakes— and, more importantly, for the sake of Elizabeth's reputation. She wished to be held in high regard, or even feared, across Europe, just as her father Henry VIII had been.

Throckmorton described his experience of being a prisoner at Saint-Germain to Smith, relaying that "the chamber in the tower I am being kept in is hung with tapestry. In the morning, I am accompanied by three or four guards to walk in the park of Saint-Germain for only an hour, in the daytime I am allowed to walk in the gallery of the house with the keeper." He further revealed that next to his chamber "was a big one, where I can walk all day and another smaller room to dine and sup in. About 6pm each night I am being locked in my chamber with one of my servants and a guard lies upon a pallet at my door."[6] It was no life for an esteemed ambassador.

When Throckmorton complained to Montmorency about his treatment and reminded him of his rank, the constable replied, "this is not a formal imprisonment; see this as a little getaway from the court to reflect on your actions."[7] Throckmorton was furious at this answer, but there was nothing more he could add. The meeting ended with no hope of a reconciliation between the ambassador and the queen mother of France.

But the matter wasn't over just yet.

At that time, there were discussions of a potential marriage between Mary, Queen of Scots, and Don Carlos, Philip II of Spain's son. It was Smith's opinion that young Mary was likely to agree to the terms of this union. However, it was a union that would endanger both France and England, elevating Spain's position in the European power play—something Catherine and Elizabeth knew all too well. Catherine realized a compromise must be achieved.

Eventually she swallowed her pride and convinced her son, Charles, to accept Throckmorton as a commissioner—which was a simple way of saying he would be demoted, and still deprived of his freedom, as severe restrictions were placed on his movement. Without French royal approval, Throckmorton could not travel the country and visit different estates in the way he was used to. It did, however, mean that he could plead his case to the French rulers in person, as well as being able to play a role in the upcoming negotiations.

On a cold morning in early November 1563, Throckmorton met Smith, accompanied by "a guard of arquebusiers, like a prisoner." They were both expected the next day at the queen's house in Monceau. They went, and after dinner they were taken to see Charles. The queen sat beside the young king throughout, as Smith began his offensive on how his colleague's treatment had been "unacceptable."[8]

In response, Catherine shouted, "You only repeat what you have already said so many times!" The matter was not of interest to her, and the two men were quickly dismissed, missing out on the opportunity to discuss other important issues.[9]

Throckmorton had not yet earned his freedom entirely, but he believed it was on its way. After all, what other choice did the French rulers have if they wished to counterbalance Spain's power in Europe?

But months passed and no real progress was made; Elizabeth and Catherine kept disagreeing on all grounds, the lives of their men still at stake as they argued their case. Throckmorton, as well as the French noblemen, were still imprisoned, though Throckmorton was given some special dispensations: as well as being granted audiences, he was finally allowed to officially correspond with Elizabeth.

It was time for the English queen to take things into her own hands.

After learning that Throckmorton—along with John Somers, secretary to Throckmorton and a skilled decipherer—had at last been granted an audience with Catherine, Elizabeth ordered Throckmorton "not to appear to be directed from me, but to seek occasion to speak with the queen mother" to ensure the ratification of the Treaty of Cateau-Cambrésis of 1559, which secured peace between France, England, and Spain, and put an end to the Italian wars that had ravaged the first part of the sixteenth century.

On February 14, 1564, Catherine sent a coach for Throckmorton. He was invited to court under the conduct of Captain La Salle. Discussions took place for days on end as Throckmorton and Smith met with various French privy councillors, who all endeavored to ensure a peaceful outcome—but who were all aware that the true power lay with Elizabeth and Catherine rather than any of their representatives.

Catherine was clearly not going to return Calais to Elizabeth, but the question of the French noblemen's release—as well as the amount of money that the French should pay for Calais—still remained unanswered. In a succession of meetings that took place between February 20 and 23, Throckmorton continued to negotiate with Catherine.

Throckmorton was a tall man with piercing blue eyes who always wore black apparel to remind everyone of his religious beliefs. He was an imposing figure to behold, even more so because he was an experienced representative of the English queen. In Catherine's eyes, however, no matter how charismatic and imposing Throckmorton might be, his personal connections with the Huguenots—the French Protestants who followed the teachings of Calvin and had been persecuted by their Catholic government—made him an enemy of the French crown, even if she allowed him to continue negotiating on behalf of the Tudor queen.

During one of their audiences, Catherine offered "120,000 crowns for the liberty of the hostages"—an insult to the 500,000 crowns originally promised in the event that Calais was not returned to the English.

"The queen does not want money, she wants the ratification of the treaty," Throckmorton responded.

"If she released the four gentlemen right now, my son the king will give her the best jewel in his cabinet," Catherine said calmly.

Baffled by such a declaration, Throckmorton replied, "Can a jewel be the compensation for the ratification of the Treaty of Cateau-Cambrésis?"[10]

Catherine was not impressed by the remark. Once more, Throckmorton was dismissed.

Nevertheless, after its war of religion France was now united again—at least for the time being. It became more and more apparent that the English had little leverage left, especially as Catherine was about to toughen her stance. Charles had been true to his word: he had given her free rein to continue in her rule of the land, and she would neither bend nor break. If the English wanted to continue the war, they would lose more than Calais—and they'd already lost a decisive battle at Newhaven, which they wished to forget.

Catherine was now in a position of strength, and when she granted Throckmorton yet another audience, she already knew that she would not budge—not even a little.

So, on April 3, 1564, Catherine met with Throckmorton. She received him alone to discuss both the hostages and the financial matter.

"My mistress, the queen of England, has agreed to accept 300,000 crowns," Throckmorton said, commencing the next round of interminable negotiations.

"This is more agreeable than the former offer. But we can only afford the sum of 120,000 crowns. We will not exceed that amount," Catherine replied firmly.[11]

The next day Throckmorton was granted another audience—this one lasting three hours. Throckmorton again touched on the issue, agreeing this time to descend to 250,000 crowns. When Catherine refused yet again, he came down to 200,000, to which she immediately replied with her usual answer: "As I've told you before, we will not exceed 120,000 crowns."[12]

Throckmorton had no other option but to accept the sum, which he finally did on April 6. Elizabeth had given him full authority in these negotiations, trusting him to have England's best interest at heart, just as she did. But now another question arose: how would this bill be paid?

Catherine offered to pay 60,000 crowns within six weeks after the treaty was ratified at Dover "with two of the hostages, Messieurs de Palaiseau and de la Ferté, because they are married and their debts will first be paid, to be permitted to return to France in the French vessel that shall bring the money. The other 60,000 crowns to be paid six weeks later at Boulogne or Calais and to be transported in an English ship under the charge of Englishmen."[13]

Her bold terms were accepted. Rejoicing at her diplomatic victory, Catherine wrote to her ambassador, the Bishop of Rennes—who served at the court of the Holy Roman Emperor, Ferdinand I—that she was very pleased of the outcome of her negotiations with Elizabeth. As a result, the four French noblemen who had been imprisoned at the Tower of London were freed and sent back to France, and Calais remained French.

Catherine had won this first arm-wrestling contest against Elizabeth.

As for Throckmorton, after experiencing a series of diplomatic humiliations, he had only one goal: to return to England.

Upon the signature of the peace treaty, Catherine consented to give Throckmorton one last audience, during which she asked if he and Sir Thomas Smith would like to go to church to thank God. They accepted the invitation, and they, with Throckmorton "on the left hand of the king and Smith on the right hand of the queen went to the Cathedral."[14]

Finally, on April 23, 1564, the peace between France and England was proclaimed, and "fires of joy were made in all places." As for Throckmorton, the provost of the merchants of Paris with the sheriffs and the principals of the same city visited him and presented him "with spices and confitures, as the manner is in such times and cases."[15] These gifts must have left a rather bittersweet taste in the English ambassador's mouth.

During this queens' diplomatic war, Elizabeth and Catherine had both learned the extent to which they would truly need one another in the years to come. They might have been rivals, but they were also united in their power, each admiring the force of the other. Both of them brave and intelligent women, they were unlike any other rulers of the age, and while this might divide them, it would also bring them closer together. But ultimately Elizabeth and Catherine would never let themselves forget that they were, first and foremost, each other's true rival. The world watched, waiting to see what they would do next.

PART I

The Making of Queens

1533–1558

I

Love and Scandals, 1533–1536

She had been waiting for this moment for a long time, and now—finally—it had arrived. Holding her head up high, she took a deep breath, ready to meet her fate.

It was a warm Thursday afternoon, and Lady Anne Boleyn was about to leave Greenwich Palace in a brightly painted brigantine. Surrounded by her ladies-in-waiting, and accompanied by around a hundred similar vessels, all garnished with banners and standards, Anne had never felt—nor looked—more resplendent in her life. As she looked out at the city around her, the sounds of drums, trumpets, and flutes rang out over the River Thames.

As the procession drew closer to the Tower of London a cannon fired a salute while, behind the official vessels, more than two hundred small boats welcomed her. Anne stared at the beautiful sight, full of awe. The Thames was flooded with boats, and the air filled with joyful clamor, and as the future queen of England arrived at the city to be crowned at last, the din increased. Despite her enemies claiming she had been rejected by the people, their presence as Anne arrived in the city proved the contrary. She did have support among the Londoners—for now, at least.

Having been received by the lord chamberlain, Anne was brought to the king, Henry VIII, who had been waiting for her at the waterside. He kissed her, and then she turned around and waved at the crowd—who applauded Anne, celebrating their new queen—before entering the Tower.

The festivities were now in full swing, and in fact they'd only just begun; as Anne's coronation was going to take place on Sunday, June 1, 1533, these celebrations were going to last for days yet. She hoped that they would be everything that she had imagined.

★

On Saturday, May 31, Anne awoke and readied herself for the formal celebrations, which included a procession from the Tower to Temple Bar. She was appareled in a royal dress, made in the French fashion, and her hair floated down over a superb surcoat made of white cloth of tissue. She also wore a coif complete with a circlet of rich stones, including rubies and diamonds.

She mounted a litter covered "inside and out with white satin," and above her hung "a canopy of cloth of gold." Twelve ladies, also clothed in gold, followed the queen-to-be, the entire procession full of splendor and glamor. The queen's mother was in the next chariot, accompanied by the Duchess of Norfolk, stepmother of the duke. Behind them, twelve more young ladies followed on horseback, all arrayed in "crimson velvet."

Three gilded coaches were next, carrying other noblewomen, and then there were twenty or more other ladies on horseback, all wearing black velvet. The Duke of Suffolk, acting as constable for the day, the Lord William Howard, Great Marshal and Great Chamberlain, and his brother, Thomas Howard, Duke of Norfolk, were all escorted by esquires wearing "bonnet furred with ermines." They were followed closely by Jean de Dinteville, ambassador of France, who had by his side Thomas Cranmer, the Archbishop of Canterbury, the Venetian ambassador being accompanied by the chancellor, while behind them were many bishops and other great English lords.[1] It was as though all the great men of Europe had descended on London in celebration of Lady Anne.

Along the streets, which were covered with tapestries and cloth of gold for the occasion, a vast crowd gathered to see the grand procession moving toward Westminster Hall, where a festive banquet was to take place.

Tomorrow would be the big day.

*

It was Whitsunday, June 1, and Anne Boleyn was about to be crowned queen of England. The London mayor, aldermen, sheriffs, and councillors left the city for Westminster at 7 am, followed by the queen-to-be at around 8:30 am.

She made her way to the high altar in Westminster, wearing a magnificent "surcoat and robe of purple velvet, furred with ermine," her dark hair draped over the luxurious material.[2] Her train was carried by the old Duchess of Norfolk, and as Anne walked toward the high altar, many ladies followed behind her.

Once at the altar she was met by Thomas Cranmer, Archbishop of Canterbury, who presented her with St. Edward's Crown, the centerpiece of the famously heavy crown jewels. The weighty crown rested on her head only briefly before it was replaced with another crown for the rest of the ceremony, one much lighter and made especially for the occasion. After the Mass had been performed, the newly crowned queen received the Sacrament and gave an offering at the Shrine of St. Edward.

Following the ceremony, a dinner celebrating the coronation took place at Westminster Hall, where all the gentlemen and gentlewomen of the country drank and ate to their hearts' content.

Anne was now officially queen of England—despite all the trouble her marriage to Henry VIII of England was creating, both in England and on the continent, as the reverberations of his divorce were felt throughout Europe.

The truth was, many enemies already had their eyes on Anne and were currently plotting her downfall. Indeed, Anne only had a few allies, including Francis I, king of France, who, despite having some reservations about the newlyweds, showed his support by sending a squire named Julien to offer a "fine rich litter and three mules, with their caparisons" as a wedding gift to Anne.[3]

★

On a summer's day a few months later, Eustace Chapuys, ambassador from the Holy Roman Emperor Charles V at the English court and one of Anne's most ardent enemies, requested an audience with Henry VIII. Unfortunately for the ambassador, however, the king was not able to attend; he had retired to a private house, as his physician and some people of the royal household had caught "the sweat," the deadly sickness. Instead, Chapuys had to settle for being entertained (and amused with hunting and feasting) by Stephen Gardiner, Bishop of Winchester, and Chief Secretary Thomas Cromwell. They took this opportunity to have a word or two on the matter of the recent marriage.

"The Holy Roman Emperor and king of Spain, your master, and the pope will eventually consent to the divorce," Cromwell said with confidence, referring to Henry's first marriage to Catherine of Aragon, dissolved so that he might marry Anne.

Chapuys, however, was not so sure about that statement. "I urge you to persuade the king to return to the right path," he replied simply.

Cromwell thanked him for his advice, assuring the ambassador that more discussions would take place within the king's Council and that all Council members were "well disposed" toward Charles V. Good relations between the nations were to be maintained, they all agreed.

But Chapuys was now starting to feel sure that Henry had realized his mistake; in Chapuys's eyes, the fact that the king had been spending time away from Anne after only a few months of marriage, seemingly busy with other matters, could only mean one thing: he had "begun to repent."[4]

Cromwell invited Chapuys for another hunting session, scheduled for when Henry would be back at court in two days' time, leaving the ambassador hopeful that everything was to be resolved, and that the affront caused to Catherine of Aragon, Charles V's aunt, would soon be amended. However, Anne was pregnant, and that only intensified matters. There would be no simple resolution to this controversial marriage.

A month passed and the pressure that Anne Boleyn's pregnancy put on all parties continued to increase. Henry met with all kinds of physicians and astrologers, all of whom assured him that the queen was bearing a son—the son he was so desperate for, and that Catherine of Aragon had not been able to give him.

But their predictions were wrong.

On September 7, 1533, between three and four o'clock in the afternoon, Anne gave birth to a daughter, and the following Wednesday, the christening of the newborn princess took place.

Once everyone had gathered in the Friars church, the baby girl Elizabeth was presented to the hall, causing all present to step forward, two by two, to acknowledge her: the citizens of London; then the gentlemen, the squires, the chaplains, the aldermen, the mayor alone, the king's Council; then the barons, bishops, and earls. The Earl of Essex bore the "gilt covered basons," the Marquis of Exeter carried a taper of virgin wax, the Marquess of Dorset bore the salt, and the Lady Mary Howard bore the chrisom, the heavily jeweled and embroidered baptismal robe of pearl and stone.

The elderly but respected Agnes Howard, Duchess of Norfolk, carried the princess swaddled in a mantle of purple velvet, while her long train was held by Elizabeth's maternal grandfather, Thomas Boleyn, 1st Earl of Wiltshire. Charles Brandon, 1st Duke of Suffolk, and Thomas Howard, 3rd Duke of Norfolk, stood on either side of the duchess while John Stokesley, Bishop of London, christened the princess.

Thomas Cranmer, Archbishop of Canterbury, was announced as godfather, while the Duchess of Norfolk and Margaret Wotton, Marchioness of Dorset, were named godmothers.

All rejoiced at the christening, clamoring, "Bid God send her a long life."[5] The trumpets sounded and the gifts were given to Henry and Anne, who was now holding the princess in her own arms. The christening had been a triumph, and while little Elizabeth was not the boy Henry had wanted, the king now had a legitimate daughter—his only heir.

For Chapuys, being such a strong supporter of Catherine of Aragon and her daughter, Henry's first child the Princess Mary, this celebration did not ring true. In his mind, the people of London swore allegiance to Catherine, not Anne. But both sides of the story were true—not surprising, considering the two queens were both charismatic women who had their own networks of support.

Chapuys was pleased when he reported the birth of Elizabeth to Charles V, informing him that "the king's mistress was delivered of a daughter, to the great regret both of him and the lady." He rejoiced in the reproaches—and, at times, the punishments—the physicians, astrologers, sorcerers, and sorceresses received after having claimed the baby "would be a male heir."[6] The Imperial ambassador wrote that the people of London rejoiced in the announcement that it was a daughter and not a son, assuring Catherine's supporters that this was surely the beginning of Anne's downfall.

Misinformed, Chapuys reported to the Holy Roman Emperor that the child was to be named Mary, like her sister, which he saw as another affront to the older princess. Yet he was wrong on this point too, and had to rectify his error in his next dispatch, explaining that the princess had in fact been named Elizabeth. Perhaps Chapuys was receiving incorrect information, due to his inability to secure direct audiences with the king himself: he was no longer welcome. It did not take long for Chapuys to complain about his treatment—or lack thereof, given that most of his audiences with the king were either dismissed, delayed, or interrupted by members of the Privy Council.

Persistent as ever, however, the ambassador was reluctant to withdraw, deciding instead to wait around in the hopes of having a word or two with anyone who was close to Henry.

Finally, on the evening of September 14, 1533, Chapuys intercepted the Duke of Norfolk after dinner and begged him for a short discussion.

Norfolk pretended to have an important meeting with the regent, but assured Chapuys that Queen Anne's brother would be with him shortly. When George Boleyn found another excuse to avoid a conversation with the ambassador, Chapuys asked to speak to Cromwell. After much persistence, the ambassador eventually obtained what he'd been waiting for: a conversation with two important privy councillors.

"I have been informed that the new-born child has been proclaimed a princess, which I found odd as the first princess has been deprived of that title because of her sex," he said.

Surprised by such a statement, Cromwell and George Boleyn glanced at each other, not sure what to say next, as Chapuys continued: "There is obviously no harm in calling her a princess, as all children of a king ought to be so called, but I thought it was then a great prejudice to the first princess."

Cromwell replied, "It is a matter of too high importance for us to discuss it with you. This is a matter you should discuss with the king directly."

Chapuys knew he had struck a nerve, and he readily agreed with Cromwell; after all, he had been trying to obtain an audience with the king all day.

The privy councillors awkwardly excused themselves, on the pretext that the king was waiting for them, as he had spent the day in meetings dealing with urgent matters that they needed to discuss.

Later, Chapuys wrote to Charles V, saying he expected that if he had asked for another audience "to speak upon the said subject, I should not have it."[7]

As for the French, Francis I continued to show support to Henry and his new wife, even sending a bearer carrying a ring for Anne as a token of his "affection" to her and the newborn princess.[8] But Francis had other things to consider and was now concerned with another important matter: the wedding of his second son Henry to the pope's niece, Catherine de Medici—also known as the Orphan of Florence.

*

The young Catherine de Medici had a very difficult start in life, despite her high parentage. She was born the daughter of the powerful Lorenzo II de Medici, Duke of Urbino, and the gracious Madeleine de La Tour d'Auvergne, and her birth gave rise to great festivities in both Rome and Florence. But her time with her parents would be cut tragically short.

The union of Catherine's parents had been a cause for celebration in the castle of Amboise, one of the most prestigious French castles that belonged to Francis I of France; the marriage of Lorenzo and Madeleine represented the alliance between France and the Papal States that Francis had desired for years.

On September 7, 1518, after months of traveling back to Italy, journeying through Chambery, Bologna, and Villa Poggio, the happy couple solemnly entered the capital of Tuscany, their new home. They were now ready to start their own family and dynasty—a dynasty based on two powerful aristocratic families and the two powerful realms they originated from. Their happy news, however, would not last long.

On a Wednesday morning—April 13, 1519, at eleven o'clock—within the walls of Palazzo Riccardi, the duchess gave birth to a healthy little girl. The mother herself was apparently "healthy and the birth has been a happy one."[9] Or, at least, this was how it seemed. Sadly, things were about to take a turn for the worse.

Three days later, young Catherine was baptized "Caterina Maria Romola," and celebrations were arranged in Florence. The next day, her mother Madeleine began to suffer from a bout of fever, described in a letter written by the Bishop of Fano as "very violent."[10] On April 22, Lorenzo was reassured by the duchess's physicians that she was doing a little better, but it wasn't long before she was unable to leave her bed.

After a few days of this terrible illness—during which Madeleine was in agony—she passed away on April 28, 1519, leaving behind her newly born daughter. She was buried at San Lorenzo, a parish of the Medici family.

In deep shock, the people of Florence donned their mourning

clothes and publicly grieved for their late duchess, weeping in the streets as they accompanied her corpse to its final resting place. Some were simply inconsolable: it was a true tragedy, both for the de Medici family and for the future of unstable Florence.

Worse news was to come.

On May 3, 1519, Cardinal Medici received word that Lorenzo, Catherine's father, was dying of wounds obtained when trying to defend Urbino from Francesco Maria, a former Duke of Urbino who had wanted his duchy back. The cardinal was told that he needed to hurry to be by his side as his final hour drew near and, sadly, Lorenzo died the next day.

Although he received a lavish funeral, a chronicler reporting the event noted that the people showed fewer signs of grief for him than they had for his late wife. The duke had many enemies, even in his own city of Florence, and his death triggered domestic troubles as well as difficulties further afield.

Now Catherine was alone in the world. As a child, she was cared for by a succession of relatives, including her grandmother and various aunts and uncles, her fate now in the hands of many people who, at times, only saw her as a pawn to advance their own political agendas after the death of the influential duke. Catherine, in contrast, was a modest girl, described as very humble and obedient. And she was already honing her survival instincts. The little duchess knew how to watch and wait, to observe affairs closely in order to protect herself from the harsh world that surrounded her. Finally, Francis I, who looked to assert some sort of dominion over Florence (and indeed, other parts of Italy) drew up a treaty with Leo X (Giovanni di Lorenzo de Medici), which involved the transfer of territory and the requirement that young Catherine should be sent to France, keeping her out of the way. The papacy, however, held the final decision on her fate, and kept delaying its judgment.

Then, on December 1, 1521, Pope Leo X—Catherine's great uncle—died of malaria. He was succeeded by Pope Adrian VI, until September 14, 1523, when another relative of the little orphan was elected to the papal chair, Clement VII (Giulio di Giuliano de Medici)—the unfortunate antagonist of both Holy Roman Emperor Charles V and Henry VIII of England. During that difficult time, Catherine was still in the care of her relatives, unsure of the future that awaited her.

Catherine was known as the "duchessina," despite being previously deprived of her title of Duchess of Urbino by the late Pope Adrian VI due to his ongoing conflict with the Medici family. Her wealth remained considerable, however, enabling her to live like a princess even if her options seemed limited.

As an infant, Catherine found herself center stage in not only Florentine diplomacy but also in European politics. As she grew older, her wealth, beauty, and papal connections meant that she was potentially a great match for any European house.

As a result, she received many marriage proposals, her suitors coming from all over Europe; from Henry VIII's bastard, Henry Fitzroy, Duke of Richmond, to James V of Scotland, prestigious suitors offered themselves to the young orphan, who was now under the protection of Pope Clement VII. Being well aware of this, Francis I of France offered his own second son—Henry, Duke of Orléans—to the duchess. Tall, melancholic, and well built, with dark hair, Henry was certainly a handsome prince; he was praised by his contemporaries for his physical attributes, and he was also said to be a good horse rider and very talented at fencing, hunting, and dancing. In other words, he had all the qualities required of a strong warrior prince.

The negotiations between Pope Clement VII and the French royal family regarding a potential union between Catherine and Henry began in 1531. On June 29, 1531, Gabriel Cardinal de Gramont wrote to Ferdinand, Charles V's brother: "There is no longer any doubt that the marriage between the pope's kinswoman and the Duke of Orléans will be concluded soon."[11]

Not fully ready to commit to Francis I, however, the pope delayed his final decision, allowing him to play a few tactical diplomatic games with Charles V—who also had his eye on the Italian territories and who had caused trouble to the papacy during their conquest, which had started at the end of the fifteenth century. Catherine's fate hung in the balance, and she anxiously awaited news of her destiny.

Italian wars had been ravaging southern Europe for quite some time when, in 1494, Ferdinand I of Naples died, creating a succession crisis. Charles VIII of France invaded the peninsula with the support of Ludovico Sforza of Milan, facing little resistance. Then, in 1527, Holy Roman Emperor Charles V led an attack against the Papal States and Rome—a conflict that resulted from the alliance made between the pope, France, Milan, Venice, and Florence against Charles V. Further disputes and battles took place between France and Spain, with both rulers trying to earn the pope's favor and support.

This dispute between Charles V and Francis I evolved into a diplomatic contest, with Catherine de Medici now the prize: not so much for who she was but for what she represented to Clement VII. Charles V soon realized that Francis I was making progress with the potential union between his second son and the young duchess, which would consolidate his conquest in Italy.

While Catherine was not royalty, the marriage contract stipulated that Clement VII would "at his own discretion, furnish his illustrious relative with clothing, ornaments, and jewels." Indeed, when she ultimately traveled to France it was as a true royal princess of great wealth, including "ropes of pearls, rings, golden belts—one encrusted with rubies—and many other fabulous gems."[12] On a fractious continent, Catherine would be a prize indeed for the family that would win her.

*

On Sunday, October 12, 1533, in the French port of Marseille, an expectant crowd gathered to witness a highly unusual event—the arrival of the reigning Pope Clement VII, who was bringing with him his young niece, the orphan Catherine de Medici. She was now betrothed to Henry, the second son of Francis I of France.

Clement and Catherine had traveled from La Spezia in considerable style, with eighteen galleys, three sailing ships, and six brigantines. When fourteen-year-old Catherine, having already been lavished with jewelry from Italian and French courtiers, set foot in France for the very first time, she was already being treated like the royalty she was soon to become.

The French court had prepared for the arrival of the pope and his niece with great care. Musicians had been hired, cheering crowds were gathering near the port, and there was much singing and feasting. The festive spirit was infectious as everyone eagerly awaited what would be the greatest event of the year: the royal marriage between Henry and Catherine. The Orphan of Florence could not wait to become a princess and to resolve her contentious identity at last. The expectation of such an alliance was all she could talk about with her ladies-in-waiting. She luxuriated in the grandeur of her party.[13]

As the ships approached there was a series of thunderous volleys, launched by rank after rank of artillery lined up on the huge fortress known as the Château d'If. This fortress had been built between 1524 and 1531 on the orders of Francis I, who, during a visit in 1516, saw the island as a strategically important location for defending the coastline from sea-based attacks. Notre-Dame de la Garde, the Catholic basilica of Marseilles, relayed the signals, and all the bells of every church in the entire Mediterranean city rang out.

The person entrusted with stage-managing the welcome and safe arrival of Catherine and her uncle was Anne de Montmorency, Constable of France, who arranged for the visitors to spend the night outside Marseilles; more preparations needed to be made for the pope's solemn entry into the city the next day.

Catherine herself would have to wait a bit longer before officially entering Marseilles; on October 23, she entered "riding a roan horse decked out in gold brocade" accompanied by a procession of "six horses, five caparisoned in scarlet and gold...twelve demoiselles with a royal and papal guard." Wearing an "outfit of gold and silver silk," she evidently cut quite the fine figure, and both her appearance and manners were impeccable. In terms of making a good first impression, Catherine's entrance certainly did not disappoint.

When she arrived at the pontiff's temporary palace she "knelt and kissed the pope's feet," a gesture that greatly touched Francis I of France, who was standing next to him with his two sons, Henry and

Charles. To welcome her to the family, he "lifted the young girl to her feet and kissed her."[14] Even at this stage in her life, she had that magic touch associated with public performance—and that sprinkling of stardust that goes with it. Certainly, she had already charmed her father-in-law.

Catherine would never forget this event, which transformed her from Florentine orphan to French princess. Years later, in a letter to her cousin Cosimo I de Medici, Grand Duke of Tuscany, she recalled "being overwhelmed with joy" and very grateful for the welcome she received that day.

Yet obstacles lay ahead. As many other noblewomen before her, and even though she had just become a member of the French royal family, Catherine would go on to face many hardships.

Her uncle, Pope Clement VII, died a year after her union to the French prince, meaning that the promises, the alliance, and the concessions made by Francis I had all been in vain. The union to the Orphan of Florence no longer seemed like an astute diplomatic move; in fact, it looked like an utter failure on Francis's part, and threatened to diminish Catherine's value, isolating her from the dynasty she had been so delighted to join.

Her fate was now completely in the hands of Francis, and depended entirely on how valuable she could prove herself to be as her own person—without the support and the network of influential relatives.

★

On the other side of the Channel, misfortune was also striking an influential woman. Anne Boleyn, Queen of England, was struggling in her role as consort, failing to produce a male heir to the crown. Her enemies loved spreading rumors that her days as queen were numbered.

When the news came that Anne Boleyn had been charged for high treason against the king, on suspicion of adultery with various men— including her brother, George Boleyn, Viscount Rochford—Chapuys rejoiced. He delighted in the news that the king was "determined to abandon her," adding for good measure that "it is still more wonderful to think of the sudden change from yesterday to today."[15]

Anne's downfall had indeed been precipitated, her enemies already gathering like vultures around her not-yet-cold body. At five o'clock in the afternoon on May 2, 1536, Anne Boleyn was escorted to the Tower of London. It was the last sunset she would ever see as a free woman.

William Kingston, Constable of the Tower of London, would later recall that "when she came to the court gate, entering in, she fell down on her knees before the said lords, beseeching God to help her as she was not guilty" of the charges made against her. But there was nothing anyone could do for her: the court had passed judgment, and she had been found guilty of high treason against Henry VIII on account of adultery—and her so-called incestuous relationship with her own brother.

★

Twenty-three years later, in 1559, Alexander Ales, a Scottish theologian who had moved to the German-controlled countries and had become a supporter of Luther, wrote to Elizabeth months after her accession. He needed to tell the story he thought to be true regarding her mother's death.

According to him, the reason for Anne Boleyn's execution was due to the fact "that she persuaded the king to send an embassy into Germany to the princes who had embraced the Gospel."[16] She had been framed, he believed, because of the political power she wielded beyond the English court.

By Ales's account, soon after Edward Foxe, Bishop of Hereford, and Nicholas Heath had been sent on embassy to the Lutheran princes in Germany, the wily Stephen Gardiner—the Bishop of Winchester and ambassador at the court of Francis I—"wrote to those friends whom he had in the court of the king of England, conspirators like himself, to the effect that certain reports were being circulated in the court of the king of France, and certain letters had been discovered, according to which the queen was accused of adultery." These letters were shown to Thomas Cromwell—"the king's ear and mind"—and then inevitably "became known to the king himself."[17] In response, Henry demanded that the facts be discovered.

Night and day, spies had dogged the doomed queen and had offered substantial bribes to her servants; "there is nothing they do not promise the ladies of her bedchamber," it was said. They reported to the king that Anne had been dancing with other men and that they had seen her kissing her brother with their own eyes. It didn't take long before it was decided and concluded that the queen was an adulteress, "and deserved to be burnt alive."[18]

On April 30, 1536, the Council was summoned to meet the king at his palace in Greenwich and, shortly after this, Anne was sent to the Tower, where her execution would take place.

In the letter to her daughter Elizabeth, Ales wrote that he remembered "the most serene queen, your most religious mother, carrying you, still a little baby, in her arms and entreating the most serene king, your father, when she brought you to him in Greenwich Palace, as he looked out of an open window into the courtyard."

Ales also remembered how angry the king was with Anne. There had been no hope for her; the court's verdict was a foregone conclusion.

On sunrise on the day itself, May 19, 1536, Anne made a short speech: "I have come to die, as I have been judged by the law; I accuse none, nor would I say anything of the ground upon which I am judged. I pray for the king, a most merciful and gentle prince. He has always been a good, gentle, sovereign lord to me." She then kneeled and muttered, "To Christ I commend my soul,"[19] before commanding her executioner, who'd come especially from Calais for the occasion, to strike.

Once the deed was done, her body was thrown into a common chest made of elm, which was then buried in the chapel within the Tower of London. Ales recalled, "She who has been the queen of England upon Earth" that day became "a queen in heaven."[20]

Ales concluded his letter by assuring Elizabeth that Anne was remembered for "her constancy, patience and faith towards God that all the spectators, even her enemies, and those persons who previously had rejoiced at her misfortune out of their hatred to the doctrine of the religion which she had introduced into England, testified and proclaimed her innocence and chastity."

One might well wonder what thoughts came into Elizabeth's mind when she read the letter describing her mother's death—a death that was to lead to great hardship and sorrow for her young daughter. Elizabeth never forgot her mother, or the lessons her death taught her. Cast out of court after Anne's demise, Elizabeth learned that her life would always be in danger, and that if she was to survive she must quickly learn to navigate troubled waters.

And Anne's death was a reminder that a royal position did not always protect a woman. This was something Catherine de Medici would also soon discover.

2

In the Shadows of the Royal Courts,
1537–1546

During her early days at Francis's court, Catherine was a discreet figure. She often found herself overshadowed by other more beautiful ladies, including Francis's chief mistress, Anne de Pisseleu d'Heilly, Duchess of Étampes, and the queen, Eleanor of Austria. This did not, however, prevent Catherine from spending time with the king himself; one of their favorite pastimes was hunting, and the French king loved his daughter-in-law's company while riding in the forest, hawking or fowling.

Catherine the Duchess of Orléans proved to be very agile and athletic, and she was believed to have introduced the women of France to the sidesaddle position when riding horses, which made Catherine as fast as men when riding. She was already an excellent horse rider but, thanks to the Amazon technique, she was now one of the few ladies who could actually keep up with the king himself. As a result, Francis often commented on Catherine's "grace while riding and hunting." During one particular hunting game, Francis was in awe of Catherine's ability to handle a crossbow. "What a great shot!"[1] he exclaimed.

Catherine also pursued her education, studying Latin and Greek as well as history, geography, natural philosophy, and astronomy—for which she showed a true passion. She also loved writing and, along with her sister-in-law, Marguerite de France (also known as Marguerite de Valois), wrote stories to be read out loud at court by their relatives, including Catherine's husband, Henry, Duke of Orléans. These interests allowed Catherine to integrate herself into court life.

But by 1536 Catherine had been married to Henry for three long years and she had not yet shown any signs of fertility, raising questions at court; despite her proximity to her father-in-law, rumors began to spread through the court about the longevity of her union with the young duke.

Things got even worse when, on August 10, 1536, the king of France's eldest son—another Francis—died suddenly after a game of jeu de paume (a precursor to tennis) in Tournon. Seven autopsies were conducted by different surgeons. Some of them believed that the young prince drank some iced water after the game, causing a dysfunction in the intestines, while other contemporaries claimed he had been poisoned, with Charles V being the first to blame (Charles was Francis's arch-enemy and fervent opponent during the war of Milan, between 1536 and 1538). However, suspicions rapidly turned to the ones directly benefitting from the young prince's death: Henry and Catherine, who were now officially Dauphin and Dauphine of France and therefore heirs to the throne of France. Catherine's Italian origin was the main reason the couple were suspected of poisoning the prince—though there was no evidence to prove it. Nevertheless, the rumors unsettled Catherine, and threatened her royal favor.

Furthermore, the fact that the couple remained childless endangered Catherine's position at court, and by 1537 she had become very vulnerable indeed. The Italian diplomat Gasparo Contarini confirmed this in a letter: "Because of the death of the dauphin, and as people doubt that Catherine could ever have children, rumours spread that Francis I himself was seeking for a divorce."[2] Catherine, who was already panicking at the idea of being repudiated and losing yet another family, decided to confront the king herself.

One of Catherine's greatest strengths was her humility, her ability to appear docile and obedient. Years later, however, she would reveal other facets of her personality that proved just how truly resilient and strong—even authoritative—she could be. But this was not the time for an expression of strength.

"I have heard that you were looking for another wife for your son. Since God himself has refused to honour me with children, and since it no longer pleases your Majesty to wait in that regard, I want you to know that I fully understand that it is such an honour to contribute to the succession of such a great realm, and that I remember how blessed I am that you have chosen me in the first place," Catherine humbly told the king. "I will accept my fate whatever you decide and regardless of how painful the decision might be for myself."[3]

Francis was touched by such a speech, and by Catherine's modesty—or perhaps he was just in a jovial mood. Either way, the king had always had a soft spot for the Orphan of Florence, who had been a good addition to the family. In response he reassured her: "My daughter, since God has chosen that you were my daughter-in-law and the wife of the dauphin, I do not wish that it should be otherwise, and maybe God will answer your wishes and ours."[4]

Catherine happily bowed to Francis, before leaving him to deal with his state affairs. She felt relieved; after all, as long as the king was on her side, she had not much to fear—at least, that's what she assumed. But Catherine still struggled to charm her own husband, who by now lived only for the love of his life, Diane de Poitiers.

*

The issue of a good noble family, Diane was born on January 9, 1500, to Jean de Poitiers, Seigneur de Saint Vallier, and Jeanne de Batarnay. She loved riding and swam regularly, and she was known for her athletic body. She was fifteen when she married Louis de Brézé, Seigneur d'Anet, Count of Maulévrier, and Grand Senechal of Normandy. He was thirty-nine years her senior, and grandson of King Charles VII of France by his royal favorite, Agnès Sorel. Louis became a courtier at the court of Francis I, where he introduced his wife to the joys of court life and where she was chosen as one of Queen Claude of France's ladies-in-waiting. When the queen died, Diane served the queen mother Louise of Savoy and then Queen Eleanor of Austria, her presence at court growing steadily over the years as she learned from these powerful royal women.

When her husband died in 1531, Diane was finally able to take control of her own affairs. She wore black and white—the typical mourning colors—for the rest of her life, and she retained her husband's finances; Francis allowed her to manage all her inherited estates without the supervision of a male guardian or relative, further increasing her influence and power at court. Now financially independent, she became her own mistress.

After Francis I invited Diane to become his sons' tutor, she developed a strong bond with the second prince, Henry, which would later develop into a romantic, and sexual, relationship. Francis might have disapproved of Diane being so close to his son, but he failed to foresee what was about to happen: just one year after Henry married Catherine, he made Diane one of his mistresses.

The pressure of providing an heir to the crown increased when Henry "fathered a child with Filipa Duci, the hitherto virgin sister of one of his Piedmontese grooms, while campaigning in Italy."[5] Henry was thrilled to learn about the pregnancy—believing it proved to everyone that, although the royal couple had remained childless, the fault was certainly not with him. In 1538, Filipa gave birth to a daughter named Diane de France, named in tribute to his favorite mistress, Diane de Poitiers. This was one of the many affronts that Catherine had to endure.

However, Diane's own position at court was not as secure as she would have liked. Francis's own chief mistress, Anne, Duchess of Étampes, could not stand Diane's influence. The two women bore great disdain for one another, so much so that the whole court was divided between them. As they were both supported by their respective lovers—Francis and Henry—this also caused tensions between father and son.

When the rumors of Catherine's possible rejection began to swirl around the court, Diane decided that she had to support the dauphine. She could not afford to risk Henry divorcing Catherine and finding a more beautiful and even younger bride if she was to remain his favorite. While Diane's relationship with Henry was an affront to Catherine, she understood that the mistress's support could help protect her, and so the two women forged an uneasy truce.

Diane understood the importance of Catherine and Henry securing the dynasty, but it seemed to her that Catherine was failing in her duty as a wife and as the future queen of France. First, there was not yet a child. And Henry felt no passion for Catherine; he liked her and appreciated her company, but he never seemed truly loving in his behavior toward her. And so, a *ménage à trois* developed, though Catherine was wounded by the two lovers, who never hid their passion and affection for one another. In fact, it caused her great pain. Years later, in a letter Catherine wrote to one of her closest councillors and secretary of state, Monsieur Pomponne de Bellièvre, her feelings were as strong as ever as she wrote, "Never did a wife who loves her husband love his whore."[6]

Diane shared advice with Catherine on sexual positions that would likely arouse Henry's passion for her, but this was not enough to spur the royal couple to engage in more physical activity together, and left Catherine distressed. As the dauphine continued to show no signs of pregnancy, the humiliations continued.

Catherine became convinced that something was wrong with her, and decided to investigate exactly how Diane and her husband engaged in their sexual relations. She ordered holes to be bored through the floor of her chamber—above her husband's room—in order to spy on the couple when in action. The sight of their intimate encounter only succeeded in deeply hurting the dauphine, however, who realized that Henry did not perform the sexual act the same way with her as he did with his mistress.[7]

Nevertheless, Diane continued to offer more advice on the matter to Catherine, and finally suggested that she should stimulate the prince before sending him to his wife's chamber. This trick apparently worked, with Catherine confirming that Henry seemed to show more passion after this course of action. The royal couple was also examined by a doctor named Jean Fernel, who offered his advice on reproduction. In any case, these interventions finally helped the couple to conceive. In June 1543, a pregnant Catherine wrote to Anne of Montmorency, Constable of France and close advisor to her husband: "Mon Compère, as I know well that you desire as much as I do to see me with children, I wish to write to tell you of my great hopes that I am with child."[8]

The pregnancy proceeded smoothly and on January 19, 1544, Catherine gave birth to her firstborn: a healthy baby boy named Francis, after his grandfather. There was a great feeling of achievement and relief not only for her and her husband, but also for the king. Marguerite of Angoulême, Queen of Navarre, wrote to her brother, Francis: "I am sure you must have been moved to tears, with a joy even greater than I saw in you at the birth of your first born."[9]

The joy did not stop there. A year later, Catherine brought a daughter into the world, Elisabeth of Valois. At this point the dauphine wrote to her cousin Cosimo I de Medici, Duke of Florence, who she had grown up with and remained close to ever since: "I gave birth to a daughter [. . .] which I hope will be the knot to shape and maintain all alliances."[10] Finally, Catherine felt safe.

Over the course of their marriage, Catherine and Henry had definitely secured the Valois line: they had ten children, seven of whom reached adulthood. Catherine's position at court was finally secured, even if she remained in the shadow of Henry and Diane's love.

*

Meanwhile, across the Channel, another princess was also being overshadowed. Upon the death of her mother in 1536, the young princess Elizabeth was stripped of her title and declared a bastard at just three years old. She had been entrusted to Margaret Bryan, lady governess to the children of Henry VIII of England, the now little Lady Elizabeth having been cast away from court with hardly anything to her name.

Clueless about what to do, Lady Bryan wrote to Thomas Cromwell. "As my Lady Elizabeth is put from that degree she was in, and what degree she is at now I know not but by hearsay, I know not how to order her or myself, or her women or grooms." She begged him "to be good lord to her and hers, and that she may have raiment, for she has neither gown nor kirtle nor petticoat, nor linen for smocks, nor kerchiefs, sleeves, rails [nightdresses], bodystychets [corsets], hand-kerchiefs, mufflers, nor begens [nightcaps]."[11]

Elizabeth was also suffering badly with her teething, which worried Lady Bryan as she hated to see the little princess in so much pain. Fortunately, Cromwell seemed to have been moved by the governess's letters, sending what was needed for the care of Elizabeth.[12] After all, only her title was disputed, not the fact that she was—and would always be—the king's daughter.

The death of Anne Boleyn had one positive result for little Elizabeth: her half-sister, Mary, no longer viewed her as a monstrous little bastard, instead growing rather fond of her. The two sisters enjoyed their time together and even became quite close. When Henry VIII, who had remarried only ten days after the execution of Elizabeth's mother, announced in October 1537 that his new wife and queen, Jane Seymour, had given birth to a son, Edward, the two sisters were inevitably even further overshadowed by the little infant—their father's much desired son.

Three days later, Edward was christened and, as part of the ceremonial procession, four-year-old Elizabeth carried out "her first official duty, bearing the chrisom on her breast." She then took her place next to her older sister Mary, who was announced as godmother to their brother.

Unfortunately, Jane Seymour—who had shown incredible kindness to Mary—died just twelve days later, on October 24, almost certainly due to puerperal sepsis. She was the first of Henry VIII's wives to be buried as queen, her funeral taking place in Windsor on November 12, 1537, only a month after the birth of her son. Henry, though devastated by the loss, immediately set about looking for another wife.

Lady Bryan, who had been caring for Elizabeth, was given the position of Lady Mistress of Edward's royal nursery. In other words, this was the second time that Elizabeth had lost a mother figure. Cromwell replaced Lady Bryan with Katherine Champernowne, also known as Kat Ashley, which turned out to be a blessing in disguise. Kat showed great devotion to the princess right up until her death, with Elizabeth recognizing her governess for "her great labour and pain in bringing of me up in learning and honesty."[13]

Years passed, and Elizabeth spent her life more or less away from the Henrician court, and she received a good education alongside her half-brother; they shared the same tutors and mentors, including the renowned William Grindal. The three siblings were mostly brought up in the royal houses of Hertfordshire, including Ashridge, Hunsdon, Hatfield, and Hertford Castle, which is where Elizabeth learned to hunt. She was thus able to be distant from the drama happening at court in those years, including the repudiation of Anne of Cleves and the execution of Katherine Howard, a relative of hers. She remained away from public attention, which was focused on the scandals dominating the court of her father.

In fact, Elizabeth was perceived as a figure of almost complete non-importance, especially on the diplomatic and political scene, and this was confirmed by Charles de Marillac—French ambassador at the English court—as he recalled her profile at court in 1539. During a discussion concerning potential marriages between Henry VIII's daughters, Mary and Elizabeth, Thomas Howard, Duke of Norfolk, told Charles, "The younger of the two was not to be spoken of, because, besides being only seven years old, the opinion of Queen Anne, her mother, was such that it was quite decided to consider her illegitimate."[14]

On July 12, 1543, Henry VIII married his sixth and last wife, the pious and caring Katherine Parr. Their marriage was a true blessing for the royal children, as the new wife and queen took a great interest in all three of them, developing a particularly strong bond with the little princess Elizabeth. She ensured that the siblings, who had been living peacefully with each other for years, were reinstated at court. This relocation, and their strong bond, brought Elizabeth back into favor.

On Thursday, June 26, 1544, during an official dinner at Whitehall followed by a reception where wine and sweetmeats were served to the guests—also called a "void"—Henry VIII officially restored Mary and Elizabeth into the line of succession to the throne, behind

Edward.[15] The two sisters sat by their father's side, and although they were still not fully legitimated, the message was clear: they were the king's daughters and could potentially inherit the throne one day.

But a person of importance was missing from this event: the queen herself. Henry was feasting before going on a military campaign in France, and he had named Katherine—along with his chosen privy councillors—as regents. They were assigned to Hampton Court.

Elizabeth missed her, and wrote to Katherine a month later, after she had been forced to stay at St. James's Palace because of fears of the plague, away from her siblings who had all returned to Hampton Court. She wrote tenderly that she had been "deprived for a whole year of your most illustrious presence, and still not being content with that, I have been robbed once again of the same good." She asserted, "I am not only bound to serve you but also to revere you with daughterly love, since I understand that your most illustrious highness has not forgotten me every time that you have written to the king's majesty." She ended her letter by praying for her father's victory over the French and for "his happy return."[16] A few weeks later, she was delighted when she finally joined her siblings and the queen at Hampton Court, where she spent the rest of the summer and the autumn.

During that time, Elizabeth experienced a different kind of court—one that was ruled by a queen instead of a king. She constantly attended Queen Katherine, enjoying seeing her exercising her royal authority through her title of Queen Regent. Katherine was the one sitting in state in the Presence Chamber, and though she "shall use the advice and council" of members of the king's Privy Council, she remained the one solely in charge.[17] During Henry's absence, her official title was "general regent of the realm."[18] Elizabeth admired the calm and measured manner in which Katherine used her new authority.

In her letters to Henry, Katherine showed great devotion as she declared her feelings: "Though you have not been absent for long I cannot find peace until I hear from you [. . .] God, the knower of secrets, can judge these words not to be only written with ink, but most truly impressed in the heart."[19] Yet in other letters, when required to make decisions for the safety of the country, she also showed her steel, such as when she issued a proclamation ordering the "examination of persons who had returned from the king's army in France," or when she forbade anyone who were from parts of London and Westminster where "the plague reigns" to "come to Court; to avoid danger to the queen, the prince, and other the king's children."[20] She signed her name confidently: she was "Katharine, the Queen Regent." In other words, she was not afraid of exercising her power as well as her obedience, something which was not lost on young Elizabeth.

Elizabeth's early years at her father's court were marked by her own devotion. Remaining mostly in the shadow of her stepmother, the young princess was protected by her, and she was also very much influenced by the queen's growing interest in Protestantism. In order to please Katherine, Elizabeth translated—on parchment, and with an embellished embroidered cover, which was also of her making—Marguerite of Navarre's *Miroir de l'âme pécheresse*, offering it to the queen as a new year's gift on December 31, 1544. Marguerite of Navarre, Francis I's sister, had not hidden her interest in the reformed religion, first publishing *Miroir* in 1531. It is believed that Elizabeth used the copy that her mother, Anne Boleyn, had kept in her own library, and Elizabeth accompanied the translation with a letter, which started: "To our most noble and virtuous Queen Katherine, Elizabeth, her humble daughter, wisheth perpetual felicity and everlasting joy."[21]

A year later, the young princess reiterated the gesture by showing her own interest in the reformed religion, translating the first chapter of Jean Calvin's *Institution de la religion chrétienne*, which had been published in 1541. The accompanying note read: "To the most high, most illustrious and magnanimous Princess Katherine, queen of England, France, and Ireland, Elizabeth, her most humble daughter, gives greeting and due obedience."[22]

For the same new year's gift exchange, Elizabeth translated her stepmother's work, *Prayers or Meditations,* and offered it to her father, Henry VIII. She wrote this work on a parchment and embroidered the cover too, and it is the only letter from Elizabeth to Henry that has survived. The young princess wrote affectionately:

And though as your majesty is of such excellence that none or few are to be compared with you in royal and ample marks of honour, and I am bound unto you as lord by the law of royal authority, as lord and father by the law of nature [...] this work which is most worthy because it was indeed a composition by a queen as a subject for a king, be translated into other languages by me, your daughter. May I, by this means, be indebted to you not as an imitator of your virtues but indeed as an inheritor of them.[23]

Elizabeth really was her father's daughter, and during her time at his court she learned the importance of showing her deference—to appear docile and perhaps even slightly fragile to get into her father's good graces. These years shaped Elizabeth's views on several important matters, including religious policies, diplomacy, and warfare, but especially, and perhaps most importantly, the art of royal authority.

In the shadows of their respective courts, Catherine de Medici and Elizabeth learned invaluable lessons, as well as benefitting from powerful protectors: Francis I for the French dauphine, Katherine Parr for the Tudor princess. They also learned the rules of the games played at court, seeing how someone could be at the top of the list of courtiers one day, and the next at the very bottom, losing their reputation—and their lives—in the blink of an eye.

3

Courts of Wolves and She-Wolves, 1547–1553

The year 1547 was a bad one for kings.

Europe lost two of its most powerful and charismatic Renaissance monarchs in the space of only two months—first Henry VIII of England and then Francis I of France—resulting in the first use of the now well-known adage expressing the continuity of monarchy, "The King is dead! Long live the King!," which was proclaimed in the two countries. With both men gone, their dynasties were left in the hands of their sons—and their female relatives were left at the mercy of the wolves of their respective courts.

The two men had had an interesting relationship. Sometimes brothers in arms and allies united against Emperor Charles V, they were also often rivals and even enemies—going to war against one another on occasion. These complexities would later be reciprocated by their eventual female successors, Elizabeth and Catherine.

★

In the early morning of Friday, January 28, 1547, King Henry VIII of England died at Whitehall Palace. Initially his death was kept secret by three of Henry's closest advisors, who themselves were plotting to seize power: Edward Seymour, the Earl of Hertford (later Duke of Somerset) and senior uncle to Edward VI; Sir Anthony Denny, the Chief Gentleman of the Privy Chamber; and Sir William Paget, the king's secretary.

Somerset's first action was to ride to Hertford Castle, where Edward was staying, to attempt to take control of the prince who was now king of England. The young Edward had been kept in the dark about his father's demise, and it wasn't until he stopped at Enfield—where his sister Elizabeth was residing—on his way back to London that the news of their father's death was announced to them both. The news hit the siblings hard; their faces were soon covered with tears and they cried "deeply" in each other's arms.[1]

For Elizabeth, this was to mark the end of a period of peace; with a vacuum of power at the heart of court, danger would be now lurking around every corner.

Henry's death was finally announced officially on January 31, 1547. On that same day, Edward and his uncle Edward Seymour, Earl of Hertford, arrived at the Tower of London, where they took up residence. Henry's body was disemboweled, cauterized, embalmed, and encased in lead, ready to be taken to the Chapel Royal at Whitehall on February 2. Twelve days later his body was moved to Windsor, and on February 16, Henry was finally buried in the vault of St. George's Chapel, next to the grave of Jane Seymour—his third wife, who had given him his longed-for and cherished male heir.

Edward VI was crowned king of England at Westminster Abbey days later on February 20, 1547, while his senior uncle, Edward Seymour, was made Lord Protector of the Realm. His new position created a potent rivalry with Edward VI's younger uncle, Thomas Seymour, Lord Admiral, and unfortunately Elizabeth would soon find herself caught up in their machinations.

After attempting first to offer his hand to Elizabeth—which she politely declined—Thomas Seymour laid his eyes on the dowager queen, Katherine Parr. He knew that Katherine had once loved him, long before her marriage to Henry VIII, and he hoped to rekindle any romantic feelings that may have remained. This he managed to do; the queen had never truly forgotten him, and Seymour and Katherine married in secret in mid-April 1547. For Elizabeth, this marriage would go on to have drastic consequences.

Elizabeth and Mary had been left with an income of £3,000 a year and a dowry of £10,000 on their marriages—though these unions had to be approved by the Council. If they were not, the women would be removed from the line of succession and their incomes reduced. Katherine was also well provided for. Henry left her £3,000 in "plate, jewels, and household things" alongside £1,000 in money and her dower in lands.[2] She chose to live at Old Manor in Chelsea, where Elizabeth joined her, and soon after Thomas Seymour joined them both.

Katherine Parr had always been a good influence on Elizabeth, both in terms of her education, which Katherine had fervently supported, and in the model of female rulership she provided for her. For Seymour, however, Elizabeth represented an opportunity, a bargaining chip that could help him to compete with his brother's growing power over their nephew, Edward.

Tall, well built, and with dashing blue eyes, a manly beard, and auburn hair, Seymour was certainly a handsome man; women were often seduced by his physical attributes and his charisma. Katherine, for one, had fallen completely under his charm, and there's no doubt that the thirteen-year-old Elizabeth was also mesmerized by him as she was often reported to be "blushing" at the mention of his name in these early days.[3] Seymour was well aware of the effect he had on the two women.

Soon after Seymour moved in, rumors surfaced that he was behaving inappropriately toward Elizabeth. Early in the morning he would come into her private chamber and, before she could even get dressed, he "struck her upon the back or buttocks familiarly." One morning, Kat Ashley—Elizabeth's faithful servant—recalled that Thomas Seymour, Lord Admiral, "strove to have kissed her [Elizabeth] in her bed."

His advances, however, did not stop there. Thomas was also seen in his nightgown "bare-legged in his slippers"—in other words, without his trousers—entering Elizabeth's chamber to tickle or pursue her in her bed.[4]

While servants and contemporaries were shocked at this behavior and thought of reporting it to Katherine herself, they quickly realized this would be in vain. Despite her pregnancy—or perhaps because of it—Katherine began to act as her husband's accomplice.

Perhaps she might have feared that she'd be completely overlooked if she did not participate in Seymour's foolish games.

During their late spring stay in Hanworth Park House—a royal hunting lodge Henry VII had used when hunting on Hounslow Heath—a contemporary remembered that Seymour had cut Elizabeth's gown "in an hundred pieces" and that the princess could not defend herself as "the queen held her, while the Lord Admiral cut it."[5] There is no doubt that Seymour and Katherine misbehaved in the presence of the young woman, and that the bond Elizabeth had always had with Katherine was now broken.

Soon enough, however, Seymour's schemes began to displease his wife. Katherine became jealous, and though she would miss her husband when he was away, she also welcomed his departure when he had to leave to spend several weeks at court; no doubt she appreciated how his time away also put some distance between him and the young princess.

Now very heavily pregnant, in June 1548 Katherine wrote to Seymour, and she tasked Elizabeth with finding a messenger to deliver the letter to him. On the outside of the letter, Elizabeth decided to add a plea in Latin—*Noli metan* (Thou touch me not)—though she then erased it and rewrote *Nolito me tangere* (Let him not touch me).[6] The message was clear: Elizabeth did not appreciate Seymour's advances, and she wanted him to stop.

But Seymour persisted. Thomas Parry—cofferer to Elizabeth—related that, on June 11, 1548, Katherine stumbled upon her husband and the princess in each other's arms, yelling, "They were all alone, he having her in his arms!"[7] She could stand it no longer. The very next day, Elizabeth was sent to live with Sir Anthony and Joan Denny—the sister of Elizabeth's governess, Kat Ashley—at Cheshunt in Hertfordshire, while the married couple went to live at Sudeley Castle. Elizabeth was confused by this decision, telling Katherine that she was "replete with sorrow to depart from your highness."[8] In spite of her feelings about Seymour, her respect for Katherine was clear.

Throughout her stay with the Dennys, Elizabeth found herself in severe pain, suffering from serious migraines and other digestive

problems. This led to unfounded rumors that she was in fact pregnant, and Somerset himself sent out his own physicians to examine
the princess, for which she thanked him, saying that he had "been
careful" about her health.[9]

It wasn't long before things took a dark turn, when Katherine died
of childbed fever on September 5, 1548, just one week after giving birth
to her only child, Mary Seymour, named after Princess Mary. Days
before the dowager queen's death, Somerset himself had congratu-
lated his brother on the birth of the little girl, despite conceding that it
would have given them "more joy and comfort if it had been a son."[10]

But Katherine's death did not seem to greatly affect Seymour—
though he had certainly been surprised by the suddenness of it.
Whitman, one of Seymour's servants, recalled that his master was "a
very ambitious man of honour; and it may so happen that, now the
queen is gone, he will be desirous for his advancement to match with
one of the king's sisters."[11]

Her death did, however, affect Elizabeth—greatly. The little protection Katherine had been able to give Elizabeth had disappeared, and
no one stood between Seymour and his ambition—except for an
entire Council and a power-hungry lord protector, who was more
than reluctant to see his younger brother gaining in influence.

Now that Katherine was gone, Seymour intended to put his plan
of marrying Elizabeth into action, inquiring of Thomas Parry, "How
many persons [meaning servants] she kept?" and "What houses she
had and what lands?"[12] As with any other upper-class Tudor marriage,
the question of wealth was a very central one, and Seymour wanted
to know everything.

As for Elizabeth, she might have blushed when Seymour's name
was mentioned, but blushing can mean many things; it could have
been a sign of shame, especially if she'd had to suffer his unwelcome
sexual advances. Despite this, she remained polite and pleasant, but this
could well have been an act of self-preservation; her way of avoiding
potential conflict with a powerful man twenty-five years her senior.

Parry asked the princess point-blank: "If the Council would like
it... would you marry him?" and she replied, "When that time comes

to pass, I will do as God shall put in my mind." Evasive answers such as this were already one of Elizabeth's strengths—one she would deploy in the future on the numerous occasions she was asked if she would ever marry.[13]

Seymour's pursuit of Elizabeth ran parallel to the younger uncle getting closer to King Edward, spoiling him with gifts. In fact, it was soon reported that Seymour was planning to capture his nephew, seeking to use his influence over him to impose a new government—with Seymour at its head. In a swift decision, Somerset ordered the arrest of his brother, who soon after was interrogated and condemned.

For Elizabeth, this marked the arrival of a new nightmare. A few days after Seymour was arrested on January 17, 1549, Elizabeth's two faithful servants, Thomas Parry and Kat Ashley, were sent to the Tower of London to be interrogated. The princess "was marvellously abashed, and did weep very tenderly a long time." Robert Tyrwhitt—Katherine Parr's former Master of the Horse—was sent to Hatfield by the Council to get to the bottom of what had happened with Elizabeth, and to discover if she was in fact Seymour's accomplice. Tyrwhitt was the perfect man for this thorny task, as he was fully aware of the rumors surrounding the princess and the Lord Admiral. He might have thought it would be easy to get a confession of guilt from the princess—but, like many others, he had clearly underestimated her.

Tyrwhitt tried to convince Elizabeth that Ashley and Parry had confessed that she had accepted Seymour's advances and marriage proposal, and he also coaxed her to come forward and tell the truth about what happened.

Elizabeth kept her nerve and expressed her surprise at their apparent confessions, calling Parry "a false wretch," but mostly she remained steely throughout the interrogation. Tyrwhitt was now making threats—reminding the princess that "she was but a subject"—but Elizabeth would not be so easily compromised. Standing her ground, she continued to remain silent, warding off Tyrwhitt's interrogation tactics and forcing him to conclude that "she hath a very good wit, and nothing is gotten of her but by great policy."[14] By "great policy," he meant that Elizabeth acknowledged her awareness of Seymour's interest in marrying her, but this was of no matter to her: she swore that she "would never marry neither in England nor out of England, without the consent of the king's majesty, your grace's [Somerset's] and the Council's." Certainly, when it came to the marriage question, Elizabeth already knew her answer by heart.

Wanting to further prove her innocence, Elizabeth went on the offensive and wrote directly to Somerset, urging him to put an end to the "shameful slanders" that suggested she was kept in "the Tower, and with child by my Lord Admiral."[15] In response, he agreed to take action against any defamation of her dignity. It wasn't long before one wolf was taken down: on March 20, 1549, Thomas Seymour was beheaded for treason. After this dangerous episode, the princess had one threat fewer to contend with. She decided to focus her attention elsewhere, on her education.

William Grindal, Elizabeth's first tutor, had died in early 1548 and had been replaced by Roger Ascham, who was extremely fond of the princess; he praised her highly in his memoirs. In the book, entitled *Schoolmaster*, he described her scholarly routine and complimented both her skills as a linguist and her great maturity.

And it was her maturity that helped shape her approach to the new king, her brother. She knew it was vital to appear obedient and humble in her communications with Edward, so that she could not be perceived as any kind of threat. In May 1549, she sent him a portrait of herself as a token of her affection, also admitting that she should "learn to follow this saying of Horace, *Feras non culpes quod vitari non potest*" ("what can't be cured must be endured").[16] She gave the impression of a stoic, stable woman, ready to support her brother in any way. She knew that even a sibling's position could be precarious, and that male interest could be deadly. She would use this knowledge to protect herself in the years to come.

*

Across the Channel, another royal woman was learning invaluable lessons, especially when it came to buying herself time against an enemy. A life-changing event compelled Catherine de Medici to fight for her rightful place at the French court. She could no longer afford to be cast out or forced to reside in the shadows of her rival, Diane de Poitiers.

On March 31, 1547, King Francis I of France died at Rambouillet, and his corpse was moved to Saint-Cloud, where he lay in state. During his funeral on April 11, Catherine—unable to hide her pain—wept greatly; she could probably foresee the hardships that lay ahead of her. After all, Francis I had been a strong and benevolent father figure to the young princess, and now she found herself alone in a court that was dominated by her husband and his powerful mistress. However, it was true that she also had new power: at just twenty-seven years old, the little Orphan of Florence was now queen consort of France.

Upon his father's death, Henry II sacked the former ministers who were loyal to Francis and instead appointed his own friends and supporters to important positions, except Anne de Montmorency who remained Constable of France. Henry was certainly making the French court his own.

The Venetian ambassador, Marino Cavalli, who witnessed Henry's accession to the throne of France, described the king as a man with a very robust constitution who could "have a melancholic mood at times" and who was "very skilful when it comes to armed exercises." The ambassador also immediately noted Diane's influence over the young king, writing that "this lady has made sure to indoctrinate, to correct, and counsel" Henry, pushing him to thrive as a successful leader of his country.[17]

Catherine was queen only in name; Diane was the queen of Henry's heart and everyone knew it. She was showered with jewels, offices, responsibilities, estates, and other honors that simply could not be overlooked by anyone at court—or beyond. For Catherine, this was a new humiliation.

As the king and queen made their royal entrances, Diane was always to be found right behind Catherine, and all too often the pageants praised only her, leaving Catherine in the wake of the mistress. In descriptions from Paris, for instance, Diane was named in the same rank as the princesses of France, seen looking "regal and proud." In Lyon, a pageant reproduced a forest with the figure of Diane the huntress carrying on her forehead the "silver crescent." In Rouen, a naiade was recited—praising Diane—and the aldermen brought jewels and other gifts made of gold to her feet.[18]

The glory of Diane, however, did not stop there.

When Henry gave Diane the Château of Chenonceau—one of the most prestigious and beautiful royal castles and part of the estate of the crown—Catherine, who thought the castle should be hers, protested vehemently. Once again Henry ignored his wife, continuing to privilege his mistress over her.

Before long, Diane was attracting the attention of the foreign ambassadors who spent time at the French court. In 1550, Edward VI of England sent his ambassador, William Pickering, to offer a compromise between Henry II and the Holy Roman Emperor, Charles V. At the time, the court was staying at the Château of Anet, which had been renovated and also given to Diane. After Pickering's audience with the king, Diane insisted on entertaining the ambassador by showing him the splendor of her castle—and Pickering was indeed very impressed by the beauty of it all.[19]

In 1552 Lorenzo Contarini, another Venetian ambassador, was also struck by Diane's influence at court. As he recalled, "she knows about everything and every single day, after dinner, the king looks for her and spends an hour and a half with her to discuss everything that has happened."[20]

As for Catherine, she was now only useful for ensuring the safe upbringing of the king's descendants—which she did well. After Francis and Elisabeth, Catherine had given birth to another daughter, Claude, on November 12, 1547, and then two years later she had another son, Louis, born on February 3, 1549, though he died a year and eight months later; Charles on June 27, 1550; Henry on September 19, 1551; Marguerite on May 14, 1553; another Francis on March 18, 1555, and twins Victoire and Jeanne, who were born and died in 1556. Catherine had certainly succeeded in securing the dynastic line, despite her continuing domestic frustrations.

Diane, now Duchess of Valentinois, was adamant that she would play a part in the royal children's life, while Jean and Françoise d'Humières were in charge of the health and education of the little princes and princesses. They both worked closely with Diane, which further enraged Catherine. Now, she perceived that a battle for motherhood was about to begin, and in this she was determined not to lose to her rival.

The education and well-being of royal children were always topics of great importance to a queen, and even more so to Catherine, whose significance at court depended perhaps even more than usual on her motherhood. But Diane also spotted an opportunity here: she saw in the royal children a means to further secure Henry's love and adoration. Henry was certainly fond of his children, and he prioritized them as much as his royal obligations would allow.

On October 20, 1548, Henry's cousin Jeanne d'Albret married Antoine de Bourbon at Moulins. After attending the wedding, Henry chose to leave his court behind to spend some time with his children in Nevers.[21] After Henry's visit, the Duchess of Valentinois directly informed Madame d'Humières of the king's desire to see the children once more, writing: "My ally, I didn't wish to let the messenger come to you without this present letter from myself, to let you know that the king will be in Saint-Germain on 12 November." She insisted that "the said Lord goes beyond what is expected of him to see my lord's children."[22]

Diane played the role of intermediary between the parents and their children, enjoying an opportunity to act as a motherly figure. In another letter she sent to her dear friend Françoise d'Humières, Diane inquired about the health of little princess Claude.[23]

Catherine was determined to fight what she saw as the appropriation of the young princes and princesses. She insisted that she visited and wrote to them frequently, and also demanded of Jean d'Humières that he write to her to let her know how her children were doing "as often as you can." She asked for portraits of them, and gave strict instructions regarding their diets, wanting to remain in charge even when she wasn't there with them physically.[24] Catherine might not have been her husband's favorite—and Diane was certainly still the one monopolizing the attention and favor at court—but when it came to the royal children, she was determined that there would be only one mother. Diane never managed to exert the same level of influence on the young charges. She did, however, manage to shape Catherine's relations with another key royal figure: the little queen of Scotland, Mary Stuart, who at the end of 1548 was sent out to the French court.

The arrival of the little queen was welcomed by all: Catherine hoped Mary would get on well with her children, and Henry became fond of her straight away. Noticing Henry's preference for her, Diane did everything in her power to build a bond with Mary too.

Mary Stuart wrote to her mother, Marie de Guise, that her "uncles were taking great care of myself, as was Madame de Valentinois." Then, in another letter to her mother, Mary revealed the influence Diane was starting to have on her: "You know how much I owe Madame de Valentinois for all the love she has shown me, and she would like her granddaughter, Mademoiselle de Bouillon, to be married to the Count of Aran."[25] But Diane also poisoned Mary's ears with stories depicting Catherine as inferior, including one that portrayed Catherine as merely the "daughter of a merchant."[26]

For Catherine, there was no doubt that the she-wolf of the French court was Diane de Poitiers. Her influence over so many courtiers, as well as the little queen of Scotland, the governor and governess of the royal children, and—most of all—Catherine's husband, now knew no limits. Throughout the first part of Henry's reign, Catherine had remained a docile and conciliatory wife, but her frustrations were mounting, and increasingly she felt that these constant insults could no longer go unpunished. If Catherine ever wished to gain her husband's respect—as well as the court's—she had to impose herself, and remind everyone that she was the true queen consort of France.

4

Struggle to Power, 1553–1558

On the evening of July 6, 1553, Edward VI drew his last breath at Greenwich. For the moment, his death had to remain a secret—at least until John Dudley, Duke of Northumberland, could execute the *coup d'état* he'd had in mind for quite some time. In preparation, he occupied and fortified the Tower of London. The idea was simple: Northumberland wanted Edward's death to remain unknown so he could obtain "possession" of his sister, the Lady Mary, who had just been summoned to visit Edward at the royal manor of Hunsdon in Hertfordshire.[1] Before Edward's death, he had also persuaded Edward to agree to change the line of succession—making Lady Jane Grey, wife to Northumberland's son Guildford Dudley, his heir.

On the afternoon of July 10, 1553, at around three o'clock, Lady Jane Grey was brought to the Tower of London to be made queen in accordance with this new line of succession. Mary, however, got wind of the plan, and successfully avoided Northumberland's trap, instead fleeing—along with a great number of supporters, such as Sir Thomas Wharton, Earl of Bath, and Sir John Mordaunt—to Kenninghall Castle in Norfolk. On her way to the castle, the rightful queen was hosted by her supporters, who offered her and her retinue shelter along the route.

As she set out very early one morning, a party from Cambridge—who opposed her cause and who had heard of her arrival—attacked Sawston Hall, the house at which she had been planning to stay. As the mob burned the place down, Mary looked back at the flames and declared, "Let it blaze, I will build a better Huddleston."[2] She went on to keep her word: Sawston Hall was later rebuilt at her own expense.

Edward had made his reasons clear for the change in succession: he simply could not have accepted England reverting to Catholicism under his sister's leadership, a real threat as Mary had always honored her mother Catherine of Aragon's Catholic beliefs. Although Elizabeth might have been a good candidate—particularly considering that, during the later years of Edward's reign, her standing had grown at court—she was also seen as being too loyal to her father's will to accept being first in line herself. Loyalty was one of Elizabeth's guiding principles; she would never betray her half-sister.

As for Mary, the Council was adamant: she and her supporters needed to be crushed. It was therefore agreed, and confirmed with a vote, that Henry Grey, Duke of Suffolk (and Jane's father), should lead an expeditionary force against Mary. In tears, Jane tried to convince her father otherwise—she did not seek conflict with the rightful heir—though her efforts were in vain.

The Council asked Northumberland, one of the most admired soldiers in the realm, to lead the forces against Mary; they assumed, given his renown, that no man would dare stand against him. Mary, however, was not a man, and she was ready to fight for her throne.

Indeed, by now support for Mary was growing throughout the country, with the public sympathetic to her plight: she was proclaimed queen of England in Buckinghamshire and soon after in Oxfordshire too. Her forces were moving toward London and, on July 19, 1553, Mary was proclaimed queen of England in the capital itself. The Council, alarmed by the tide of support for Mary, turned its back on Northumberland, issuing a proclamation that he should "dismiss his army and not to come within ten miles of London, or else they would fight with him."[3] Consequently, he was arrested in the town of Cambridge by the queen's order. Mary had won. Lady Jane Grey's fate was not yet sealed, but being part of such a *coup* could hardly be forgiven.

Elizabeth—who had been staying in Hatfield, away from the power struggle between her half-sister and her cousin—was now ready to support her sister publicly. After all, reestablishing Mary as the right-ful queen of England would further legitimize her own position as rightful heir to the crown, as well as honoring her father.

Ten days after Mary had been proclaimed queen, Elizabeth entered the City of London, riding through Fleet Street on her way to her new town palace at Somerset House. Escorted by 2,000 horses, "with spears and bows and guns," Elizabeth certainly knew how to mark the occasion.[4] Wearing green and white, the Tudor colors, the young princess was reminding everyone of her own dynastic claim to the throne, as well as her support for her half-sister. She would meet her sister on July 30, demonstrating her allegiance to the new queen by bringing so many of her followers with her.

On August 3, 1553, at around five o'clock in the afternoon, Mary arrived in Wanstead, where she changed apparel into a beautiful and regal "gown of purple velvet French fashion," adorned with gold, pearls, and gemstones. Then—accompanied by many gentlemen, squires, knights, and lords, all in velvet coats—she finally proceeded to pass through the city in celebration.

In Aldgate, she met with the Lord Mayor and his brethren. Sir Edward Hastings, Master of the Horse, the Lord Mayor, and Mr. Recorder all knelt in front of Mary, welcoming her: "In token of loy-alty and homage, we most humbly welcome your highness to this your highness's city and chamber of London."

"I heartily thank you and all your brethren aldermen of your gen-tleness showed unto me, which shall not be forgotten," she replied.

Meanwhile, all the streets of London were filled with citizens rap-turously acclaiming their new queen: Mary I of England's reign had just begun.

*

Elizabeth took her place behind her half-sister, witnessing Mary's glory firsthand. The Tudor line had now been rightly reestablished, but the *coup* had given her pause: Elizabeth would never totally forget how rapidly the English people could turn their back on a claimant to the throne, or how easily they could be swayed one way or the other. She saw now that loyalty was something a monarch had to work constantly for, and that once obtained it could not be guaranteed. For a woman whose loyalty to her own family had always been unwavering, it was a difficult lesson to learn.

Northumberland and some of his supporters were beheaded, a clear message that such rebellion would not be tolerated. Meanwhile, Lady Jane Grey and her husband Guildford Dudley remained imprisoned in the Tower, while Jane's father was pardoned—for now. It was prudent, Mary felt, to be seen to show mercy as well as strength. Now Mary was free to make her mark and express her religious preferences: the Mass was soon reestablished, but Mary also sought peace between Catholics and Protestants, and commanded everyone to remove inflammatory terms such as "papist" and "heretic" from their vocabulary.[5]

In truth, however, Mary's religious convictions continued to be a driving force. As the weeks of Mary's reign passed, Elizabeth encountered more pressure to convert to Catholicism at her sister's behest. Elizabeth resisted, which Mary saw as a personal affront, perhaps forgetting her own treatment under Edward's reign.

In early September, Elizabeth sought an audience with Mary at Richmond Palace; in tears, the young princess begged for her sister's understanding. She swore to her sister that she refused the conversion not because of disobedience but rather out of ignorance. She then asked for books and a priest, swearing that she would inform herself and attend the Chapel Royal.

On September 8, 1553—a day after Elizabeth's twentieth birthday— the court celebrated the Feast of the Nativity of the Blessed Virgin Mary. As promised, Elizabeth appeared, though she complained all the way to the church that her stomach ached, a recurrence of the ailment that had plagued her when she resided with the Dennys, another tumultuous time. Nevertheless, her attendance at Mass seems to have pleased her sister. By the end of the month, at the queen's coronation, Mary and Elizabeth seemed closer than ever; on the eve of Mary's big day, Elizabeth joined her at the Tower of London, and she sat beside her at the coronation banquet.

These good relations, however, did not last long.

In officially reestablishing Catholicism as the religion of the country as Edward had feared—and in restoring Catherine of Aragon's memory as rightful queen consort of England—Mary had legitimated herself. In doing so, she had antagonized her younger sister, a fervent supporter of her father's reformed religion, even if Elizabeth had tried to please her by taking part in the religious ceremonies. But Catholic sentiments occupied Mary's mind more than ever, and she even contemplated removing Elizabeth from the line of succession—though some of Mary's advisors disputed the wisdom of this course of action: the young princess carried Tudor blood. Elizabeth knew that tensions were rising, and asked for permission to leave the court. Her request was granted. For some time at least, there would be peace.

Mary had other things on her mind too. Now aged thirty-seven, she had a clear goal: to marry and secure heirs of her own. In her eyes, her husband had to be a warrior king, one who would help her restore Catholicism in England and who would also honor her Spanish origins. With this in mind, she was sure that the future Philip II of Spain was the one for her.

For the people of England, however, even the idea of such a match was an outrage. It didn't take long before rebellious subjects rallied, with rebellion engulfing the south and southeast. One particular force—led by Thomas Wyatt and supported by Henry Grey, Duke of Suffolk—was already gathering in Kent, ready to march to London, leaving Mary with no choice but to confront the rebels.

So, on February 1, 1554, she rode from Whitehall to the City, guarded by soldiers in armor, and addressed a crowd in Guildhall. "On the word of a prince," she said to her people, "I cannot tell how naturally the mother loveth the child, for I was never mother of any. But certainly, if a prince and governor may as naturally and earnestly love her subjects, as the mother doth the child, then assure yourselves, that I being your lady and mistress, do as earnestly and tenderly love and favour you."[6]

Though it is not known for sure if Elizabeth was present at the speech itself, she certainly heard of her sister's success with it and she would never forget the use of such powerful rhetoric, which combined the strength of a king with the motherly love of a queen.

Mary continued her speech, rather twisting the truth when claiming that she never "intended to marry outside of the realm" but that, thanks to her Council's advice and consent, she now saw that an alliance with Philip II would be the best possible outcome for England as a whole.[7] Mary had always felt strongly about her Spanish roots, so no doubt marrying outside of England was always one of her greatest desires, but her benevolent speech assuaged the fears of her subjects.

When Wyatt's army reached the city, he'd therefore already lost the support of the citizens of London, and Mary's troops easily defeated his. The leaders of the rebellion—including Wyatt—were imprisoned and then executed at the Tower of London. This time Mary showed no mercy.

A series of retributions took place in the aftermath, sealing the fate of Guildford Dudley and Lady Jane Grey. At ten o'clock on Monday, February 12, 1554, Guildford was beheaded on Tower Hill, and his wife, Lady Jane Grey—who was only seventeen—watched, knowing she was next. When she saw the block on Tower Green, Jane showed great courage; frightened, she said to her executioner, "I pray you dispatch me quickly." She then laid her head on the block, ready to die, and muttered, "Lord, into thy hands I commend my spirit!" And with that, the axe fell.[8]

For Elizabeth, watching from afar, Jane's death was a cause for concern. It showed that Mary could be utterly merciless. And Elizabeth was right to be worried. Behind the scenes, machinations were beginning. Simon Renard, Holy Roman ambassador to Mary's court, urged the queen to arrest Elizabeth; he had no doubt of her culpability in the recent rebellion and was adamant that, while she was still alive, she represented a danger to Mary's life and rule. The fact that she had not attended Jane's execution, Renard believed, was proof of this. Elizabeth had claimed ill health, but royal doctors certified that she was fit to travel. Nevertheless, Elizabeth agreed to return to court, but what should have been a short journey of about five days actually took over ten as Elizabeth did indeed fall ill, delaying her entry to the capital until February 23—the same day that the Duke of Suffolk, Jane's father, was beheaded.

Elizabeth wore white as she traveled, while her hundred horsemen—who were riding in front of and behind her—were attired in red velvet coats; it was an impressive sight, and Elizabeth knew it. She passed through Smithfield and Fleet Street to Whitehall, where she was supposed to meet Mary—but this time the queen refused her an audience. Instead, the princess was lodged in a remote, secure corner near the privy garden. Evidence against her was growing—there was no point in denying that the rebels had at least tried contacting her about the *coup*—but what remained to be proved was her actual knowledge of their conspiracy, and whether or not she supported them.

On Friday, March 16, Elizabeth was charged with involvement in the conspiracies against the queen, and although she denied it vehemently, she was placed under house arrest. In just one moment, Elizabeth had gone from being the heir to the throne to being a potential traitor to the crown, and now her fate—her very life—was hanging in the balance. She then begged for the opportunity to write to her sister to remind her of a promise she once had made: that she would grant Elizabeth an audience to plead her cause if there was any suspicion of treason against her. This initially was deemed impossible, but eventually the Earl of Sussex capitulated.

Elizabeth poured her heart out in the letter she hoped would save her life. In it, she reminded her sister of the promise she'd once made to her: "that I be not condemned without answer and due proof. Which it seems that now I am, for that, without cause proved, I am by your Council from you commanded to go unto the Tower, a place more wonted for a false traitor than a true subject." Elizabeth also swore, "I protest afore God that I never practised, counselled, nor consented to anything that might be prejudicial to your person any way or dangerous to the state by any means."

She continued by appealing to Mary's sisterly feelings, insisting, "I pray God as evil persuasions persuade not one sister against the other [. . .] with humbleness of my heart because I am not suffered to bow the knees of my body, I humbly crave to speak with your highness.

Which I would not be so bold as to desire if I knew not myself most clear, as I know myself most true." She ended her letter, hoping to demonstrate her allegiance by not insisting further on her own rank, signing it instead, "your highness's most faithful subject that hath been from the beginning and will be to my end, Elizabeth."[9]

The letter did not work. An audience was not granted, which meant Elizabeth was about to spend some of the worst weeks of her life as prisoner of the Tower of London. The next day, she was escorted by water by the Marquess of Winchester and the Earl of Sussex. Despite the popular belief that Elizabeth arrived at Traitors' Gate, she actually landed at Tower Wharf, entering the Tower across the drawbridge to the west of the fortress. She begged for a delay in which she might prove her innocence, but she was immediately rebuked and told that this was simply not possible.

Elizabeth remained in the Tower until May 19, 1554—the anniversary of Anne Boleyn's execution. Even then, however, her daughter was not free; she was once more put under house arrest, this time at Woodstock.

It was during her journey from the Tower to Woodstock, however, that Elizabeth realized just how popular she had become. It seemed that Mary's slights against her had only increased the esteem in which she was held by the English people. Her first stop was Richmond, where she stayed only one night, and then she rested at Windsor, in the dean's lodging, before being invited to Sir William Dormer's house at West Wycombe. Finally, she was hosted by Lord William of Thames in his residence at Rycote in Oxfordshire. Everywhere she stayed, people—especially women—showered her with gifts.

Elizabeth then traveled through several small villages around Oxfordshire, and at Wheatley people gathered to get a glimpse of her, screaming out, "God save your Grace!" Elizabeth was overwhelmed by the support she received wherever she went—and it was probably then that the idea of royal progress, and her own potential rulership, entered her mind.

Although Elizabeth's life was no longer in immediate danger, it didn't mean Mary had given in; she was still determined to impose

Elizabeth's conversion to Catholicism. In the end, Elizabeth showed just enough allegiance, obeying Mary and attending Mass when ordered to do so, to appease the tensions with her sister. Her time at Woodstock lasted less than a year and, during that time, Elizabeth was reminded again of the value of loyalty.

However, there was little doubt that Elizabeth's own popularity continued to grow among the English people while Mary's was clearly diminishing. Elizabeth represented a bright future, the hope of a better England, while Mary was increasingly perceived as an "evil" queen, led by a religious fervor and burning any subjects judged by the Marian regime to be heretics. Perhaps biding her time, Elizabeth made little comment on these events, which surely troubled her, choosing instead in August 1556 to pledge her complete allegiance to her sister, writing, "and like as I have been your faithful subject from the beginning of your reign, so shall no wicked persons cause me to change to the end of my life."[10] In many ways, the tumultuous reality of court life was preparing her for what was to come: a life and reign full of dangers, conspiracies, and victories. But at what cost?

As for Mary, her reign would continue to be challenging. Through her marriage to Philip II of Spain she found herself dragged into the Italian wars, facing the prospect of defeat by France, and by Catherine de Medici—who was to help orchestrate the decisive victory against England.

★

Catherine's precarious situation in the French court echoed Elizabeth's, but their positions remained quite different. Despite feeling undermined, she remained queen consort, not simply a princess in line to the throne. Her biggest challenge remained Diane's ascendancy, but despite Henry's reliance on Diane de Poitiers's counsel—as well as that of his chief minister, Montmorency—a shift in power would soon occur.

Catherine had been steadfast in her devotion to Henry, and despite his devotion to his mistress he had taken notice of this, starting to trust his faithful wife in matters of state. When Henry was elsewhere, he entrusted his wife with the position of regent both in 1548 and in 1552. Catherine's powers were nevertheless quite limited, particularly as Diane saw the nomination as a direct affront to her and used her influence with the privy councils to ensure Catherine had little in the way of real power. In 1548, Montmorency was made co-regent at Diane's suggestion and, during Henry's campaign in Germany in 1552, Diane effectively named Chancellor Bertrandi as co-regent, forcing Catherine to report to him.

"All I desire is to fulfil and obey my lord and husband's wishes," Catherine responded prudently.

By now she was resigned to fighting for what was hers, and when rebellions erupted in Paris during Henry's time in Germany she did not hesitate to make the important decisions. She ordered the arrest of "the two preachers who have been complaining about my king's actions and decisions" and ensured further rebellion was quashed swiftly.[11]

In 1557, things took a darker turn. Due to the war against Spain—and therefore also against England—all of France's troops were being utilized on different fronts: in Italy led by the Duke of Guise, and in Flanders led by Montmorency himself. Meanwhile, Henry was in Compiègne, striving to build a bigger army there to support the constable. Spanish and English troops were engulfing northern France, and the king had no choice but to ask for help from his wife, his regent, who had stayed in Paris. He explained to her that he needed more money—and that the survival of France depended on it. It was the opportunity Catherine had waited for, a chance to show her true potential as leader of her country.

On August 14, 1557, she went to the Parlement of Paris, urging them to fund her husband's army. She knew it would be a request that they did not wish to hear, and that its success depended entirely on her. The Venetian ambassador, Giovanni Capello, had requested to be present and, impressed by Catherine's oratory, he recalled, "with the most imposing form of words, she exposed the needs of the moment." In her speech, she stirred the hearts and minds of everyone present with her straightforward but strong words:

My dear lords, I am come to you because the blood of France is also my blood. We know that during times of war many sacrifices have to be made and that for some cities the cost of war is so great that it is almost unbearable. However, I would not be presenting myself to you if I, and your lord, my king, did not need you in this difficult time […] I do not doubt the confidence, trust, and affection you have for your king, my lord and husband. And in this moment in need, he needs you to grant him 300,000 crowns, 25,000 to be paid over the next two months, to ensure the victory of France and of my king over his enemies. I will not impose myself while you deliberate but please do know that I am asking this with my heart and my love for my king and this country.

After concluding her speech, Catherine left the room and waited patiently in a chamber next door.

She did not have to wait too long, however, as the parliamentarians soon asked her to return, immediately agreeing to the queen's urgent request for funding.

"Your Majesty, we have also made the decision that a hundred notables of the city will now give you 3,000 crowns each so you can support his Majesty more swiftly."[12]

Catherine thanked them wholeheartedly, knowing that she'd just achieved the impossible; somehow, she had touched the spirits of both the parliamentarians and the Venetian ambassador. When her achievement was reported across Europe, and Catherine's oratory praised, she was finally recognized for her political astuteness.

Catherine was thrilled, and knew that her success would be appreciated by her husband. She boasted to her cousin Cosimo de Medici of how "honoured" she felt that her husband "trusted her with such duties." Capello, the ambassador, further noted, "Everyone talks about the prudence of the queen and how well she proceeded in this enterprise."[13] Finally, Catherine was worthy, growing into her regency.

Thanks to Catherine's plea to the Parlement of Paris, Henry was able to fund his campaign and, ultimately, defeat his enemies. It was reported that "when the realm looked as if it was about to collapse, after great defeats, [and] lost territories, France recovered and was now stronger than ever. The French army repelled the attacks and made his enemies tremble."[14] Without Catherine, such a show of military might would have been impossible.

French troops may have been defeated in Saint-Quentin and elsewhere, but in 1558 they finally won back Calais, the city that had been occupied by the English for over two hundred years. This was pure victory, and it was seen by all as Catherine's doing. But across the Channel, Catherine's name had become infamous. The defeat of Mary I of England was something for which Elizabeth, in the years ahead, would never truly forgive Catherine.

Back in France, by 1558 the royal couple seemed closer than ever. Henry saw his wife in a new light, and Catherine asserted that she was more in love with her husband than she'd ever been. But Diane was not pleased by Catherine's rapid ascent. It was clear to her that there wasn't enough room for both of them, and while she appreciated Catherine when she agreed to remain in her shadow, Diane was far less agreeable when the queen finally became ready to perform her role as queen consort and regent at court. She might not have matched Diane's beauty, but Catherine showed she didn't need to do so: she outranked the duchess when it came to far more important qualities of intelligence, prudence, and valor.

★

The year 1558 was a bad one for Mary I of England. She not only lost Calais to the French—despite Spain winning the overall war against France—but her health also deteriorated rapidly. On November 17, she died suddenly at St. James's Palace, aged forty-two, during an influenza epidemic. After years of struggle, Elizabeth would finally succeed her sister and ascend the throne of England. Across the Channel, Catherine de Medici was paying close attention to the rise of another, younger, queen. Neither woman knew yet that, for the next three decades, their fates would be intertwined.

PART 2

Crowns of Thorns and Fire

1558–1564

5

When Death Brings Glory, 1558–1559

The queen was dying, and everyone knew it—including Mary's husband, Philip II, who had chosen to remain in Spain, away from his ailing wife.

Eight days before Mary's death, Gómez Suárez de Figueroa, first Duke of Feria, was sent by Philip to London. His mission? To approve Elizabeth as successor to Mary and to ensure that she would maintain good relations with Spain—strengthened, it was ventured, by a possible union with Philip himself. Even when his wife was in the throes of death, there was always diplomatic business to attend to.

The next day, November 10, 1558, Feria sought out Elizabeth at Brocket Hall to assure her of Philip II of Spain's assistance and support. During the dinner, Elizabeth and Feria "laughed and enjoyed [them]selves a great deal," but it wasn't long before Elizabeth turned abruptly to business. As they talked, she invited him "to speak freely" in his mother tongue.

Feria was so delighted by this invitation that he seemed to forget he was speaking to the future queen of England. "Your highness needs to understand," he said, "that in reality she owes her claim to the throne, not to your sister, the queen, nor the Council of this country, but solely to the king of Spain."

"It is the people of this country who have put me in the present position," Elizabeth retorted in irritation, "and I will not acknowledge that your majesty or the nobility of the realm had any part in it."

Before Feria could add anything further, Elizabeth shrewdly

continued, "I am well aware that the reason why the queen has lost the affection of the people is because she has married a foreigner." Before Feria could respond, Elizabeth leaned forward and whispered, "I will not make the same mistake."[1]

Feria was lost for words, and outraged by Elizabeth's arrogance he wrote immediately to Philip, warning him that "she is a very vain and clever woman. She must have been thoroughly schooled in the manner in which her father conducted his affairs, and I am very much afraid that she will not be well disposed in matters of religion." He finished his letter convinced that "she is determined to be governed by no one."[2]

Little did he know just how true that statement was.

*

On Thursday, January 12, 1559, Elizabeth left the Palace of Whitehall and set out on a ravishing ship. The destination was the Tower of London.

This time, Elizabeth was preparing for her own coronation. She was neither a prisoner, nor under a threat of being one: instead, she was the rightful heir to the throne of England. The daughter of the unfortunate Queen Anne Boleyn had come quite some distance.

On a cold, bleak Saturday at two o'clock in the afternoon, Elizabeth was carried in a litter covered in yellow cloth embroidered in gold, lined with white satin, and borne by two robust mules. The litter was, of course, open on every side so that the people lining the streets could see their new queen as she passed by, going from the Tower to the Palace of Westminster. Elizabeth was followed by earls, barons, dukes, and all nobilities of the country—all well dressed and sitting proudly on their horses. Her ladies were dressed in crimson violet with various linings, given as livery by the queen herself, with gold necklaces as headpieces and a vast array of sparkling jewels adorning their outfits. Pageants floated along the streets, filled with people acclaiming their new queen. At Gracechurch Street, a pageant portraying both King Henry VIII and Queen Anne Boleyn could be

seen by all. Elizabeth was proud of her mother's lineage and inherit-
ance, and intended to celebrate it, reaffirming Anne's reputation; in
matters of family, Elizabeth bore the same courage and resilience as
her mother had done before her.

Elizabeth finally arrived at Westminster Abbey the following day,
where everything was prepared for the much-anticipated coronation.
She was conducted directly to the very spot where Henry III of
England—known as the rebuilder of the Abbey—had been crowned
himself and where he still lies buried: at the east end of the abbey is
the high altar, and St. Edward's Chapel and the shrine of the royal
saint can be found right behind it.

In front of the altar were two thrones: St. Edward's Chair with,
beneath it, the Stone of Scone—used in the inauguration of Scottish
kings until 1296, when it was seized by Edward I—and a chair of
estate. Behind the altar, there was a traverse in which the future
queen could change into the special dress required for the ceremony.

While coronation ceremonies were usually undertaken by the Archbishop of Canterbury, this time someone else would have to step in
and perform the important duty; Archbishop Reginald Pole, a fervent
and devout Catholic who had served under Mary, had died on the
same day as the late queen. A new appointment could not be made
until Elizabeth herself was crowned queen of England. So it had been
decided instead that the Roman Catholic Bishop of Carlisle, Owen
Oglethorpe, would be at the helm of this important ceremony.

Oglethorpe led Elizabeth up to the stage, where he asked the public if they would have her for their queen.

"Yea, yea!" the audience shouted as the trumpets, drums, organ,
and bells all resonated together in celebration.

After this, the service began, but Elizabeth now seemed uneasy.
She gestured to William Cecil, who was not too far behind her, and
then handed him a little book "to deliver to the bishop."[3] Elizabeth
would not be a passive figure in her own coronation; she had to show
Oglethorpe that she was going to be the one writing the script.

At first the bishop refused the book, but after glancing at the
queen—who was staring at him intently—he understood that this

was not a suggestion but an order. Elizabeth would swear the oath in the usual form, but it seemed that the service itself would have to be slightly altered—though the exact nature of these changes remains unknown.

The rest of the service passed without incident, and once it was concluded Elizabeth withdrew into the traverse for the anointing, slipping into the gold and silver coronation robe.

There was gold everywhere: Elizabeth leaned down on gold cloth cushions laid on a gold carpet for the anointing. Three crowns were placed on her strawberry blonde hair in quick succession, the audience cheering each time.[4]

Herself arrayed in gold from head to toe—from the heavy gold of the royal crown now atop her head to her golden shoes—Elizabeth now held the golden scepter in one gloved hand, the golden orb in the other. With her hair cascading down over her robe, her crown seemed to glow with flames. She was magnificent. Finally, it was time for Elizabeth to embrace her destiny; she walked to the throne on the stage to be acclaimed by her people as their consecrated monarch.[5]

Next it was time for the coronation Mass. Once again, Elizabeth ensured there were alterations to the proceedings to suit her desires. For one thing, the Epistle was read twice—once in Latin, and once in English—illustrating that she was already breaking with Catholic tradition, where it was read only in Latin. The Gospel, too, was read twice, again in both languages. Elizabeth was giving clear messages to everyone present: the country was under her own authority, not just that of the pope and the Catholic Church. Bishops across the land, including Oglethorpe, were stunned by Elizabeth's bold attitude, which established from the very moment of coronation what they would be forced to live with in the years to come.

Afterward there followed the sumptuous coronation banquet. As she surveyed her guests, her kingdom laid out before her, Elizabeth had never been so happy. Still wearing the crown, and still holding in her hands the orb and the scepter, she smiled broadly as she greeted everyone who came to offer her their congratulations. She had every reason in the world to feel both joy and relief: she had been crowned on her own terms but, more importantly, after years of hardship and uncertainty, Elizabeth was finally tasting hard-won glory.

★

In France, Henry II—along with everyone in his court—had his eye on the new developments in England. For him, the accession of Elizabeth to the throne changed everything. Most significantly, it meant that the alliance between England and Spain might be diminished. He wished keenly to take advantage of this turn of events.

So, before the end of December 1558, he personally wrote to congratulate Elizabeth:

> You know how sincere and perfect is my amity and the affection that I have always felt towards you. You have already had sufficient proof and security of it. I deeply regretted the war that had sprung between the late queen of England, your sister, and myself and the great and incredible damages I have received from her. I am glad to hear that you are now the present queen and I am hereby assuring you of my continuing affection for you.[6]

Elizabeth, surely surprised by Henry's good wishes, particularly given his stance and treatment of so-called heretics since the beginning of his reign in 1547, decided to play the game and meet his good wishes with her own: "Monsieur, my good brother, I am glad to acknowledge the sincere and perfect amity and affection which you have shown towards me. I most heartily thank you and do assure you that I shall do my part and respond with sincere amity."[7]

This was the first time that Henry, Catherine de Medici's husband, and Elizabeth had exchanged letters. Peace between the two realms was at stake, and the tone of their correspondence suggests that they both knew it.

Yet questions remained. Would Elizabeth turn her back on Spain and remain neutral on the rivalry between Henry and Philip II of Spain? And, more importantly, would she agree to make peace and end the conflicts raging between the three crowns: France, Spain, and England?

The three countries had been at war since 1551, fighting over the numerous territories in Italy—including the Kingdoms of Naples and Sicily and the Duchy of Milan. Henry II of France and Philip II of Spain were truly their fathers' sons, reproducing the same wars and continuing the same old rivalry as the years went on. These battles were hurting all participants, with heavy costs in lives and resources, and there were no clear winners. England had lost Calais, France had lost numerous towns in northern France, and Spain had been busy severing its relationship with Rome.

Immediately after her coronation, Elizabeth decided to send her commissioners to France to defend her interests in the peace talks, choosing three men who had served her father before her; these men had supported his marriage to her mother, Anne Boleyn, and they also had diplomatic experience in France. She thought, therefore, that Richard Cox, Bishop of Ely; Nicholas Wotton, Dean of Canterbury; and the Lord Chamberlain, William Howard, Baron Howard of Effingham, were the right men for the task of defending England's interests on the continent.

Elizabeth's instructions to these men were crystal clear: "Do not conclude anything with the French that may diminish in any point the said old amity with Spain." More importantly, they were to "ensure that Calais is restored to the English crown as it is ours."[8]

While Elizabeth had refused Philip II's hand, she was determined to ensure peaceful relations with him as well as with Henry—but she was adamant that this would not be achieved at any cost. Calais was a matter of pride for the young English queen, and she needed to recover it in order to restore honor to England.

The topic of peace was an increasingly fraught one, too, because now Scotland had been dragged into the conflict, due to its alliance with France through the marriage of Francis, Dauphin of France, and Mary, Queen of Scots. To add to the existing grievances, upon the death of Mary I of England this royal couple had taken up the title, coat, and arms of England as their own, a move that had certainly offended Elizabeth, who complained that "the world is not ignorant of the great injuries offered to us there in France, by taking our arms, style, and title, so many manner of ways, by using seals and commissions into Scotland at this present, with the arms of England and the style of England."[9]

In was clear that this could not go on, and the representatives of each nation agreed that an assembly was required as soon as possible. Only one question remained: where? Cambrai, near the northern border between France and the Spanish Netherlands—and not too far from Dover and Calais—seemed like an appropriate venue. The problem was that the city had been ravaged by the many battles that had raged there in recent years, and many soldiers were still stationed there. They needed a location close to this region, but not so close that it reminded them all of the past trauma, and of the differences that still existed between the three realms.

Christina of Denmark, daughter of King Christian II of Denmark and Norway, dowager Duchess of Lorraine, was brought into the peace talks. Christina had intervened in various diplomatic incidents throughout her first marriage to Francis II, Duke of Milan, and then during her second marriage to Francis I, Duke of Lorraine, and was a woman who understood the art of making peace. She suggested Cateau-Cambrésis, which was only fifteen miles away from Cambrai—a perfect place, she said, for the peace talks to proceed. The Bishop of Cambrai owned a castle where the dowager Duchess of Lorraine could reside when in northern France, and it was agreed that this would be an ideal setting for the meeting between the realms.

The ambassadors journeyed in early February, and on the cold and snowy morning of February 11, the first official meeting took place. In a dark but spacious room they gathered, with the English ambassadors sat at the end of the table, the Spanish representatives on both sides of the table, and the French opposite the English at the other end.

William Howard began the discussion. "My mistress, Queen Elizabeth, wants everyone to know that she does not wish to see her interests being separated from the king of Spain's. She wishes peace between all Christian princes, but her first duty as queen of England is to give back Calais to her people."

"The king of France will never give back the city to the English," retorted the Constable of France, Anne de Montmorency.

Charles, Cardinal of Lorraine—a fervent and devout Catholic, who was sitting on the right side of the constable—barked at the English that "it will cost the lives of a thousand men and mine with theirs before France gives Calais back to you." He stormed out of the room, followed quickly by the constable.

The English, infuriated by the scene that had just occurred, asked for a private discussion with the Spanish representatives.

Nicholas Wotton expressed surprise: "I am so shocked by the stubbornness of the French"; Antoine Perrenot de Granvelle—one of the Spanish commissioners—politely remarked, "I told you that the return of Calais was going to be an issue. Their reactions are hardly a surprise."

Eventually, the French commissioners returned to the table, though the tension in the room was now palpable; it was as though they were all still on the battlefield, anticipating what their enemy's next move would be while also plotting their own.

Wotton was the first one to break the silence, taking a moment to remind the French that the English had a legal right over Calais, a fact much disputed by the French. This dispute threatened to overshadow all other peace talks.

Eventually Anne de Montmorency halted the arguments, which were going absolutely nowhere, with an announcement: "As it stands, the city remains in the hands of the king. Let's move the talks on to other topics and we will come back to this issue another time."

The Bishop of Ely, however, would not have it. "What is your exact proposition?" he asked.

"That we leave things as they are for now and that we will discuss this later on, after other issues regarding the peace have been resolved," Montmorency replied, his tone hardening even more as he added, "I don't see how it is possible for anyone to conceive that a city surrounded by French territories could be separated from French sovereignty—especially after being reconquered recently."

"Elizabeth will not abandon Calais,"[10] said the Bishop of Ely simply.

In response, Montmorency—followed swiftly by the Cardinal of Lorraine—once more stood up and left the room.

The first official meeting had led to no conclusive resolutions for the peace treaty, and the English had started to realize that recovering Calais was going to be a much—*much*—harder task than they had expected.

Days passed, during which the different parties barely muttered a single word to one another. Nothing of much importance seemed to be happening. It was clear that a compromise needed to be found, and fast, but how?

After several days, the Cardinal of Lorraine conjured a nice trick to convince the English to give up on Calais for the time being. "For now," he said, "Calais will belong to the king of France. However, the eldest daughter of the dauphin of France should be promised to the eldest son of Queen Elizabeth and Calais will be part of her dowry. This way, Calais will eventually come back to the crown of England without being a humiliation for France."

"The problem with your suggestion, Cardinal," Wotton retorted, "is that the dauphin and dauphine of France have no children as yet and that our mistress, the queen of England, is unmarried. We cannot accept an arrangement based on your fantasising."[11]

Tensions persisted, and with them came the increasing fear that war would erupt again between the three realms.

The dowager Duchess of Lorraine had had enough of these trifles over a single city, and so on March 3, she invited all the commissioners to her chamber. As the one who had suggested Cateau-Cambrésis, she was the host of the negotiations, a remarkable fact given that the majority of the participants were men. The number of women present at the negotiations remains uncertain. However, it is pretty safe to assume that the duchess was the only woman in attendance with real political influence.

Once more, the English refused the cardinal's proposal, and in

turn a violent dispute erupted between the French and the English—
bringing up, yet again, the hundred-year war that had deeply tarnished
their diplomatic relations. The French threatened to leave the talks
entirely and go back to court, where they would inform the king that
the negotiations had failed and that the war, therefore, was not over
at all.

"Enough!" shouted Christina. Shocked by her outburst, all parties fell
silent, and she took advantage of this as she asked, "My lords, I am sure
we can find a compromise that would benefit all parties, can't we?"

Granvelle—who was supported by Fernando Alvarez de Toledo,
Duke of Alba—declared his agreement. "Our host is right. Let's discuss what may be an easier topic: the alliance and marriage of
Elisabeth of Valois, eldest daughter of Henry II and Catherine de
Medici, with our king Philip II of Spain, as well as the alliance and
marriage between Marguerite of France, Henry II's sister, to Emmanuel Philibert, Duke of Savoy."[12] This was indeed an easier matter to
resolve; both parties were pleased with such an arrangement, which
would ensure peace at least between Spain, France, and the Duchy of
Savoy.

The question of Calais, however, remained a thorn in everyone's
side.

Fortunately, Christina had an idea. She summoned the Spanish and
French commissioners, to whom she suggested "to avoid humiliating
France but to ensure peace with England, what if the king of France
were obliged to give back Calais but in four, six or seven years, and if
he doesn't he should be financially penalised?"[13]

The proposition was attractive, and both parties conceded. The
English, however, remained unconvinced.

Several private talks took place between Wotton and Anne de
Montmorency. Though what they actually discussed is undocu-
mented, this proposal cannot have been far from their minds. Then,
on March 12, everyone reunited in the dowager duchess's chamber,
ready for the next stage of the discussions.

Wotton declared that the English had accepted that "Calais will
remain French for eight years. After this period, the king of France

will have to restore Calais to the English or pay 500,000 crowns to England." He grinned and added, "England will keep the four prisoners arrested at the end of the war. The prisoners will be freed once Calais—or the money—is given to England."

The constable looked pensive for a moment before replying, "Obviously, any English attack on France or Scotland will free the king of France of this commitment to give back Calais."

The English commissioners agreed. It was time for the treaty to be drafted.

And so finally the Peace of Cateau-Cambrésis was signed between England and France on April 2, 1559, and then between France and Spain the next day. The agreed signatures did not mean, however, that the agreement was fully ratified; further steps needed to be taken before peace would be fully secured by all parties and for the ratification to be complete.

On April 21, Henry II sent Sieur de la Marque to the English court for the first ratification of the treaty.

"I imagine that you know what arrangements have been concluded between our respective deputies in the matter of the peace," he told Elizabeth. "I am now waiting to receive your oath of the treaty. Please find mine in the hand of my bearer [Sieur de la Marque]. My son, the dauphin, and his wife, the dauphine, will also send theirs to you."[14]

Mary, Queen of Scots, composed a joint letter with her husband—Francis, the dauphin—to Elizabeth, though she also insisted on sending another letter of her own. In it she wrote earnestly, "Our very dear and loved sister and cousin, how pleased we are to hear that the peace, amity, and reconciliation has been concluded between yourself and our very dear and honoured lord and father the king, between our realms, countries, and subjects for the common good of our three realms. Please find our bearer Sieur de Leddington, who will offer you our oath for the ratification of the treaty."[15]

Elizabeth, however, was not about to be duped; she knew that this monetary arrangement with the French would pose future complications and—as was often the case when it came to diplomatic and political matters—she was right. Nevertheless, she could not afford to go to war against France just because of Calais. So, she signed the treaty and sent her oaths back to Henry.

In her letter to the king of France dated May 3, she thanked the dauphin and dauphine for their oaths but chose not to reply directly to them, implicitly making the point that the matter was between herself and the French ruler, and that she would not fully give up on Calais—not yet, at least.

With the peace finally having been approved by all parties, there were celebrations all over Europe. Henry and Catherine de Medici in particular had great reason to celebrate: their eldest daughter Elisabeth was about to become the queen of Spain.

This was a thought that particularly warmed Catherine's heart. She rejoiced in the idea of having placed her daughter in one of the most prestigious and powerful courts of Europe. After all, Elisabeth would now be able to serve as her mother's eyes and ears, and as she was very close to her daughter, she must have suspected that this prospect could give her diplomatic advantage in the years to come.

On June 15, the representatives of Spain—the Duke of Alba, William the Silent, Prince of Orange, and Lamoral, Count of Egmont—arrived in Paris. Elisabeth of Valois, the shy young daughter of Catherine de Medici, was now to become queen consort of Spain, and Catherine herself could not have envisioned a better or brighter future for one of her favorite daughters.

On June 22, Elisabeth married Philip II of Spain by proxy at Notre-Dame. The whole court attended the religious ceremony, acclaiming the new alliance between France and Spain. At only fourteen years old, Elisabeth showed dignity befitting a queen when, after the ceremony, she was asked to lie down on a bed, with her right leg bare, next to the Duke of Alba, who had his own left leg bare, in order to symbolize the consummation of the marriage. After the official union between the two, Emmanuel Philibert, who had attended the ceremony, and Marguerite de France signed their marriage contract as witnesses.

The celebratory tournaments and festivities began a few days later on June 28. The Palace of Tournelles—not far from the Grand Rue

Saint-Antoine—adapted its premises so that it could host the jousting tournaments that were to take place the next day; triumphant arches, galleries, and platforms had all been erected in anticipation.

Despite the air of jubilation, however, Catherine was feeling increasingly anxious—confiding in her ladies-in-waiting about ominous feelings that she had been turning over in her mind. She was of course happy for her daughter and she fully embraced the new alliance with Spain, but she just couldn't shake off a feeling that something bad was yet to come. In 1552, she had been warned by a famous astrologer—Simeoni, also known as Lucas Gaurico—that her husband would die in a duel around his fortieth year. He had also predicted that Henry would die of a wound that would blind him.

Henry was now forty years and three months.

Catherine had always been superstitious, and now she was convinced that something terrible was about to happen to her family. She started to have frequent nightmares, and on the morning of the jousting event she was burdened with great anxiety, inquiring constantly about the whereabouts of the king and moving about constantly, seemingly unable to sit still.

The tournament commenced on Friday, June 30, and Henry was determined to show the Spanish—as well as anyone else at his court—what a great warrior king he was. After all, he had always excelled at jousting and hunting, so he had no reason to think that this occasion should be any different. He enjoyed any opportunity to show his prowess to all at court, and, more importantly, to his lover, Diane de Poitiers. He was even wearing her colors of black and white. He had no reason to share Catherine's anxieties.

The first joust took place between the king and his new brother-in-law, the Duke of Savoy. Jokingly, Henry shouted to him, "Make sure your knees are tightened because I'm going to hit you so hard; you are about to fall off your horse!"

This is exactly what happened: Henry hit the duke in the chest, and the blow knocked him straight off and to the ground. Henry was not humble in his victory either; he removed his helmet and smiled widely at the audience in a show of triumph.

His next opponent was Francis, Duke of Guise, and this time, though the duke took the hit, he didn't lose control. This time it was a draw.

The audience cheered, enjoying the royal spectacle.

Catherine, who was sitting not too far from Diane, was not so cheerful. She was full of anguish at having to witness her husband fighting so violently against his opponents. In fact, at one point she even stood up and walked to the end of the stage. "My lord," she pleaded, "please, stop now. You have had your fun. Please let's put an end to the game."

"I am just starting!" exclaimed the king, wiping away the sweat that was pouring out from under his helmet.

Catherine glanced at Diane, who remained silent for a moment. Then, with a smile, Diane encouraged her lover to continue fighting for her honor, clearly enjoying the fact that he was doing so while wearing her colors.

Henry's next opponent was a young and dashing courtier, Gabriel de Montgomery, and although Henry was showing signs of fatigue, he was also in a frenetic mood, spurred on by his previous victories.

As the two riders approached each other, Montgomery hit the king violently in the chest. Henry fell off his horse, but seemed unhurt. Catherine gasped at this sight and begged, yet again, for the tournament to end.

Henry, however, was unfazed. He got to his feet straight away and shouted, "Let's have another round!"

"Sir, your majesty, are you sure?" Montgomery asked tentatively.

"It's an order!" the king snapped, clearly irritated.

As he got back on his horse, the king made sure to leave his visor slightly open, so that he could look over at Diane and see if she was still encouraging him. Of course, she was.

Not far from the favorite sat Catherine, silently consumed with fear as she held the hands of her ladies-in-waiting. She kept thinking of the prophecy, reliving the nightmare that had shown her husband's face covered in blood.

This time, as the two riders confronted one another, Montgomery's lance landed straight in the helmet of the king, who fell clean off his horse, blood spilling out of his visor.

The crowd screamed and, in the gallery, Catherine fainted. As his squires approached the king and removed his helmet, the blood continued flowing—by now it was all over both his face and body. The men leaning over the king could see immediately that some fragments of his adversary's splintered lance had pierced Henry's eye.

The king was still breathing—but only just.

"Let's carry him to the castle of Les Tournelles!" exclaimed Montmorency.

The squires did as they were told, picking up and carrying the king to his chambers. He was brought to a bed and joined by both Catherine and Diane, one woman standing on each side, both sobbing. The Duke of Guise was also present, and he did what he could to help, applying vinegar to the king's face and hands.

"Bring Ambroise Paré at once," ordered Catherine, between her sobs.

Only the most famous and talented surgeon could do something to help the king now; only Paré could have the slightest chance of averting the nightmare that was unfolding in front of the king's powerless wife and advisors. The sight of the king of France in such agony was too much for most to bear. Francis, Henry's eldest son, could hardly look at the wound and Mary, Queen of Scots—horrified by the sight of so much blood—quietly asked if she could leave the room.

Ambroise Paré had had a rapid ascent to fame. Born in Laval in 1509, he had followed in his father's and brother's footsteps by becoming a barber. He had, however, higher ambitions: he was determined one day to become a surgeon (though some might say the differences between the two professions were slim at that time). He learned a great deal from his other brother, Jehan Paré—who was a surgeon in Vitré, Brittany—and it was there that he first treated wounds requiring more skills than a barber could offer.

Ambroise recalled his brother's sagacity when treating a patient: he "always showed great caution when treating them." He sought to do the same.

Paré then moved to Paris, where he worked in the only hospital in the capital, Hôtel Dieu. In 1536, he followed the Maréchal de Montjean to the battlefields of Italy where, at the time, the war between France and Spain was raging. This was where he conducted military surgery—and Catherine hoped this skill that would be invaluable for Henry as he writhed in agony.

During his time on Italian soil, Paré saw a large number of horrific injuries caused by gunfire, the most common remedy being to cauterize the wounds with fire—a practice Paré found absolutely barbaric as well as completely unhelpful. So, he developed an unusual, and successful, method to heal the soldiers in pain: he cauterized the wounds using boiling sambuco oil. Once his remedy was proven to be successful, Paré promised himself "never again so cruelly to burn the poor soldiers wounded by arquebus."[16] From this moment, he became a pioneer in the treatment of serious wounds.

However, Paré had not yet been granted the title of official surgeon and, despite having worked for the king at various military camps over the last decade—and his discovery of an extraordinary alternative to cauterization with fire—he had not actually been nominated as a royal surgeon either.

The official royal surgeons had been trying to ease the king's pain by removing some of the splinters found in his eye, and they had also applied some mixture made with egg whites to the wounds, but they hadn't done much more than that. In truth, they had no idea what they should be doing. Could Paré offer a better solution?

Paré was tall, with a mix of dark and silver wavy hair, and when he entered a room he commanded immediate respect and admiration, exactly as he did when he entered the room where the king lay dying. He proceeded with a thorough examination of the king's eye.

"Bring me the lance and give me every detail of what actually happened," he said, after a silent inspection of the wounds. He turned to Catherine and added, "Your majesty, would you consider ordering the execution of three or four prisoners so I could practise my operation on them before trying what I have in mind on the king?"

"Straight away, Paré," she replied, before turning to her guards. "You have heard him." Off they went to execute the unlucky men.

Soon, the doctor was practicing on the corpses laid out in front of him, assisted by some gentlemen and gentlewomen of the court who were eager to witness such an extraordinary event; after all, the operation Paré was performing, right in front of them, was the very first of its kind.

When throwing the lance in the first two corpses' eyes, he missed the target entirely. On the third, he tore open the face instead. "You can get more corpses if needed," Catherine assured him. Finally, on the fourth victim, Paré managed to reproduce a wound similar to that of the king's.

After hours spent examining the wound, and imagining how the body might possibly have been affected by it, Paré was full of despair. Avoiding Catherine's teary eyes, he muttered, "I am sorry, but this is a lost cause. I cannot save the king."[17]

Henry did not die straight away; for ten days he stayed alive, in agonizing pain. He took his last breath on July 10, 1559—leaving behind a wife, seven children, and his royal favorite.

In the last days of Henry's life, Catherine had ordered Diane to leave both his bedside and the court. The Duchess of Valentinois already knew that the life she had enjoyed was coming to an end. Upon hearing the news of Henry's death, Diane wrote to Catherine, begging for "pardon for my past offences against your person," and humbly signing the letter, "your most obedient and loyal subject."[18] With this letter, she also sent back some crown jewels that Henry had gifted to her during her time at court. For the first time, true power lay with Catherine, and Diane was anxious about the queen's reaction. Would she take everything away from her? All her lands, titles, and castles? Would she even take away her life?

Catherine, however, must have been feeling generous. She decided to leave the duchess with everything she had acquired over the years, including all her lands, titles, and castles—that is, all but one. Catherine took back the castle of Chenonceau, one of the most prestigious royal castles in France. It would be hers and hers alone. Diane had no choice but to retreat to the castle of Anet, where she would eventually die in 1566. Catherine had—eventually—defeated her rival.

But despite this personal—and, to some extent, political—victory, Catherine could not hide her sorrow. She could not hide her tears in front of her ministers or ladies-in-waiting. The pain of losing her husband, who she had loved deeply in spite of his flaws, was just too strong to bear. She felt that she was now all alone again in this very hostile world, as she had been as a young orphan. This time, her enemies were watching her every move and, worse, they were surrounding her royal sons. The survival of the dynasty depended solely on her, and her ability to navigate the troubled waters that were now flowing through a treacherous court.

*

Unsurprisingly, all princes and princesses of Europe diligently offered their condolences to the widow, who was only forty years old. Her son, Francis II, and his wife, Mary, Queen of Scots, became king and queen of France. For Catherine, losing the love of her life—even if she was not the love of his—was an unfathomable pain and she wrote of her "extreme sorrow" in correspondence with Philip II's sister, Joanna of Austria, princess of Portugal.[19]

Another queen also offered her most sincere condolences. When Elizabeth I was informed of the king of France's injury, she "showed a great displeasure and sorrow." She swore to Gilles de Noailles— resident ambassador at her court, who had just broken the news to her—that she wished that "there had been no spear in France" so that the king would have never been injured.[20]

At the news of Henry's death, Elizabeth first wrote to his successor, Francis, expressing her sorrows and hoping that the alliance with France "continues in strength."[21] The queen of England chose not, however, to write to either Mary, her cousin, or Catherine, the new dowager queen of France—at least not yet. She was asserting her status as queen regnant and therefore choosing to only write to her equal. Nevertheless, she had suffered losses in her own life and surely understood the pain that Henry's family must be feeling.

Catherine was mired in grief but, thinking of her children, her mind turned gradually to more practical matters. Her husband was dead, yes, but she was the mother of a king—as well as three little princes and two little princesses—who she meant to protect. Though her position was changed, through her family she knew she had the potential to forge strong and durable diplomatic alliances all over Europe in order to guarantee Henry's legacy.

It took until September 1559 for Elizabeth to acknowledge Catherine's new role at the French court. She sent a special envoy, Sir Peter Mewtas, to once more offer her condolences to the French king, but this time she included a letter to Catherine herself. It was the first letter of many that Elizabeth wrote to the woman who was about to become her French rival—and perhaps her greatest rival of all.

Catherine was touched by Elizabeth's words of condolence. "We thank you affectionately for the letter you have presented to us through your bearer, Sir Peter Mewtas," she wrote back. She also used this letter to share her personal sorrows with Elizabeth, while also approving the alliance between England and France. In her correspondence, she had mastered the art of diplomacy, mixing the personal with the political to obtain the confidences of her correspondent and, in doing so, establishing herself as a political player. A powerful woman herself, Elizabeth could respect this.

"We are suffering a great and lamentable loss with the death of our late lord and husband, the king. We are glad to hear that you want to continue the good amity and peace with our son, the king," she wrote, before swearing that all she wanted and prayed for was "to increase the common good, peace and tranquillity between our realms, estates, and countries, as we have just declared it to Sir Mewtas."[22]

Meanwhile, Francis II and Mary ascended the throne of France; on September 21, Francis was crowned in the Cathedral of Reims, where all the kings of France had been anointed before him. Catherine attended wearing a black dress—as was tradition, she would mourn her husband until her death. As for Mary's coronation, it would take place at a later date, as the Salic law—which prevented women from ascending to or having any rights over the throne—baldly stated that the coronation of a queen consort was not of the same importance as that of a king.

Shortly after her son's coronation, Catherine decided against taking the title of Queen Dowager of France, the usual one for a woman in her position. Instead, she insisted on being called Queen Mother—a title that suited her and her political ambitions, aligning her more closely with her son and his new power while perpetuating a maternal image. After all, he was only a boy of fifteen, and Catherine knew he would require her assistance to navigate the complex world of the court. Legally, he was considered king in spite of his tender years, but his health had always been fragile, and the question of who would help the young king exercise his power had already been asked more than once.

Much to the queen mother's horror (and despite Francis's own devotion to Catherine), Mary's uncles, the Guises, considered themselves the frontrunners in this contest, and were already taking over the most important offices in the French government, to the immense pleasure of their very young niece. They chose to cast away Anne de Montmorency from court and office; he had been too influential during Henry II's reign for their taste. Catherine was unhappy with this turn of events, but she nevertheless assented, deciding to bide her time.

One thing was clear, though: Mary was about to become a thorn in both Elizabeth's and Catherine's sides. Nor was peace going to be so easily attained.

6

Fight for Peace, 1559–1560

Sir Nicholas Throckmorton was an experienced diplomat. He had been assigned to the French court since May 1559 as Elizabeth's first resident ambassador, and following the death of Henry II Elizabeth had to ensure that Throckmorton's position was not compromised. So she wrote to the new king, Francis, insisting "that our trusted ambassador should stay at your court as long as it pleases us."[1] No one objected to the suggestion. Elizabeth was particularly pleased with her choice as Throckmorton was so loyal to her, as well as stubborn and resilient—qualities needed to navigate the tricky game rules of the French court.

The fourth of eight sons of Sir George Throckmorton, Sir Nicholas Throckmorton was the cousin of the last queen consort of Henry VIII, Katherine Parr. He had met Elizabeth when she was only a teenager, when serving in his cousin's household. He was a staunch Protestant who had been waiting for Elizabeth to become queen for years so that he might see his religion honored.

Although publicly he supported Mary I, he had been tried for conspiring against her in the Wyatt Rebellion, despite swearing that he had no involvement whatsoever in the enterprise. After being sent to the Tower of London, where he was held for a year, he then fled to France before being called back and pardoned by Mary in 1557. When Elizabeth ascended the throne in 1558, Throckmorton shrewdly positioned himself as a loyal and devoted councillor to the new queen, rapidly gaining her trust and winning the French embassy in the spring of 1559.

Being a Protestant ambassador at a devout Catholic court proved to be even more complicated, however, than even he had anticipated.

Following the death of Henry II, Throckmorton paid particular attention to the attitude and actions of the newly appointed king and queen of France and reported his observations back to Elizabeth. For the past eight months they had been adopting the title, style, and coat of arms of England as their own, something that infuriated Throckmorton's mistress. If they continued to use the title, style, and coat of arms of England, it could well cause a diplomatic incident. Unfortunately, this proved to be the case. When their seal was finally produced, both Francis II and Mary officially used the English title—introducing them as "Francis and Mary, By Grace of God, King and Queen of France, Scotland, England and Ireland."

In September 1559, the royal couple invited Throckmorton for dinner—almost certainly so that he would have to face the humiliation that the new king and queen of France were falsely declaring themselves to be his true masters. The message was more than clear when Throckmorton was served his dinner in silver dishes bearing the usurped insignia.

After the dinner he wrote to Elizabeth: "I'm afraid the king and queen of France are determined to cause you offence and use your legitimate title. It appears that this obstinacy is pursued more by the queen, Mary, than by her husband."[2]

This was a blatant affront to Elizabeth's authority, but it was also a punishment to the English for supporting the reformist rebels—referred to as the "Lords of the Congregation"—who had taken up arms against Mary Stuart's mother, Marie de Guise, as dowager queen of Scotland. Meanwhile, the Scottish Protestant Reformation had begun. Among its leaders were Mary's illegitimate half-brother, James Stuart, as well as the preacher John Knox, who abhorred female rule—especially if the women were Catholics. Elizabeth may have been a female ruler herself but she shared the rebels' dislike of Catholic power at such close proximity.

Mary Stuart insisted that her husband, the king of France, must send troops to Scotland to vanquish the rebels and protect her mother.

The Scottish Congregation, led by the rebels, were now fully determined to ensure that Catholic France was no longer in control of
Scotland, and so made a pact of assistance with William Cecil, Elizabeth's principal secretary. At this point, the Peace of Cateau-Cambrésis
was not yet officially ratified, and Elizabeth wanted to avoid conflict
at all costs—at least, officially—in case there was ever any chance of
England getting Calais back.

By February 1560, the matter was still unresolved. Then, on the
25th, Throckmorton was invited to dinner by Mary's uncles Charles,
Cardinal of Lorraine, and his brother Francis of Lorraine, Duke of
Guise. Of rather short stature and with a perfect straight Greek nose
and thin lips, Charles did not have his brother's charisma, but he did
share the same determination to promote his family's interests above
all else. Soon, the trivial dinner conversation turned into a session of
remonstrance.

"My mistress, the rightful queen of England, finds it very worrying
that the king of France has sent some troops close to the Anglo-
Scottish border. Are we at war again?" Throckmorton asked.

"Not at all," Charles replied. "France is the ally of Scotland and our
queen, being also the queen of Scotland, is simply defending her realm."

"The problem, you see, Cardinal, is that it is hard for the English to
fully understand the true intentions of the French when the king, and
especially the queen, of France also bear the arms of England. This
could be seen as a hostile act."

The conversation continued in a similar vein, with all the preju-
dices of both sides against their rival thrones clearly in play.
Throckmorton knew he needed to be cautious—the peace that had
only recently been secured was fragile. But he also knew he could not
appear weak.

"We want to preserve the Treaty of Cateau-Cambrésis but we won't
be duped, and we won't ignore the actions of the French at our northern border, nor how the king and queen of France used our mistress's
title, style and coat of arms," Throckmorton warned his hosts.

The cardinal snapped back, "Likewise, as we know that your mistress, your queen, is supporting the rebels in Scotland—helping them

to overthrow our sister, the dowager queen of Scotland, and our niece, queen of Scotland and of France."

"She's simply defending her northern borders," Throckmorton replied.

"Well, if this is her only intention I'm sure your mistress, the queen, will have no problem reaffirming her accord to the French rulers. After all, we have done nothing other than treat you well, as you are a representative of her crown, and I can assure you that the king has you in great esteem. On the matter of the title, the king and queen of France were using the title before the treaty was signed. If this was such a problem, why has your queen agreed to signing it?"[3] The cardinal grinned and, before the ambassador could reply, he added, "Do I need to remind you that my niece, the queen of Scotland and France, is the great granddaughter of the late King Henry VII of England and, as such, has legitimate rights to the English crown?"

Throckmorton, of course, could not deny Mary's bloodline. "While she is indeed a descendant from that house, she ought not to bear these arms without any differences, using them in the same way as her own, and employing them on seals, using the title of Queen of England..."

The cardinal interrupted him. "How about your mistress, the queen of England, using the title of queen of France?" he asked.

The trick here was to preserve peace while making it clear to the French that this usurpation of title was simply not acceptable. Throckmorton remained calm and composed. This, obviously, was a completely different matter.

"Cardinal," he said, clearing his throat, "you know as well as I do that the kings of England have long justly borne the arms of France. Besides, the coat and arms are not entirely similar—ensuring that it causes no offence to the French monarchs. The fact that the king and queen of France are adamant in bearing the title of England makes my mistress, the rightful queen of England, suspicious of their true intentions regarding her realm and herself."

"What a strange fear to have," the cardinal replied, frowning. "Haven't we just signed a peace treaty with England?" he asked.

"Furthermore, when Francis and Mary chose to bear the arms of England, France was at war with England—so it was within their rights to do so."

"They were at war against the late queen, Mary, not Queen Elizabeth," Throckmorton pointed out, "and bearing the title, style and coat of arms of her kingdom during peace time is an insult to her."

The cardinal scratched his nose, seemingly pondering what to say next, and eventually replied, "The peace and amity with England is important to the king. Tell me what would satisfy the queen. As for the injuries done to the French, we will forget them."[4]

Throckmorton—who was startled by such a sudden change of attitude—promised that he would pass this message on to Elizabeth, as well as reassuring the cardinal that England was also determined to preserve the peace.

Before long their conversation came to an end and Throckmorton left the meeting, quite satisfied with both the outcome and with how he'd handled himself. He hadn't won much yet, but he felt he'd made a strong case for Elizabeth's legitimate rights to the English throne.

Later that day, Throckmorton was invited to accompany Francis, Duke of Guise and brother to the cardinal, to meet the queen mother and Mary. During this meeting, Catherine dominated the conversation and, as a result, her young daughter-in-law; she didn't let her say much, always interrupting her and insisting that the French rulers wished for nothing more than to have peace with England.

"You can assure your mistress that we only have good opinions of her," Catherine said calmly. She then turned to Mary with a meaningful look—a sign that she was waiting for her to support her stance on the Anglo-French alliance.

"Yes, the queen, my good sister, may be assured to have a better neighbour in me, being her cousin, than in the rebels, and so pray I you signify unto her," Mary said.

This allusion to the rebels was probably not what Catherine had in mind, but nevertheless the show of support would do for now.

Both queens then adjourned, leaving Throckmorton amazed at having witnessed firsthand the new power play at the French court.

Catherine might only be queen mother, but she was certainly not going to let her son's wife be a dominant figure at court. For too long, Catherine had been in the shadow of more beautiful and charismatic women, but not this time. She would make sure of that.

The next day, Claude de l'Aubespine, secretary to the king, went to meet Throckmorton, assuring him of the king's "total determination to preserve the peace with England and to satisfy the queen of England, his good sister and cousin."[5] However, the specific details of that satisfaction still needed clarifying; the English ambassador was left with many promises but very little in the way of evidence to back them up. Nevertheless, the meeting showed that Catherine had convinced her son to pursue his alliance with Elizabeth.

In March 1560, the king sent a letter to Elizabeth assuring her that he was more determined than ever to pursue the amity between their two kingdoms, and Catherine also used this opportunity to dispatch a letter to Elizabeth. In it she explained, "I did not want you to receive the letter of the king, my son, without this letter from me."[6] It was certainly a token of Catherine's true desire to seek peace with the English queen, but it was also a way to demonstrate her power, which she felt matched Elizabeth's.

What was clear to Throckmorton, though, was the growing power of the Guise family, and this was a cause for concern. The Guise family were already one of the most powerful houses of France—if not Europe—thanks to their lands and to the Duchy of Lorraine, an independent state with a strong influence on its neighbors. The power of Francis, Duke of Guise, and his brother Charles, Cardinal of Lorraine, had increased exponentially now that their niece Mary was queen. For many Protestants trying to survive in the realm, the Guise influence over the royal couple—and especially over the young king—was too much to bear. They feared that their radical Catholicism would eventually mean a harsher stance on heresy and the Protestant community in France. And they were right to fear this.

The question throughout the land was now this: how to counterbalance the Guise influence on the young king?

A group of provincial aristocrats—led by Godefroy de Barry,

Seigneur de La Renaudie, from Périgord—decided to take action. Several influential Huguenot gentlemen, including Charles de Castel-nau de Chalosse, Bouchard d'Aubeterre, Edme de Ferrière-Maligny, and Jean d'Aubigné, father of Aggripa d'Aubigné—a famous French Protestant poet—joined the group, discussing how they could kidnap the king to ensure he stayed away from the Guises. Gaspard de Col-igny, who would later be a leader of the Huguenots, chose not to get involved and convinced other nobles in Normandy to do the same. The risk was just too great.

Unfortunately for the plotters, rumors of the conspiracy reached Charles, Cardinal of Lorraine. The Guises had to act fast, transferring the king and court from the castle of Blois to the castle of Amboise, a far more defensible site.

The Guises ordered the whole village to be on the alert—explaining that the very life of the king depended on it—and as soon as the con-spirators arrived in the city of Amboise in early March 1560, they were arrested. Those who managed to flee with La Renaudie plotted to storm the castle and, on March 17, they attacked. Their forces were easily defeated.

Two days later, La Renaudie was finally caught, and was drawn and quartered without trial, his flesh later displayed at the gates of the town along with a placard reading: "La Renaudie, leader of the rebels."[7] Even more horrifically, all of his followers—around 1,000 men in total—were hanged on iron hooks on the façade of the castle and from nearby trees. Others were drowned in the Loire or left in the hands of the people of Amboise.

Catherine attended the executions with Charles, her second son, by her side. While she did not wish to persecute Protestants at that time, she supported the decision to have the rebels executed as they had committed high treason against her son, and he must be pro-tected at all costs. She did not avert her gaze even once throughout the grizzly proceedings and, when Mary showed signs of disgust, Catherine glared at her—a queen, Catherine believed, should not show any weakness. She had after all mastered her own emotions throughout her marriage, despite the humiliations she had endured.

Throckmorton reported the outcomes of the conspiracy to Elizabeth, but what interested him more was how the Guises had used the
unfortunate event to their own political advantage. "On 11 April," he
wrote, "all the pardons for those who were not active in the conspiracy were proclaimed with trumpets at Amboise. The house of Guise
have been warned that the conspiracy has not ended and have ordered
that the townspeople and countrymen are forbidden to go armed
during the king's stay at Tours."[8]

There is no doubt that installing so much control over the popula-
tion enabled the Guises to grow their own military power, to the
extent that they were now fully in charge of the safety of the French
royal couple. Elizabeth knew that this threatened conflict on the
question of religion, and she realized that she must continue in her
support of the Scottish rebels in order to protect Protestantism—even
though this posed a great risk to relations with the French, who were
not fools and who realized these were her intentions. Elizabeth knew
that she could not afford to let her guard down: she did not wish to
see any French vessels approaching her immediate neighbor. So she
sent yet more money and supplies to the Scottish rebels—hoping this
would prevent France from taking over Scotland through Mary
Stuart.

Marie de Guise—Mary Stuart's mother, who had been acting as
queen regent of Scotland for six years—struggled to subdue the
rebellion. Mary wrote to her mother, sympathizing with her difficulties and praying "that God will assist you in all your troubles." She also
swore that the French would support her and that the queen mother
herself "had wept many tears on hearing of your misfortunes."[9] In her
last letter to her mother, Mary Stuart insisted, "My husband, the king,
will send you sufficient aid, as he promised me to do, and I will not
allow him to forget it."[10]

Marie de Guise eventually died—with the struggle for power in
Scotland still unresolved—on June 11, 1560. Mary was devastated, and
she was now more determined than ever to crush the rebels in Scotland. It was a wish she would never see fulfilled, as Spain intervened
in the conflict between England, France, and Scotland.

The peace treaty that had finally been signed by all parties a year earlier was now under threat, even if the reality was that Spain could not afford to go to war again so soon. Philip II sent two special envoys, one to the French court and the other to the English. The Cardinal of Lorraine took this opportunity to offer a special alliance with Spain against both Scotland and England, but while this was attractive enough in terms of restoring the old faith in both countries, it was just too risky for Philip to alienate Elizabeth.

Throckmorton ensured that he followed M. Schantonet, the special envoy to the French court, everywhere he went, assuring him that, "if the French gave up the arms and style and revoked their forces, the queen would dissolve the league between her and Scotland."

"We are definitely pushing for such a resolution,"[11] the Spanish ambassador replied.

Furthermore, it became clear to Throckmorton that Philip had joined forces with his mother-in-law, Catherine, to undermine the Guises' power at the French court. If the family managed to get their hands on the three crowns of Europe—France, Scotland, and England—their power would directly rival Spain's. It was an abhorrent thought for the Spanish king who was left with no other choice but to support England and Elizabeth.

Despite Throckmorton's warnings to Elizabeth regarding the French preparations for war, revealing that "a Frenchman named Vincent, servant to Monsieur d'Oysel, has been of late at Leith with two ships, and put into the town thirty barrels of powder and 10,000 crowns," and despite the fact that other towns seemed to be equipping for combat, negotiations between the three crowns and the Lords of the Congregation continued to take place. The outcome, eventually, was good for England.[12]

On July 6, the Treaty of Edinburgh was signed. It was supposed to be a coda to the Treaty of Cateau-Cambrésis, but in reality it was a totally new document that established the victory of England and the rebel lords over Mary Stuart. Francis and Mary were required to officially recognize Elizabeth as the rightful queen of England, as well as renouncing the use of the arms and title of England. French and

English troops had to leave Scotland at once. But perhaps the most insulting part of the agreement for Mary was that the rebels demanded that the council of nobles become the official government of Scotland, and that she remain an absentee ruler. France also had to admit that, ultimately, Elizabeth's involvement in the rebellion was only as a means to an end in order to preserve the Peace of Cateau-Cambrésis. It was a slap in the face for the French rulers, who never fully took part in the negotiations and who were essentially forced by Spain to agree to all the clauses. It was a huge win for Elizabeth, who had shown all her European counterparts that she was a powerful political player.

Elizabeth thanked Philip for his assistance herself, saying she could not deny that she had received "many proofs of his regard for her, both before her accession to the throne and since." Indeed, she considered him her "very dear brother" and thanked him "greatly for all his support to ensure that the peace between me and the French has been concluded."[13]

However, the matter was far from being resolved. Francis and Mary now had to ratify the Treaty of Edinburgh, though they hoped that by delaying this, they would never have to do so and accept the treaty's humiliating demands.

Throckmorton complained to the Cardinal of Lorraine, who was the first advisor to the royal couple. "I hope that the king and queen of France will ratify the treaty soon and that it will be sent to me so I can dispatch it to my mistress, the queen of England."

"There must have been a misunderstanding," the cardinal replied, grinning. "The king thought he had to send his through his ambassador at the English court, Michel de Seurre, not through you."

"It was never agreed this way!" Throckmorton said, furious; this was clearly going to create yet more delays and complications.

The cardinal continued to give him empty promises that the peace treaty would soon be resolved and ratified. "I am particularly saddened that, because of all these complications, the rest of my house has fallen into your queen's disgrace," the cardinal lied. "All we have ever wanted is amity with England." These delays were causing more damage to

Elizabeth and Mary's relationship, damage that might never be repaired. Catherine, meanwhile, was watching closely. She attended all negotiations and discussions whenever Throckmorton had an audience with the royal couple, but remained strategically silent on the issues under discussion. It was clear that she did not wish to officially support her son and his wife in a matter that could endanger the peace with England. Throckmorton continued to appeal to Mary to sign the treaty, but in an audience in September, she called his bluff:

"I am the nearest kinswoman she has, being both of us of one house and stock, the queen my good sister coming of the brother, and I of the sister."[14] Smiling sweetly as she took her leave, Mary was once more insisting on her own dynastic rights to the English crown. Perhaps, Throckmorton considered, the tensions between the two cousins was too great for peace to ever be truly achieved. Catherine, who had accompanied Mary to the meeting, once more remained silent. Undoubtedly, she took note of the ways in which Mary behaved, and how careless she was when it came to preserving peace with one of her neighbors. Surely, this would not have been an attitude she admired, but Catherine despised Throckmorton, who had challenged her authority many times. She was content to watch him struggle.

*

In the autumn of 1560, Francis had started feeling rather unwell, delaying the French king's consideration of any and all important matters, including those with England and Scotland. One evening, in mid-November, he had just come back from hunting near Orléans when he started to feel dizzy and complained of a buzzing in his left ear. A few days later, when at church, he collapsed, suffering from a terrible headache. Soon after, he was assigned to bed. It is likely that the king was suffering from a severe ear infection, but at the time, the source of his illness remained a mystery.

Catherine could not stand seeing her son in such a state, and in late November, a completely heartbroken queen mother wrote to her former sister-in-law, Marguerite de France, Duchess of Savoy. "I am so saddened by the misfortunes and woes that God has sent me after so much suffering with the death of my late husband, the king. Now the sight of the king, my son, in such pain causes me extreme grief."[15] Clearly, Catherine was bracing herself for the worst. She and Mary were nursing Francis night and day, and she insisted that his food was tasted before all his meals—Catherine was losing faith, as well as trust in anyone and everyone at court. Heavy discharge from Francis's ears continued to affect him, and, in order to relieve the pressure from the fluid appearing in both the king's ears, the royal doctors insisted on operating on him. The operation seemed to be a success but, just as the doctors started to hope that the king would shortly recover, Francis became feverish. And then, finally, the worst happened: Francis II died on the evening of Thursday, December 5, 1560.

*

In the space of just eighteen months, Catherine had lost both her husband and her eldest son, two much-missed kings. Charles, her second son, was next in line but at nine years old he was too young to rule alone. Catherine, mindful of the way the Guises had sought control of her departed son, knew that she had to move fast to become the one who would rule in his name. With this in mind, Catherine wrote to her eldest daughter, Elisabeth, queen of Spain.

"God has taken your father from me, and has now taken your brother, that I have loved so dearly, away from me. I am left with three young sons and a divided realm. I have now to preserve my authority, not for myself, but for the preservation of this realm and for the common good of all your brothers, all of whom I love."[16]

On December 21, 1560, as mother of the young king, Catherine was granted by the Estates General the title of "Gouvernante de France." With this title, Catherine essentially matched Elizabeth as a ruling queen, this time exercising royal power on behalf of her nine-year-old son, Charles IX.

Finally, at forty-one years old, it was her time to rule.

7

The King in All But Name,
the Virgin, the "Gouvernante,"
and the Widow, 1561

Mary Stuart's life had been turned quite spectacularly upside down. A moment ago she had been the queen of both France and Scotland, as well as holding on to the title of the queen of England, but now she was mere queen of Scotland. She had never been in such a precarious situation, and now the Guises were panicking at the prospect of losing all their recently acquired power.

Charles IX was the new king of France. As he was only nine years old, however, and very close to his mother, it was clear that Catherine's diplomatic role was to grow. Nevertheless, she had to move fast if she wanted to gain control over both the government and the French court.

As Charles was still a minor, it wasn't long before the question of a regency arose. Of course, as a woman in France, she could not hope for the official title of regent; the Salic laws of the fourteenth century had ensured that royal women could not be made queen regnant or effectively rule over the realm. This did not prevent women—such as the she-wolf, Blanche de Castille—from becoming powerful figures at court. No such woman, however, had ever wielded as much power as Catherine now did in France.

Her first move was to ensure that she could moderate the Guise influence, so with this in mind, she outright rejected their proposal to offer Mary's hand to the young king. In all honesty, Catherine had already had enough of the younger queen when she was married to her late son; she felt Mary had shown her little respect over the last decade. She reinstated Anne de Montmorency as constable of the realm—forgiving him for his past offenses when he'd been an agent of her rival, Diane de Poitiers. She hoped that this would secure his loyalty. She was correct.

To ensure she wouldn't contravene the Salic law, Catherine was named "Gouvernante de France"—in other words, she could rule on behalf of her nine-year-old son without being given the official title of regent, even if she was essentially acting as one.

She ordered the creation of a huge seal in order to celebrate her new position, which depicted her standing proudly, the scepter in her right hand and her left hand raised with the "index finger pointing upwards in a gesture of command." In this seal she was finally portrayed as the woman she felt she really was: the ultimate ruler. Inscribed beneath her portrait was "Catherine by the Grace of God, Queen of France, Mother of the King."[1]

Marc-Antonio Barbaro, the Venetian ambassador at the French court, reported back on Catherine's ascent, noting that the queen mother's will was "considered supreme above anything else. She is the one who has the upper hand in all negotiations, to the extent that her authority will be fully preserved and in the Council there will be no other master but herself."[2]

Giovanni Michieli, Barbaro's predecessor, also praised Catherine "for her incredible intelligence, consideration, and ability to undertake any type of negotiations."[3]

Eventually, Catherine also gained the support of the Estates General, who had been impressed by the skills praised by the ambassadors.

Her reign had finally begun.

*

In order to rule her entire kingdom effectively, Catherine also had to show favor to some Protestant nobles to ensure their loyalty. She decided to name Antoine de Bourbon, king of Navarre, who was a prince of the blood (so would be in line for the French throne if the Valois kings died without any heirs), general lieutenant of the realm.

She was sure that such an appointment would not compromise her own rulership, as she told Sébastien de l'Aubespine, Bishop of Limoges and ambassador to Spain: "The position that the king of Navarre holds here is beneath mine and under my authority."[4]

Michel de L'Hôpital—who was made chancellor on April 1, 1560—worked with Catherine to register the Edict of Romorantin, which was designed to protect Protestants from the Inquisition. This apparent toleration of Protestantism, however, had to be handled carefully, as Catherine did not want to alienate her Catholic ally, Philip II of Spain—especially after he had helped her to undermine the Guises' power at court. She also hoped that an increase in compassion would erase memories of the Amboise conspiracy of 1560, and peace and stability would ultimately prevail. In this, however, she was mistaken, though her actions did at least allow her to consolidate her power and to secure peace with the Protestant states of Navarre and England.

Mary quickly understood that her glorious time in France was finally over and, on her first day as widow, the young queen returned her crown jewels to Catherine de Medici. She certainly did not wish to alienate her mother-in-law, and she desperately wanted to avoid having any kind of confrontation, knowing she now depended on the older woman's kindness. Catherine, in turn, ordered a full inventory of the items that were handed over to her—a sign of her distrust toward her former daughter-in-law, as well as her now complete domination of her.

Mary chose to leave her grand royal apartments, instead retreating to a private chamber to mourn the death of her husband. She knew she needed to plan what came next for her and what sensible steps she would need to take. After all, Mary knew she had lost the support of Catherine when the queen mother sided with Elizabeth and Philip II on Scottish matters and the Treaty of Edinburgh.

However, the problematic treaty still needed to be ratified, and Mary was now more determined than ever to make sure this didn't happen, seeing it as her last chance of retaining a crumb of power. Nor were her uncles ready to give up maneuvring for her, and for themselves. As a young widow who was also queen regnant of her own realm, Mary was still a great match for any prince of Europe. The Guises—who were now thinking about their own political future as well as their niece's—knew that they needed to get closer to Spain if they were to succeed in making a match. They therefore began negotiations for a potential marriage with Philip II's son, Don Carlos, who had remained unmatched. This was the perfect opportunity to ensure Mary's continued importance on the European political scene while also offering a possibility of overshadowing her two other rivals: her former mother-in-law, the *gouvernante* of France, and her cousin, the virgin of England.

However, an alliance between Scotland and Spain through Mary and Don Carlos would jeopardize what Catherine had been trying to achieve. Her ultimate goal was to marry all her children off to different European rulers so that her bloodline would eventually control all of Europe. She would not tolerate any interference from Mary.

By April 1561, therefore, Catherine was more determined than ever to undermine Mary's marriage proposal to Don Carlos, and complicit in this she had one of the best allies at the Spanish court: her daughter, Elisabeth, queen of Spain. Philip II was very fond of his third wife—so fond, in fact, that he never missed an opportunity to show his affection for her in public. She was, he said, everything he had ever wanted in a wife, with all the qualities he sought: Elisabeth was pious, humble, devoted, and submissive. But what he took for submission to himself was largely submission to the will of her mother, who had for years advised her daughter on how to be a good wife to the king of Spain—particularly on the thorny question of how to avoid having to deal with any rivals to her husband's heart.

"I've heard rumours that there is some jealousy among your ladies," Catherine told her. "The trick, my dear daughter, is when you find yourself alone, in your private chamber, spend all your time playing with them; in front of people at court, do the same."[5] Catherine feared that if her ladies-in-waiting did not like her daughter enough— and that if some sort of rivalry emerged because of this—they would seek Philip's favor instead. Catherine dearly loved her daughter, and did not wish to see her overshadowed by a favorite, the fate she had suffered with Diane. And on a political level, the newly appointed regent desired to maintain Philip's allegiance.

The other person working relentlessly for the queen regent at this time was Sébastien de l'Aubespine, Bishop of Limoges, who had been accredited to the Spanish court in 1558 and who had proved to be a loyal confidant and advisor to both Elisabeth and her mother. With slightly crossed eyes and an imposing beard, Limoges had the stature and appearance of a statesman. Always composed and diligent, he took his role very seriously, watching over Catherine's eldest daughter as if she were his own child.

With her two agents in place at the Spanish court, the queen mother of France was confident that she could speak her mind about the potential union between Mary and Don Carlos. She just might have a shot, she thought, at sabotaging it.

"While it is clear that my son, the Catholic king of Spain, is worried about the new position of the king of Navarre at the French court, for religious reasons, you must make him understand that my allegiance to him and Catholicism has not wavered—and never will."

She then ordered Limoges to "Prepare my daughter for the part she will have to play in these discussions. What is at stake is too high not to have everyone playing their part." The aim was to convince Philip himself that the match was not a good one, and that, perhaps, France could offer him a much better option.

"I am determined," Catherine said, "if the marriage negotiations of my daughter, the queen of Scotland, with Don Carlos, have been progressing as much as we think they have, that we have to do everything in our power to slow it down and delay it indefinitely. For that, I am prepared to offer another potential bride to Spain: my little daughter, Marguerite. This will help me achieve what I want."[6] For Catherine, there was nothing more important than consolidating and securing her sons' dynasty as well as protecting their family legacy. All her actions now were driven by this potent mix of maternal instinct and personal desire for power.

While the queen regent was resolved to maintain and preserve the

Catholic faith in her realm on behalf of her son, as well as developing strong relations with other Catholic powers, she was also shrewd enough not to antagonize those who did not share her faith—especially the ones that shared a common goal. This was the case for Elizabeth, the virgin of England, who—like Catherine—did not wish to see a union between Mary and Don Carlos. In her eyes, nothing would be more abhorrent.

In a letter on the matter, Catherine swore to Elizabeth that no other French monarch had been more determined to "continue and increase the amity and alliance that exists between this crown and yours, that truly pleases us, assuring you that it is one of the things in this world that we desire most—and our actions will prove it."[7]

The regent signed, "your good sister and cousin, Caterine," as protocol required, though this also propelled her to the same regal rank as Elizabeth—certainly a sign of the esteem in which Catherine held herself.

Elizabeth responded with a letter through Throckmorton, destined for Catherine, stating that she would also maintain the "alliance between our two realms."[8] While she kept it short, the two queens knew that—at least for now—they had a common goal in mind: to hinder the marriage negotiations between Mary and Don Carlos.

At Elizabeth's behest, Throckmorton was diligently gathering any and all relevant information that could potentially sabotage the negotiations. He was received by Gaspard de Coligny, who had been Admiral of France since 1552 and who was now also a Huguenot leader. Both men showed a great deal of respect for one another and, in a private conversation, the admiral spoke plainly.

"The marriage between Mary and the prince of Spain is very likely to take place, and it seems that it is so greatly advanced that it will not be broken. I don't think that the king of Spain esteems the marriage for Scotland only. He has eyes on England," he said. "That marriage will bring great danger to religion and to England—and for France, if both England and Scotland fall into the hands of the king of Spain."

Throckmorton agreed that this would be a terrible outcome. "Thank you for your honesty, Admiral," he replied. "I can assure you that my mistress, the queen of England, will employ all her help to the promotion of God's true religion and that she will do all in her power to prevent the match."[9]

★

Months earlier, a rather important figure in European politics—and a close relative of Catherine's—had foreseen this necessary alliance between Catherine and Elizabeth. Lucrezia de Medici, Duchess of Ferrara, daughter of Cosimo I de Medici, Duke of Florence, and cousin to the *gouvernante* of France, had been watching the political situation closely. Cosimo and Catherine had grown up together when Catherine was a young orphan; born only two months apart, their familial bond was strong, and Lucrezia venerated the queen mother of France.

In order to strengthen the dynastic alliance between the Medici and Este families, Cosimo's daughter had been promised to Alfonso d'Este, Duke of Ferrara, and in February 1561, she finally entered the duchy. Unfortunately, the young Medici did not survive long enough to enjoy her role as Duchess of Ferrara; she would die of pulmonary tuberculosis on April 21, of that same year.

In early January 1561, before departing for Ferrara, Lucrezia had chosen to visit her kinswoman, Catherine. She met with her at Orléans, where the French court was residing because of rumors that the plague had hit Paris. During her time there, Lucrezia showed her appreciation of having two queens ruling neighboring countries. Dressed in her favorite black, silver, and gold attire, and wearing plenty of jewelry—especially rubies, which adorned her chest and her hair—Lucrezia invited Throckmorton to her lodgings for dinner on January 6.

"Please sit next to me, ambassador," she said as he entered the room.

Throckmorton was pleased to be received so gracefully. However, he had not anticipated such familiarity.

The duchess spoke plainly. "I owe your mistress, the queen of

England, great love, not just because she is a Christian and virtuous queen, but also because she has set forth in her realm the true service, glory, and honour of God, and I trust other princes in all Europe will follow the good example she has thus set."

Throckmorton nodded, showing appreciation of this statement.

Lucrezia continued, stating that "God has blemished the fame of the great men of the world through the doings of a weak woman. All the greatest princes of Christendom desire her in marriage. Yet your mistress has done what neither her sister nor ancestors could do, for by the occasion of her religion she has obtained the amity of Scotland. Please know that many who are not of her religion are persuaded that the Lord has prospered her—even the queen mother, my dear cousin, a virtuous and sage lady herself."

Throckmorton was surprised by her frankness, but he was also very pleased. "My mistress, the queen, will be more than pleased to hear this," he told her. "She will most thankfully accept your good affections."

"You should go and find the queen mother, ambassador," she replied. "You should offer her some persuasions, there being no means so certain for a perfect amity between France and England." She continued, "After all, there was another cause which would convince your queen and Catherine to pursue a good amity. There was an old acquaintance between your queen's mother and the queen regent, when the former was one of the maids-of-honour of Queen Claude, sister of Renée of France, my own mother-in-law and dear friend to Catherine de Medici herself. They were friendly towards another. There is no reason for Elizabeth and Catherine not to continue that friendship."[10]

The mention of Anne Boleyn stunned the English ambassador; it had never crossed his mind that the reputation of Elizabeth's mother in France could be used as a diplomatic tool to reinforce Anglo-French relations. "I will not forget to mention this to my mistress," he replied before quickly taking his leave.

Elizabeth's reply to Throckmorton did not mention his private audience with the duchess; the queen must have wanted to wait a little longer before deciding upon her alliance with the queen mother of France. She was still quite unsure of Catherine's true position on England.

Despite Elizabeth's caution, Lucrezia was right: at this precise moment in history, the *gouvernante* and the virgin had more reason to be united than divided. This was to prove true when Elizabeth and Catherine were finally united in undermining the Guises' scheme of marrying their niece to Don Carlos, Prince of Spain.

The marriage negotiations were finally abandoned in mid-1561: Philip II of Spain had decided against marrying off his son to the Scottish queen. Mary was now seen as an enemy—or, at the very least, someone Catherine and Elizabeth would need to keep a watchful eye on. Other questions remained: would Mary stay in France or return willingly to Scotland? And would she finally sign the Treaty of Edinburgh?

James Stuart—1st Earl of Moray, half-brother to Mary, Queen of Scots, and member of the Scottish Lords of the Congregation— traveled to France in spring 1561 to talk to Mary about eventually returning to Scotland and ruling alongside the Congregation. Once in Paris, James desperately sought a secret meeting with Throckmorton to discuss his sister's actions and behavior. He found the English ambassador in his lodgings and asked for a private audience. Throckmorton was delighted to accept.

"I am here to warn you on a few matters regarding my sister, the queen of Scotland," James began.

An intrigued Throckmorton was all ears; he even grabbed some paper and a quill to write everything down. He had no doubt that this intelligence would be invaluable to Elizabeth.

"She is not disposed to ratify the Treaty of Edinburgh," James told him. "She has told me directly that she will defer it until she comes to Scotland, and she has already ordered that the estates of the realm should not be assembled, and that no matters of importance are to be ordered or answered during her absence." James paused for a moment before revealing that his sister was "not glad of the kindness and concord that currently exist between England and Scotland. She fears the queen of England is preferred to herself in her home country."

Upon hearing this declaration, Throckmorton could not hide his grin. There was little doubt that, as things stood, Elizabeth was favored in Scotland—at least by the Scottish Lords of the Congregation.

James continued, "My sister is careless of the amity of France as she is of England. She is pursuing an alliance with a powerful foreign prince as she hopes that it will turn the balance of power upside down." James also warned Throckmorton that rumors were circulating in Lorraine regarding Elizabeth's own religion. "The Cardinal of Lorraine and my sister, the queen of Scotland, commented on the cross and candles in the chapter of your mistress, the queen of England. They said that she was not yet resolved of what religion she should be."

"The testimony of my mistress's conscience bears witness to the religion she professes," Throckmorton replied. "Beyond religion, the queen of England has been making peace with her neighbours. Constable Anne de Montmorency himself told me just the other day that my mistress was the happiest princess and her standing the best in Christendom. She has had great honour of her enemies, and has honourably kept promise with her friends."[11]

Elizabeth herself had promised that "we do not mean, nor ever meant, to make changes of the order of religion."[12] For two and a half years now, thanks to the 1559 Acts of Uniformity and Supremacy, Elizabeth had ensured that a compromise between Catholicism and Protestantism had been found.

James Stuart agreed. Elizabeth was a wise ruler who knew—at least, for now—how to preserve peace in her country while also "defending God's religion."

As James took his leave, Throckmorton was left with more pressing matters to consider. For one thing, Mary was still showing no sign of accepting the treaty, creating an avalanche of problems for England and for the much-needed peace in Europe.

A few weeks later, James returned to Scotland. He had convinced his sister to put him in charge until her return, but she had refused to allow him any power regarding the ratification of the treaty.

For Catherine, the delay only emphasized what had become evident during the marriage negotiations between Spain and Scotland: Mary could not be trusted. She was no longer welcome. "The Scottish queen cannot leave France fast enough," Catherine asserted.[13] So, in spring 1561 preparations were made for Mary to return to Scotland by sea, though both Catherine and Elizabeth still sought a resolution to the treaty before her departure. In late May, Mary fell ill with the ague, further delaying any discussions. Finally, in June, Mary accepted the invitation of the king and the queen mother to visit them at court, with a diplomatic dinner planned for the 18th, which would bring together the queen of Scotland, the French rulers, and the English ambassador.

During the dinner, Throckmorton did not hold back. "My mistress is glad to hear that your health has improved, Madam," he started. "She, however, thought that with the ratification of the treaty being such a pressing matter, she would renew her demand."

"Being not in perfect health as yet, and though I remember all the things you have recited previously, I delay my final answer to this until the matter has been scrutinised by the Estates and nobles of Scotland. I intend to leave soon for my home country," Mary said. She glanced at Catherine as she said this, who could not hide her pleasure at the announcement of Mary's impending departure. Mary then continued, smirking as she said, "As the matter touched them as much as it touches me, I would not proceed with the ratification without their advice. I am sure you understand my position, ambassador?"

Throckmorton's blood was surely boiling, and it was through gritted teeth he replied, "I am not desirous to fall into the discourse on how those terms first began, but may I suggest that there could be no better occasion offered to put away the former unkindness than by ratifying the treaty? I would also like to remind you that the Estates of your realm have already consented to the treaty, and all it needs now is your signature."

"Not everyone has consented to it, Sir Nicholas!" Mary snapped. Then, after taking a moment to regain her composure, she smiled and continued, "Once I am among them, I will enquire if they are all of the same mind. I desire nothing more than the amity between our two countries."

"I am sure that my mistress, the queen of England, will use similar means to you to induce you to be of the same mind," Throckmorton threatened.

"I trust that the queen will not encourage any of my subjects to continue in their disobedience against their rightful queen, nor to take upon them things not appertaining to subjects. And though there is a greater number of a contrary religion than I desire, there is no reason why subjects should give a law to their sovereign, especially in matters of religion," Mary replied, before taking a sip of her wine.

"Your realm, Madam, is in no other case than the other realms of Christendom are. You have been away from your realm for a long time. Your mother, a woman of great experience, had kept your realm in quietness until she began to constrain men's consciences."

"God commands subjects to be obedient to their princes," she shot back.

"Only if those things were not against his commandments," Throckmorton replied.

The tension in the room was palpable. Both Charles and Catherine had remained silent during this verbal sparring; no doubt Catherine was fascinated to see how far Throckmorton would push the queen of Scotland into revealing her true goals for Scotland, and—in consequence—for England. The queen mother had certainly not been unaware of her former daughter-in-law's real ambitions, and felt vindicated as she finally heard her reveal them.

"Well," Mary finally said, "I will be plain with you and tell you what I would want all the world to think of me. The religion that I profess I take to be most acceptable to God, and indeed, neither do I know, nor desire to know, any other. Constancy does become all folks well, but none better than princes, and such as have rule over realms, especially in the matter of religion. And though I am young and not greatly learned, I have this matter of dispute by my uncle, my lord cardinal, and I find therein no great reason to change my opinion."

"You should be more conversant with the Scriptures," Throckmorton replied, "and that if peradventure you are so partially affected by your uncle's arguments, you could not indifferently consider the other party. I also have to tell you that your uncle, the cardinal himself, confessed to me that there were great errors and abuses in the Church and great disorders in the ministers and clergy, insomuch as he desired that there might be a reformation of both."

"I have heard him say the like," Mary agreed. Catherine was watching the two protagonists with the utmost attention.

"All I hope for is a unity of religion throughout Christendom," said Throckmorton with a sense of finality.

"I hope so too," came the response, "but I am not one of those who change their religion every year. I do not wish to constrain the faith of any of my subjects, but I trust that you will not support that your mistress, the queen, constrains mine. All I wish is a good and perfect amity between my cousin, the queen, and myself."[14]

In the end, as Catherine must have noticed, the matter of the ratification had been rather expertly buried by Mary Stuart, who once more avoided giving any clear answers to her English counterpart.

★

Elizabeth continued to consider the matter. In July 1561, she ordered her ambassador in Scotland, Thomas Randolph, to "deliver my letters to the Three Estates of Scotland. They need to press the queen of Scotland to ratify the treaty before returning."[15] The Tudor queen also sent letters to the French court for Charles IX, Catherine, and Mary. In these she complained about her cousin's behavior toward Catherine, hoping that Mary would be "showing her kindness, honour, and friendship" to her kinswoman.[16]

Elizabeth was impatient, and as a result was ready to make things more difficult for Mary. On July 14, the Tudor queen informed Charles and his mother that she would not grant "a safe-conduct to the Queen of Scots, on account of her not ratifying the Treaty of Edinburgh."[17]

Mary, who feared that Elizabeth would use her navy to stop her ship on its way to Scotland, finally outlined the reasons for her refusal. "The Treaty of Cateau-Cambrésis, from which the Treaty of Edinburgh stems, specifies nothing respecting me as queen of Scotland, and refers solely to the king of France and the queen of England. The form of the second article must be altered before I can ratify it. I have already agreed and proved my sincerity by withdrawing my troops from Scotland into France. Since the death of my late husband, I have never used the arms of England and Ireland, but I refuse to order that the ones that exist in private houses be defaced."[18]

In response, Elizabeth swore that she consented "to suspend her conceit of all unkindness, and assure you that I am fully resolved to unite a sure bond of amity, and live in neighbourhood with you as assuredly in the knot of friendship as we are in that of nature and blood."[19]

Mary still refused to ratify it, however, and went yet further—she now stated she would never do so.

Finally, to Catherine's utmost joy, the Queen of Scots was ready to leave France; on August 14, Mary embarked on a vessel from Calais to her native Scotland. "Farewell, my beloved France, farewell. I do not think I shall ever see you again," Mary said, weeping as she departed.

A month after Mary's departure, a scandal over Elizabeth's legitimacy erupted both in France and abroad. *Regis Angliae Henrici hujus nominis octavi assertion septem Sacramentorum adversus Martinum Lutherum* had just been printed in Lyon with a preface written by Gabriel de Saconay, a fervent Catholic, and it had been sent to the French court and beyond as a separate document. The book and the preface, which was circulating at court and all over France, defamed Elizabeth and her parents even more so—especially Anne Boleyn, who was referred to as Jezebel—a term that would later on be attributed to Elizabeth herself in other propagandist pamphlets against her rule. Throckmorton had to work quickly and nip the scandal in the bud before it could further undermine his queen.

In an audience with the French rulers and their closest advisors, granted to Throckmorton at the end of September 1561, Anne de Montmorency, Constable of France, was in total agreement. "This book is pure defamation and needs to be suppressed!" he shouted at their meeting. "The author should be punished. We have to do the best we can to defend the queen of England's reputation."

Catherine agreed. "This is indeed an outrageous book and we will react accordingly."

Satisfied with their reactions, the English ambassador took his leave and met with one of his closest allies in Paris: Admiral Coligny.

"How did the queen mother react to the news of Saconay's book?" Coligny inquired.

"She showed outrage and said that the French rulers will supress it," Throckmorton replied.

"I am glad she has made so good an answer, and I hope this will satisfy your mistress, the queen of England," Coligny said.

Before taking his leave, Throckmorton asked Coligny to pass on the message to the king of Navarre to ensure that the banning of the book was enacted throughout the whole of France.

"I am sure the king of Navarre will do so with pleasure. The queen of England need not fear the king of Navarre's good affection towards her in this or any other matter,"[20] Coligny promised him.

When Elizabeth received this news, she was naturally pleased that the French rulers and their advisors were supportive of her. However, she knew things weren't always as straightforward as they might appear, and she still instructed Throckmorton to continue to "investigate and ensure the suppression of Gabriel de Saconay's lewd and slanderous book. I want the author of the preface to be punished for slandering not only me but also both my parents, King Henry VIII and Anne Boleyn."[21]

On this, Catherine was in full agreement with the English queen, and indeed would now personally oversee the situation, as she wrote to Elizabeth. "The printing of the book that has defamed the late king of England has been suspended and it has been forbidden to sell it or send it throughout the realm for sale. I can assure you and the queen of England, my good sister, that I will continue to do all in my power to ensure that the book remains censored."[22]

★

At four o'clock in the afternoon on October 6, Henri Cleutin, Seigneur d'Oysel—representative of Mary in France and mediator between Elizabeth and the Queen of Scots—was invited by Francis, Duke of Guise, to the Hôtel de Guise. The Guises had been watching Mary's situation play out and were keen to avert a total breakdown in the relationship between their niece and the other ruling women.

"The way I see it, Monsieur d'Oysel, is that your role is to ensure that there is a perfect accord between the queen of England, and my niece, the Queen of Scots, who is a widow. The principal point of the past unkindness between the two queens, and consequently between the queen of England and ourselves, was the bearing of arms and using the title of the realm of England by my niece," the duke explained.

D'Oysel agreed. The damage that this had caused between the two cousins seemed almost irreparable.

"Throckmorton might perceive by Saconay's book," the duke continued, "that all were not of the same opinion of the lawfulness of the queen of England's title, and that she has no cause to resent the matter either against the Queen of Scots, or us, being her uncles. We have in the past made good of our niece's title, seeing both divines and others of quality did allow it. But we have to be excused, because then there was a war between England and France." The duke paused for a moment. Then, looking more serious than ever, he continued, "If the queen of England should die without issue, I will support the queen of Scotland's lawful heir to the crown of England. For she is descended from Queen Margaret, eldest sister of King Henry VIII."[23]

Mary's claim to the English throne was still very much on her uncle's mind.

D'Oysel reported his conversation to Throckmorton who, in turn, diligently informed Elizabeth of the discussion. The scandalous book had already reminded Elizabeth that the legitimacy of the Tudor queen could be easily contested in the Catholic realm. It could just as easily happen again. The only way to prevent this, Elizabeth knew, was to finally secure the ratification of the Treaty of Edinburgh. It was the only way to ensure that Mary would not betray her by plotting against her.

While Catherine and Elizabeth had shown a common front against Mary's ambitions to ally with Spain and challenge Elizabeth's legitimacy, there were other tensions elsewhere in their kingdoms that threatened to spill into new hostilities. The growing schisms between Protestants and Catholics across the lands were about to bring the two queens into direct conflict.

8

The Lying Game, 1562–1564

Throckmorton could not have been happier. After all the hardships he had endured at the hands of the queen mother of France, in 1564 he finally received the letter he had been waiting for from Elizabeth. For in this letter was confirmation that he could finally return to England. The request had been made often during these last years of tension, and repeatedly denied, and then postponed due to the continued uncertainties. But now he was free to go.

> Once you have secured your safe-conduct from the French rulers, which I believe they will grant you this time, you will be able to return to England. Before you do so, ensure that the French king and his mother have agreed to revoke all ships of war from the seas so your journey is as safe as it can possibly be.[1]

With Throckmorton finally out of the picture, could Elizabeth and Catherine start afresh? Since 1561, when Mary returned to Scotland, new conflicts meant that the two queens had been at each other's throats. Throckmorton himself had experienced firsthand what it meant to be caught in the firing line, but the dawn of 1564 seemed to mark a new beginning. But what had prompted this animosity between Elizabeth and Catherine—the two queens who in previous years had never stopped declaring their good intentions toward one another?

★

Catherine de Medici found herself in the crossfire of the conflict between Catholicism and Protestantism in the early 1560s, striving to rule on behalf of her son, and determined to defend his interests and the crown's, while enemies hid around every corner. The pressure was strong from each side of the religious debate—the Huguenots and the Catholics, represented in France by the Guises—each of whom sought favor. For Catherine, finding a way for them all to coexist was paramount.

On January 17, 1562, the Edict of Saint-Germain—also known as the Edict of January—came into force on Catherine's order, stipulating that the practice of the reformed (Protestant) religion would be legal, but only under specific conditions: that it was celebrated during the daytime, outside of towns, and with participants unarmed. This was, in many respects, a way to avoid a repeat of the situation in Amboise almost two years earlier. Catherine knew she needed to appear tolerant if she was to attract support from both sides of the religious divide.

However, this edict sparked great discontent among Catholics, who saw it as a disavowal of their own religion. Francis, Duke of Guise, who was leader of the most radical and fervent Catholics, returned to court with just one goal in mind: securing the abolition of this heresy.

For Catherine, it was clear that his return meant that her authority would be challenged. But she had a tactical mind, and she was also willing to resort to political machinations if this was what was required to secure the legitimacy of her son's position. She was more than ready to confront the duke and his grievances. But she never had the chance to do so: fate was about to intervene.

Early in the morning of Sunday, March 1, Francis, Duke of Guise, made a stop at Vassy while on his way to the French court. A small town in Champagne, not far from Joinville, this was one of the residences of the Guise family. Indeed, Vassy was a fortified town; it protected a royal castle that had been given to Mary Stuart as dowager queen of France, which in turn she had offered to her uncle, Francis. Earlier, in October 1561, a Protestant church had been established in the town, creating great scandal among the faithful Catholics of Vassy and beyond. The townspeople begged Francis to remedy the affront that the establishment of this church had caused to the reputation of their home.

That morning, the duke—accompanied by his wife, Anne d'Este, who at the time was a close friend to Catherine de Medici, and his brother, the Cardinal of Guise, and two hundred of his men on horses—decided to address this slight, confronting the Huguenots who were praying at their church. Since the church was within the ramparts, the Duke of Guise claimed it was an affront to the new Edict of Saint-Germain, which firmly stipulated that the reformed religion could not be practiced within town boundaries.

"Go and enquire why they are contravening the Edict!" the duke ordered three of his men.

At the steps to the doors of the church, inside which six hundred Huguenots were praying, an argument flared between the Guises' men and the Protestants, with both stones and insults being thrown at the party of the duke. One of the duke's men—whose identity still remains uncertain—became unable to keep his temper and, along with several other Catholics, charged on the unarmed Huguenots. Between 25 and 50 people were killed, including 5 women and a child, while 150 others were injured.

This was a massacre, led by the Guises.

News of the incident spread quickly around the whole country. While fervent Catholics welcomed the news, seeing the Duke of Guise as a triumphant hero defending the true faith within the borders of France, the Huguenots saw this affair as a declaration of war. If violence was what the Catholics wanted, then violence was what the Huguenots would give them. The first French religious civil war had just begun.

At court, Catherine received the news with despair.

*

Catherine was soon confronted with another major political event: a meeting of the Council of the Roman Catholic Church, the purpose of which was to reply to the doctrinal challenges of the Protestant Reformations. The 19th Ecumenical Council was due to be held on January 18, 1562, and it was to be an important meeting: the balance of power in Europe was at stake.

With the reformed religion gaining more and more followers in Switzerland, parts of German countries, and in Scotland—as well as the return to the Protestant faith in England—France was struggling to contain the heretical ideas within its borders. Catherine knew this, of course, but there was little she could do without alienating her allies. She valued the king of Navarre's influence at court to counterbalance the Guises'. But perhaps her political games were costing her the stability of her realm.

In early March 1562, before the news of the Vassy massacre had reached their ears, Throckmorton and Admiral Coligny met in secret near Fontainebleau. Coligny admitted to Throckmorton that he had just had a very important conversation with Catherine that he needed to share with his English ally.

"The queen mother has confided in me," Coligny started. "She admitted that she would welcome a strong reform of the Church, especially that the Catholics should stop imposing their laws upon Protestants."

Although Throckmorton remained silent, he was intrigued by this revelation. He could not imagine a woman as discreet as Catherine revealing so much to the admiral.

> She even suggested that the queen of England and the other Protestant princes should send their delegates to the Council, in order to state and name their grievances to the assembly and explain the abuses committed by the Roman Catholic Church. In her opinion, it would allow us to ask for a free General Council, where all parties may be impartially heard.[2]

Throckmorton was curious about Catherine's motivation. Indeed, in his letter to Elizabeth, he expressed his concerns: "Is there any way for your Majesty to have proof that the queen mother was speaking sincerely, seeing that she and the king of Navarre were bent to advance Papistry and overthrow the Protestant religion, not only in France, but in other countries?"

He continued, "After all, the queen of Navarre, the Prince of Condé, the admiral, and all his house have been forced to retire from the court. These proceedings in France greatly discourage the Protestant states of Germany to hope for any good in this common cause."[3]

In her response to Throckmorton Elizabeth stated that, while she valued Catherine's advice, she would "not send any ambassador to attend the Council where the pope is head, his Legate President, his Cardinals assistant, and all having a voice therein to take an oath to maintain his authority. No decree can be hoped for other than that which the pope shall like."[4]

While Elizabeth and Throckmorton were concerned with whether or not they should send delegates to the Council, Catherine was now dealing with the aftermath of the massacre in Vassy.

She was deeply concerned with the repercussions of the massacre, particularly on the fragile peace that had been established between the two camps. As a result, she had written to the Prince of Condé, begging him "to help me to preserve this realm and to serve the king, my son." She wrote, "I have ordered that arms should be laid down but I have not been obeyed, which greatly displeases me. I need you to obey me and not take up arms. It would lead to the total ruin of the realm."

Her request fell on deaf ears. Condé's reply was simple: "My honour would suffer greatly if I were the first one to give up arms."[5]

It seemed that Catherine and Charles could not avoid a descent into war. On April 2, Condé joined forces with his long-term Huguenot ally, Admiral Coligny, to take the city of Orléans, a former well-positioned Catholic stronghold that allowed them to remain not too far from the capital. Within a few days, Rouen was also in the hands of the Huguenot forces. On April 8, Condé confirmed that his loyalty and allegiance to the king and the royal family remained unchanged, and that the ultimate aim of the Huguenots was to free them from the Guises and their influence.

Overseas, Elizabeth was watching. This growing instability gave her the perfect opportunity not only to support the Protestant cause on continental Europe but also to regain what England had lost: the city of Calais.

And Spain had its own part to play too. In this first French religious civil war, Spain was supporting the Guises. With Elizabeth and the German princes behind the Huguenot forces, it was rapidly becoming a great European contest between Catholic and Protestant powers.

★

The situation worsened, with Protestants and Catholics massacring each other in almost every town in France. In Sens, three Catholic monks were viciously attacked, and their throats cut. In Tours, two hundred Protestants were drowned. The violence engulfed the whole of France. So many cities—such as Nîmes, Bagnols, Béziers, Montauban, but also Annonay, Tournon, and Bourg-Saint-Andéol—either openly joined forces with the Huguenots or were conquered by them; nowhere was untouched by the conflict. The Catholic armies prevailed in the northern cities, and Paris remained a significant Catholic stronghold.

Throckmorton requested an audience with Catherine, seeking to relay Elizabeth's response to the recent events.

"My mistress, the queen of England, is quite upset that you have not succeeded in quieting the troubles in your realm," the ambassador stated baldly.

"I have appreciated your queen's amity since the start of the trouble and thank her for it," began Catherine. "However, to appease the troubles, Protestant leaders should not have left France and allied themselves to Protestant princes. Instead they should have retired to their houses and avoided all public assemblies and preaching until I could guarantee their safety. They refused. They have therefore left me no choice but to bring them to reason by force," Catherine solemnly concluded.

"This is unacceptable," Throckmorton warned. "You were content that the Edict of January should be enforced throughout France, except in Paris..."

Catherine interrupted him; she did not appreciate having her authority contested. "I have to remind you, Sieur Throckmorton, that I have made the same offer to both parties, the Prince of Condé did not accept it, nor would it be acceptable to the Guises. I know many gentlemen of the reformed religion who would be content to live according to their consciences in their own houses, amongst whom are Mr. De Pienne, Knight of the Order, Mr. De Santefoy, Mr. De Vigean and others, who have now retired from their Huguenot leader."

Throckmorton decided to take his leave, since he could see that nothing conclusive could possibly come from this conversation. But before he left, he felt compelled to tell the queen mother his own mind.

"It would seem very hard that the Prince of Condé and so many others, thousands of Protestants in France, who profess his religion, should live privately in their houses without exercising their right to attend divine service, and be deprived of teaching, preaching, the administration of sacraments and baptism, and of Christ's body; for how could they be married or buried if they have no ministers appointed them for this matter?"[6]

Catherine, who had already turned her back on Throckmorton, remained silent. No doubt this man's insolence, lecturing her on how to keep the Protestants of her country, infuriated her. But she didn't show her displeasure. Instead, she chose to give him the silent treatment, simply waiting for him to leave the room.

The truth was that Catherine had no answer to give. For once, there was so little she could actually do.

Meanwhile, Throckmorton started to fear for his own safety. Paris was not exactly sympathetic to the practitioners of the reformed religion, and he had already received death threats while staying in the city.

With this in mind, he wrote to Elizabeth: "While I'm content to expose myself to hazard in France as I have done before, the people of Paris have now sworn to destroy me, which I fear all the more given that the authority of the king, and his mother, can be no sanctuary. I am not making these claims to be rid of your Majesty's service, but given the circumstance I think that any other person would do better service here than me."[7]

Elizabeth was left with no choice but to bring him home. "I believe that you are in great peril from the fury of the people, especially those of Paris. I am therefore determined to revoke you from thence. I have spoken to the French ambassador, Paul de Foix, and have written to the king and queen mother, and I have sent you the letters to send to them to ensure your safe return. Please do assure them of my amity towards them."[8]

While Elizabeth had granted Throckmorton's return by late July 1562, the process was to take much longer, and in the midst of a civil war, Throckmorton found himself stuck in France. Elizabeth did, however, send a replacement for him: Sir Thomas Smith. The transition between the two ambassadors would take over eighteen months to complete, creating some rivalry between the two men, and some unexpected camaraderie too, during desperate times.

Anne Carew—Throckmorton's wife, who was residing at the English court—reported to her husband any information she thought could prove useful for his safe return. After all, knowledge was powerful, and could be used as a bargaining tool. Especially if one knew the decisions that might be made by the English government.

"The queen seems well disposed and has now returned to Hampton Court. It is said she is receiving secret guests. I have heard no more. A way to prove your affection to the queen and remain in her good grace once you have returned would be to buy in Paris two partlets [garments worn over the neck and shoulder to fill in the low neckline] with sleeves,"[9] Anne wrote to her husband.

Elizabeth loved gifts, and she was often won over in this way, but who were these secret guests?

*

The atrocities intensified in France and, while Frenchmen were engaged in murderous conflict, foreigners were continuing to send their troops to support one side or the other. Philip II of Spain was very keen to demonstrate his strength and in particular his authority beyond the borders of his own realm; the conflict occurring in France was the perfect opportunity to do so. He agreed to dispatch "10,000 foot soldiers and 3,000 cavalrymen" to France, which greatly pleased the Guises—and, to some extent, Catherine, who knew that through her daughter Elisabeth, queen of Spain, she had a staunch ally.[10]

For her part, Elizabeth concluded a military and political alliance with Louis, Prince of Condé; on September 20, they signed the Treaty of Hampton Court, which agreed that—in exchange of Le Havre for the English—Elizabeth would send 6,000 men to fight alongside the Huguenots. This obviously had to be agreed in utmost secrecy, as in exchange for the return of Calais, which would take place in a few more years, Elizabeth had already agreed never to declare war against France as part of the Treaty of Cateau-Cambrésis. Supporting rebels and the Huguenots was in itself a breach of that promise, and she knew it. But she also knew something else: that the French would never give back Calais without strong leverage. She felt it was the right time to show to all the European leaders what Elizabeth was made of, as a queen and a ruler.

In a letter to Phillip II, Elizabeth was blunt: "I have great compassion for the young king of France, seeing that he is so advised by his subjects that his authority could not direct them to an accord. I fear that thereof might follow a universal trouble to the rest of Christendom, considering the quarrel were discovered and published before the matter of religion."

She went on to explain her most recent actions: "What touches and concerns me most is that the house of Guise is the principal head of one party. They daily increase their forces and I cannot forget that they were the ones who evicted Calais from this crown. I wish nothing more than that quietness is achieved in France and this division is brought to some accord. However, I will fortify my ports as I see fit to ensure the safety of the borders of my realm. I intend to live in peace with you and the king of France and save my right to Calais."

She ended her letter to Philip by reassuring him that peace was not far away. "I shall be found most ready to revoke my force and live in perfect rest as I did before these troubles began."[11] But this was a lie: she was just about to send "400 soldiers to Le Havre" and the rest to Normandy, with more on their way to assist the Huguenots—who were about to suffer an unpleasant defeat.[12]

In September 1562, the Catholic forces launched an attack on the city of Rouen, which they won. Upon hearing the news of their victory, Antoine de Bourbon, king of Navarre, arrived at the walls of the city with 30,000 men. His intention was to reconquer the city and to find a compromise between all factions—the radical Huguenots, the radical Catholics, and his own party, a more open-minded Catholic one, which he saw as being more apt to compromise. But the conflict was to claim his life: having been hit by an arquebus on October 15, he died of his wound a month later.

The Prince of Condé—brother to the late king, Antoine of Navarre—continued the war—further defending Protestantism at all cost. For that purpose, he was more determined than ever to forge an alliance with Elizabeth.

★

Catherine was not unaware of Elizabeth's real intentions toward France, her informants having already disclosed Elizabeth's actions. Consequently, the queen mother ordered that any English boats approaching Normandy be either entirely destroyed or, at the very least, their passengers arrested.

When Throckmorton complained about the treatment of the boats, falsely protesting that they were tradesmen and not soldiers, Catherine lied in turn:

> I have heard about your complaints regarding the English ships that have been arrested in Brittany and the ill-treatment of the subjects of the queen of England, my good sister. I can assure you that I did not know anything about it and that it greatly displeases me to hear such news. I will write to the duke of Étampes to ensure that reparation and restitution are in order.[13]

She never did write to the duke, who was in charge of the royal forces in the region.

Yet Throckmorton had a more pressing matter to deal with: his own safety. Charles de Cossé, Maréchal de Brissac and Governor of Paris—eldest brother to Artus de Cossé-Brissac, known as Monsieur de Gonnord—had been instructed to keep an eye on the English ambassador and remove him from court, because of the rumors that Throckmorton was plotting with Admiral Coligny and the Prince of Condé.

There was no time to waste: Throckmorton needed to escape the city, and find shelter in one of the territories previously won by the Huguenots. It was now far too dangerous to remain in or near Paris, as the Catholics were slaughtering any Protestant they could find.

He informed the Maréchal de Brissac of his intentions: "I need to go to Bourges and for this I will have to go through St. Mathurin, Montargis, and Gien."

"I cannot allow you to travel that way," Brissac replied, before pausing for a moment. He knew this could be Throckmorton's only chance to be safe. "If you go by Chartres, Bonneval, Chateaudun and Blois, I will guarantee that you get there safely." These Catholic cities were dangerous, but with a safe-conduct from the Maréchal, Throckmorton should be protected until he reached the Huguenot town of Bourges.

The real destination, however, was not Bourges but Orléans, where Admiral Coligny was residing.

Later, Throckmorton reported back to Elizabeth. "I arrived at the admiral's house in the middle of the night, around 2 o'clock. The Prince of Condé is also staying here. They both told me to tell you that their chiefest trust, next to God, was in your Majesty."[14]

He went on to describe the state of the town and of the Huguenot forces: "There are 1,200 horsemen, 5,000 footmen. The Prince of Condé has had nine or ten cannons and culverins made within the town, and they will make seven or eight more. They have fortified all the weak places with platforms, ravelines, and parapets."

He did not spare Elizabeth the difficulties they were facing: "They have a good store of powder, but they had some misfortune caused by a fire. Besides, the plague is very rife here and their numbers are daily diminished."

In this letter he also warned Elizabeth that Catherine and Charles had taken back the town of Bourges and were trying to win over some of the Huguenot supporters. Sir Peter Mewtas—a special envoy sent by Elizabeth to assist Smith and Throckmorton in these troubling times, in the hope of convincing the king and queen mother to put an end to the war—had just arrived at Dieppe and was on his way to meet with the royal family.

Throckmorton ended his letter by insisting on what mattered most to him: "I have served you for three years and six months. I hope you will deliver me from my charge by a speedy revocation." Once again he appealed for his freedom, so often promised but not yet delivered.

Meanwhile, Catherine was furious that the Maréchal de Brissac had allowed the English ambassador to join the Huguenot stronghold of Orléans. "I remind you that in this country you are under the authority of the king, my son and mine," she stated. "The Maréchal de Brissac was responsible for your safety and you convinced him to go against his duty, which I highly disapprove of."

Catherine felt she was losing her grip on Throckmorton, and she was concerned that his actions would undermine her own relations with Elizabeth. "You should not fear to come in perfect safety to our court at any hour or any season," she told him. "You do not need anything but your name and the name of the mistress you serve. No need for an official safe-conduct. We still honour and value our amity towards your mistress, the queen of England, as long as she reciprocates it."[15]

But this was a lie. No envoy in any country could simply travel around its territory without an official safe-conduct. Catherine knew this, and she wanted to force Throckmorton to make a mistake. She had lost all trust in him since discovering he was closely involved with Admiral Coligny and the Prince of Condé, and was enabling English forces to join the Huguenots.

Throckmorton was shrewd in his reply to Catherine: "I beg you not to be angry with me if I refuse to leave where I am without an official passport. I am only obeying my mistress's directions."

A few weeks later he repeated his request for a safe-conduct, understanding only too well the lying game Catherine was playing. After all, the queen mother was under great pressure to restore stability and prosperity to France, and he knew he was collateral damage in that campaign. Elizabeth's support for the Huguenots had only served to complicate the situation further, and now Catherine needed to put an end to Elizabeth's interference.

Throckmorton warned the queen mother that her refusal to grant him an official passport would "force the queen of England to see this as an insult to her and her authority and cause Anglo-French relations to deteriorate."[16]

Yet Catherine continued to refuse his request—insisting that he did not need one as he was serving her good ally, the queen of England. It was a stalemate.

In the meantime, Throckmorton was at least able to report to Elizabeth that the Huguenot forces were growing. As he'd told her, there were about "6,000 footmen and near 2,000 horsemen." He also continued to complain about "the queen mother's evil stand against him. Even Smith warned me not to fall into her hands."[17] Nor was there any sign of his safe-conduct.

Now, for the first time, he was well and truly stuck.

★

After their great victory in Rouen, the Catholics had the recovery of Orléans in their sights. In February 1563 the forces led by the Duke of Guise marched to the city—buoyed by their success, they were more determined than ever to crush the Huguenot army. After some promising victories—notably, the assault on the neighborhood of Portereau—the Duke of Guise felt he could let down his guard. On the evening of February 18, he rode back to his camp with some of his men, including a young man named Jean de Poltrot, Sieur de Méré. Poltrot was believed to be a Huguenot sent to the Catholic side to spy on their endeavors, who had then been turned by the Duke of Guise to become a counterspy for the Catholic forces. That night, he revealed his true allegiance. Poltrot had been working for Admiral Coligny for a few years, and now in his twenties he was ready to serve his original master.

That evening, the Duke of Guise was not wearing his usual coat of chain mail—an omission that didn't go unnoticed by Poltrot; the soon-to-be assassin removed himself from the group and ran ahead of them to hide in the bushes. As the duke rode past Poltrot's hiding place on his horse, Poltrot fired his arquebus, hitting the duke in the back. With the deed done, he then ran to find his own horse and fled as fast as he could. The duke died of his wound six days later.

When the news of the Catholic leader's death finally reached Paris, Catherine felt simultaneously mortified and relieved. The Duke of Guise had been a burden for a long time and had often undermined her authority. She promised his widow Anne d'Este, however, that his death would be avenged, and that she had never before been so determined "to employ all the means she could" to this effect.[18] It was the least she could do to prove herself worthy of Anne d'Este's friendship, which had been constant despite any grievances Catherine might have had with her husband.

Poltrot was eventually caught, at which point he was questioned by Catherine herself, who wanted to know who had ordered the assassination of the Duke of Guise. Poltrot first accused the admiral before retracting his declaration, pleading an impulse of his own to avenge what had happened in Amboise in 1560. Catherine had hoped to bring a truce between the two camps, but she knew that this could not be achieved with Poltrot walking free. She agreed to his execution, and on March 18, 1563, Jean de Poltrot was sentenced to be drawn and quartered. The duke's assassin was dead.

The next day, Francis, Duke of Guise, was given an almost royal cortège "composed of twenty-two town criers ringing bells, important citizens carrying burning torches, and representatives of the Church and nobility, [who] all processed through Paris."[19] He was celebrated as a military and war hero, his death allowing—to some extent—a possibility of a truce between the warring factions: no one wanted to see more death and destruction. And so it was to be: at his funeral, the Edict of Amboise was concluded. Freedom of conscience was granted to the Huguenots, though the nobles were mostly favored, able to practice their religion more openly than the lower classes: noblemen could hold services within their estates, while the lower ranks had to keep their worship services inside their homes. But Paris and its surrounding areas remained free of Protestantism—ensuring the prosperity of Catholicism anywhere near the king and the royal family.

Despite the peace treaty, however, neither party set down their arms entirely. Elizabeth still sought the return of Calais, and she and Catherine were still in disagreement over the treatment of the French prisoners who had been left in the Tower of London as a bargaining tool, ensuring the return of Calais to the English within eight years if no war was declared between the two countries.

Catherine fired the first shots. "I am surprised to hear that Antoine Duprat de Nantouillet, Provost of Paris, who has just replaced his father in your prison, has been so harshly treated by your guards," she wrote. "I am astonished that you deemed it right to make his treatment harder and will let my ambassador at your court, Paul de Foix, explain to you how displeased I am with this present situation."[20]

Elizabeth was not in the mood to be lectured by a mere queen mother, and therefore did not hold back in her response. The tone was no longer amicable or equable; using the royal "we," she reminded Catherine of her higher status:

We have found both your letters strangely written and your requests not to be granted by us in a manner as they be made and grounded when you shall, good sister, have better considered on your indignity of this matter, and remember what charge God has laid upon us princes for administration of justice, we doubt not, but you will use some other speech towards us to acknowledge no superior under God, and in demonstration of amity towards any prince our neighbour, being thereto friendly provoked, we mean to be inferior to none.[21]

Catherine must have screamed at the lack of respect in the English queen's tone. But, for now, given the recent events, she simply chose not to reply to Elizabeth's condescending letter.

Nevertheless, Catherine remained determined to see Elizabeth fail in her enterprise of helping the Huguenots and, eventually, regaining Calais; now, the queen mother had a plan to turn Condé against the English. She pushed into his arms the beautiful, enigmatic, and fervent Catholic, Isabelle de Limeuil. Their passionate affair, much disapproved of, helped Catherine to gain some influence over the Huguenot leader. De Limeuil was a faithful agent of Catherine's, and understood the importance of her mission to turn Condé against Elizabeth. Unfortunately for the lady, she found herself with child and—shamed by what had happened out of wedlock—was forced to leave court. She was later sent to a convent, chosen by Catherine as a means of protecting her friend from any further humiliation.

But Catherine's plan had worked. After his dalliance, Condé was now more open to a potential alliance with the queen mother—in other words, he was ready to betray Elizabeth, exchanging Le Havre, which was in the hands of the Huguenots, for Calais.

Elizabeth sensed the trouble brewing and, in April 1563, she ordered Smith to pass on "an extract of a special article betwixt her and Condé, by which it appears how I may avow the keeping of Le Havre and how the prince is bound to do nothing prejudicial to her. I need assurance that I have his hand and seal as well as the admiral's."[22]

Neither Condé nor the admiral agreed to such an article.

Miraculously, Catherine's plan seemed to be working, and her stance on Calais tightened as her letter—dated May 17, 1563—to Paul de Foix, her resident ambassador at the English court, stated: "We have been astonished that the queen of England dared to ask for the restitution of Calais, saying that only then would she give back Le Havre—which we could never accept. Ask for another audience with her and explain where we stand and that we want a clear answer if she is willing or not to restore Le Havre to us."

She continued by dismissing complaints about the loss of English ships in the Channel: "You will tell the queen of England that we also wish to see restored the many French ships and vessels that have been arrested and attacked at sea by her ships. Our subjects have simply retaliated the attacks launched by the English."[23]

Catherine would do anything and everything in her power to regain Le Havre by force. She had also managed to unify the factional leaders by claiming that only the French should occupy France—an argument that both sides could agree with, as they conspired against the English in their territories. Both Coligny and Condé asked Elizabeth again to return Le Havre. Furious at their betrayal, she replied that it was "her right as compensation for the loss of Calais" and that she would keep Le Havre "despite all of France."[24]

If Elizabeth wanted war, Catherine decided she was more than happy to oblige. Montmorency, at the head of the royal army, joined forces with Condé to launch several offensives against the English in Le Havre. As early as June 1563, Catherine was expressing delight at their attacks: "I have been more than pleased to hear about the bravery and the duty that our people have undertaken." By this point, other foreign troops, such as the Swiss, had been pushed back elsewhere.[25]

France was united again, and Catherine was finally regaining the kingdom belonging to her and her son. He had just come of age and had taken on the mantle of ruling France—though the one who continued to wield power was, of course, Catherine herself. Timid by nature and only thirteen years old, the young king simply did not have broad enough shoulders to bear the misery of France. He was happy, therefore—at least for now—to let his mother handle his affairs. After all, she was the one who had been successfully preserving their dynasty since the death of Henry II.

But Catherine's true victory in this tumultuous time remained her achievement in uniting the Catholics with the Huguenots—a unity that was not likely to last, but which did at least allow her to show Elizabeth her power. She was the English queen's equal after all. And she was convinced of their victory over the English.

She was right. On July 23, 1563, the French forces besieged Le Havre, forcing the English troops to retreat. This was a fatal blow for Elizabeth's hopes in France.

But Catherine had work to do to ensure there were no reprisals. Three days later, she complained to Smith that there were too many English ambassadors present to negotiate the restitution of Calais, and expressed particular outrage that Elizabeth had allowed Throckmorton to be one of those ambassadors, especially "given all the ill intentions he has borne against us."[26] Catherine had still not forgiven Throckmorton's involvement with the Huguenots and still blamed him greatly for the capture of Le Havre in the first place. He would be punished, and this would serve as a reminder for Elizabeth: never again get involved in French business. Throckmorton hung in limbo for months, fearing for his life and apparently no closer to gaining his longed-for freedom. In early January 1564, he was finally granted an audience with Catherine in the garden of a French royal palace. He was unsure what to expect, but the meeting began pleasantly—for Catherine, it was all about confusing her enemies. They never knew what to expect next with her.

"You can tell me anything you wish to," the queen mother said, after a lull in their conversation, which lasted over two hours.

For a while Throckmorton seemed pensive, and remained silent, but eventually he decided to speak his mind. "I truly believe that both realms need one another and that preserving peace between France and England is paramount," he said.

"I wish nothing more than preserving the peace between us," Catherine replied. "God has separated these two realms with a large and beautiful moat so that we shouldn't fear to offend one another from time to time."

Throckmorton emphasized once more the importance Elizabeth placed on the English regaining Calais, while also making Catherine aware that England "would not have intervened in France if we hadn't been asked to do so by Frenchmen." He wished to dispel any remaining hard feelings.

Catherine knew that his words were true to an extent, and in truth she had no appetite for further conflict, but she also knew that she needed to remain firm on Calais. In the end, she won the argument. She got her hostages back for the modest sum of 120,000 crowns—far from the 500,000 crowns the French monarchs had agreed on back in 1559 and 1560. This, she thought, was a way to make Elizabeth pay for her foolish decision to become involved in French matters in the first place. The costs of failed diplomacy were high. Nevertheless, having finally had this one-to-one informal meeting granted, Throckmorton had renewed hopes that his release was nigh. And he was right. The months of his ordeal had taken their toll, and he could not wait to return to his homeland.

The resolution of this long-drawn-out affair also marked the end of a difficult arm-wrestling match between the two powerful queens, and a new shift in Catherine and Elizabeth's relationship. Now that they had both demonstrated their ability to lie to each other, it was finally time to find a way of forging a stronger alliance. Spain's involvement in the first religious war had proven to be a threat to Catherine's endeavor to bring peace to France. As for Elizabeth, her relations with her Scottish cousin were about to become even more complicated. To obtain peace, Elizabeth and Catherine were going to need each other.

Fortunately, Catherine had exactly what she needed to exercise some diplomatic power: three sons of age who were king and princes of France.

What could be more appealing than that to a single English queen?

PART 3

Mothers Know Best

1564–1584

9

Charles, the Boy King, 1564–1569

In 1564, Elizabeth was about to turn thirty-one years old. For over a decade—both prior to and during her reign—she had repeatedly turned down the hands of possible suitors, including such esteemed figures as Philip II of Spain and the Protestant prince, Eric XIV of Sweden, who sought to woo her. Her own court was filled with favorites, each more handsome than the next. Robert Dudley, Earl of Leicester, and Christopher Hatton, who would be knighted by the queen in 1577 and who had remained a loyal councillor for years, were the most highly favored of the potential suitors.

Over decades, Dudley and the queen had developed a close—and some would say even intimate—friendship. What is known for sure is that Dudley had always had a special place in Elizabeth's heart. No matter how many times they argued, which was a frequent occurrence, they remained until his death in 1588 close friends with strong feelings for one another. Yet not even Dudley could tempt Elizabeth into marriage. As early as 1559, in a private audience granted to the French ambassador at the time, Gilles de Noailles, Elizabeth was very clear: "I have no intention to marry,"[1] she told him.

In her 1563 parliamentary session, when pressured again by her advisors to marry, in order to secure her realm, Elizabeth ignored their request and instead focused on presenting herself as a motherly figure to her country—a mother, rather than wife:

"And so I assure you all that though after my death you may have many stepdames, yet shall you never have any a more mother than I mean to be unto you all."[2]

However, many suspected that, in keeping her options open, and receiving male interest from both inside and outside the borders of her realm, Elizabeth was playing a long game, never quite extinguishing anyone's hopes and therefore keeping everyone close. In saying she didn't want to marry, she somehow presented herself as a challenge, almost a quest: who would convince the queen to marry and co-rule?

Across the Channel, another woman was certainly convinced that Elizabeth could be snared, if she was pursued properly. Yes, Catherine—on behalf of and through her sons—was planning to court the stubborn English queen. Maybe Elizabeth had finally met her match.

★

With the situation in France remaining unstable, Catherine was now determined to maintain good relations with Elizabeth. After all, the disputes that had divided them previously had left them both vulnerable and at the mercy of other enemies, particularly Spain. There was no better way to secure their union, Catherine believed, than through a dynastic alliance.

As early as January 1564, Catherine started to woo Elizabeth on behalf of her thirteen-year-old son. Charles was frail but he was also a handsome teenager, dark blond with hazelnut eyes. She believed he had a chance with Elizabeth—especially if the right arguments were made on his behalf. Paul de Foix was carefully instructed on his mission: he was to convey the proposed match to Elizabeth.

So, on a very cold winter afternoon, de Foix was granted an audience with Elizabeth, and he certainly did not waste any time in getting in the queen's good books. "You need to be assured how much you are admired for your greatness by my French masters," he told her emphatically.

Elizabeth was pleased with the sentiment, but she was no fool; she knew that with flattery often came unpleasant requests, and no doubt this situation would not be any different.

After a moment of consideration, therefore, she carefully replied, "I am pleased to hear that the good affection between your masters and myself is mutual," before abruptly changing the subject, hoping to avoid learning the true meaning behind de Foix's compliment.

"Tell me about the meeting between the French king and the queen mother with the queen of Spain, Elisabeth, which took place at the Franco-Spanish border earlier this year."

Without giving him a chance to answer, Elizabeth continued, "The queen mother must be happy for the great graces that she has received from God, to see together a king of France and queen of Spain, her children, elected to such a high degree of honour that there is none higher in Christianity."

This time, Paul de Foix seized the opportunity to interrupt the queen. "The queen mother's grace would be increased if we would see the king accompanied by a great and virtuous queen such as yourself. Even Monsieur Cecil and I talked about it and agreed it was a suitable match."

Suddenly, the real motive for de Foix's visit was clear.

"But you see, dear ambassador," said Elizabeth, smoothly intercepting his approach, "Cecil has also written down some difficulties that such a marriage would pose to my crown. I do not wish to go now into details because they are only excuses, but one of them I see to be relevant."

"And which is it, your Majesty?" de Foix carefully inquired.

"The difference of age,"[3] Elizabeth said bluntly, without looking at the ambassador's blushing face, before putting an end to the conversation altogether. After all, if she was going to be courted, she would want any union to last.

And so the first round of courtship was unsuccessful, but across the Channel Catherine was not too dismayed by the response. In a few years, she believed, Charles would no doubt become a strong man—and therefore a far better suitor.

★

Catherine was not a woman who accepted rejection easily, and in the following months she continued her courting of Elizabeth in their correspondence, exercising her talent for flattery.

"I desire nothing more but to strengthen our alliance through a closer bond and I would consider myself the happiest woman on Earth if one of my children made of a well-loved sister a very dear daughter, to the great honour, wealth, and greatness of our states."

The union would have other benefits too, she felt: "Our two countries are such close neighbours that it takes only three hours to go from one to another."[4] It was, Catherine imagined, the best and most obvious match one could imagine.

Catherine asserted that, despite being a great king, her son would accept the invitation to meet in person before any match was made—a request Elizabeth made to all her suitors. In 1561, Eric XIV of Sweden had almost visited the queen at the English court, but a storm had made his trip impossible—and in truth, Elizabeth was relieved that the meeting did not happen. Then another suitor contemplated the queen's request: Archduke Charles, son of Holy Roman Emperor Ferdinand. There were issues, however, regarding their religious differences. Charles was Catholic, and his refusal to make the journey to England until he was granted the right to practice Mass in private stalled the negotiations. Elizabeth was adamant: she had no desire to marry a man based only on what she could see in a portrait.

When Paul de Foix officially reopened the potential marriage negotiations between Charles and Elizabeth, some time later, he offered the queen two letters: one from Charles's own hand and one from Catherine's. They both stated their unique "desire to make a dynastic alliance" with Elizabeth.

The English queen blushed "several times" and seemed to be genuinely flattered as she read their letters, her eyes smiling. She was even a little abashed. Unusually for her, the queen stammered as she said, "Your masters are giving me a great honour." She paused, not looking De Foix in the eye, and then—as she finally looked up—she muttered, "I am not worthy of it." Clearing her throat and speaking louder, she insisted, however, that, "I will continue to reciprocate your master's affection throughout my whole life, as if I had been born the queen mother of France's daughter."[5]

Elizabeth, too, knew how to flatter Catherine—and how to play the courting game. Catherine was rather surprised by this coy rejection of her request; perhaps she did not imagine that Elizabeth was as skilled in the art of correspondence as she was herself.

As Paul de Foix considered her words, preparing his reply, he was interrupted by the queen. "If only it had pleased God that I was ten years younger to be able to make this alliance come true." She paused. "But I think the queen mother and the king have been misinformed about my age and would eventually be displeased with me, especially in the light of the king's great youth, which would leave me feeling old and unattractive and alienated from him, just as the late queen Mary my sister had been from the king of Spain."[6]

The audience ended, yet again, in a defeat for France. Furthermore, this allusion to her age and appearance was possibly just a ruse to make them try harder. While Elizabeth had always been conscious of her appearance—especially after suffering from the scars left by smallpox when she caught the virus in 1562—now in her early thirties, the queen was confident in her charisma and ability to draw male attention to her court.

*

While it was certainly clear that the difference in age was an obstacle, Catherine was determined to continue putting pressure on Elizabeth; she ordered Paul de Foix to inquire as to what Elizabeth's people and her privy councillors would make of an alliance with her son. Surely they would approve such an illustrious match? She was about to be disappointed. De Foix revealed that it was quite the opposite, and that the "English nobility feared that the greatness of the king threatened this realm with servitude and oppression."

Without the support of the English nobility, Catherine found herself short of arguments to continue the courtship. She was, however, relieved when she was told that Elizabeth "has declared many times that she would not marry someone from her realm."[7] In other words, Catherine's sons had still a chance to convince the Tudor queen.

After much thought, Catherine deployed what she hoped would be her strongest argument yet, one she knew could not possibly be ignored by Elizabeth. "Tell the queen, my good sister, that she needs to understand that she is leaving her realm in great danger if she does not secure a dynasty through heirs of her own, which is more than necessary for the common good and peace of the realm."[8]

She even teased Elizabeth's pride further: "Remind her that without a strong alliance, such as the one my son, Charles, offers, Mary, her cousin, will be called to the crown of England without any difficulty."

Surely, despite all her protestations on the question of marriage, a threat to her nation's security was something Elizabeth could not allow. Indeed, Catherine knew that Elizabeth viewed Mary as a threat, especially now that she had married the Catholic, Henry Stuart, Lord Darnley—son of Lady Margaret Douglas, daughter of Margaret Tudor and granddaughter of Henry VII of England—and Catherine did not hesitate to use this knowledge to her own advantage. Their alliance further challenged Elizabeth's legitimacy to the English throne, and Catherine knew it.

And yet still the trick did not quite work. Elizabeth held firm. She hoped that Charles and Catherine would support her nevertheless and that, therefore, they ultimately would not "prefer the cause of the Queen of Scots before hers."[9]

Catherine made no response on this point, preferring to remain ambiguous. This, she was sure, would be a more persuasive tactic, leading Elizabeth to believe that her only option was to strengthen her position as queen of England by choosing Charles as her husband, and uniting both realms. Catherine claimed that she desired "not to favour any party" and this time she meant it. She had no intention of getting involved in the dispute over Mary's recent marriage, but she was shrewd enough to use the marriage between Mary and Henry as a means to convince Elizabeth to forge an alliance with France.[10]

However, the alliance between Mary and the Catholic English gentleman Henry Darnley was a match that posed many problems, not just for Elizabeth: Mary's half-brother, James Stuart, Earl of Moray, for one, was infuriated by this Catholic alliance. By mid-August, a rebellion led by James had grown in Scotland. The rebels raged that it was utterly unacceptable to have a Catholic couple in charge of the realm. A Catholic woman at the head of the realm—on her own, no less—had already been difficult enough to accept, but now a king and queen of Scotland who were both of a different faith from the Kirk? This was just too much to bear.

The rebels asked the English crown for support—support that was indeed granted in the form of money, given in secret, but was ultimately insufficient.

Moray showed gratitude while still asking for more. "I wholeheartedly thank you, your Majesty, for your continuous generosity and favours to myself and my friends. We hope we can continue to rely on your support."[11]

Elizabeth was willing to continue giving, but not at all costs. After all, she could not completely jeopardize her relationship with the Scottish and French crowns, and needed her support for the rebels to remain secret.

Consequently, some further financial aid was honored, but no English soldiers were dispatched to Scotland. The risk of a greater dispute was just too high. Even if in Elizabeth's eyes Mary had betrayed her by marrying an English subject and kinsman without royal consent, she would not declare open war over this.

For Mary, it had never been a question of trust nor of betrayal, but instead a question of freedom. No one could dictate whom she should or should not marry—ironically, a desire she shared with her English cousin. Perhaps Elizabeth understood this; nevertheless, she could not tolerate it without jeopardizing her own position. Mary was furious.

During an audience granted to John Thomworth—a gentleman of Elizabeth's Privy Council, who had been dispatched for a short period of time as special envoy to the Scottish court—Mary screamed out in frustration: "Princes are subject immediately to God, and to owe account or reckoning of their doings to none other!"[12]

Yet for Elizabeth, this claim did not stand. After all, Mary had chosen an English subject to marry and *he* had to obtain royal approval, which he had not sought. As a means to punish him and Mary for this insult, Elizabeth ordered the imprisonment of Darnley's mother—Lady Margaret Douglas, Countess of Lennox—in the Tower of London. If they wouldn't listen to her, someone else would have to suffer the queen's wrath.

French diplomats and special envoys—including Michel de Castelnau, Sieur de Mauvissière, fervent supporter of the Guises and of Mary—implored Elizabeth to release the countess on their behalf. The English queen continued to refuse such requests, keeping the countess prisoner until an unforeseen and tragic event occurred in 1567.

By mid-autumn, the rebellion had been crushed and Moray himself had fled to England. While Elizabeth publicly condemned his rebellion, she granted him refugee status in the north of England.

But even with Moray gone, Mary and Darnley continued to face contestation within their realm. This wasn't just about the fear of having the Scottish Protestant Reformation revoked; it was a case of old rivalries between different clans. While Mary was pregnant with her firstborn son, James, whom she gave birth to on June 19, 1566, the situation kept worsening in Scotland as these tensions simmered. She lost the support of some of her nobles, and Darnley ended up showing his true colors: the man was violent, abusive, and a drunk, leaving Mary increasingly isolated. Perhaps Elizabeth suspected that it was a bad marriage: she certainly continued to assert her intention to remain unmatched herself.

In November 1566 she addressed her parliament on the matter, having received multiple requests for her to marry or at least settle the succession. She could hold off the conversation no longer, but she was keen to ensure it was had on only her terms.

"Was I not born in the realm?" she asked passionately, addressing the men before her. "Were my parents born in any foreign country? Is there any cause I should alienate myself from being careful over this country? Is not my kingdom here? Whom have I oppressed? Whom have I enriched to others' harm?"

"I need not to use many words," she continued, "for my deeds do try me."

As a single woman standing in front of a delegation of both Houses, Commons and Lords, she illustrated just how much she despised being commanded: "The second point of your petition was the limitation of the succession of the crown, wherein was nothing said for my safety, but only for yourselves." She paused before staring at them sternly. "A strange thing that the foot should direct the head."[13]

The shock rippled through the room. Not only had all the men been scolded by the queen, they had also been referred to as the "feet," an insult usually reserved for women, the so-called lesser sex. Nevertheless, they pressed her further on the question of her marriage.

This time, Elizabeth showed no mercy, having by now endured eight years of such questioning. She was just as determined as ever to do things on her own terms. Some people called it indecision, but perhaps it was sheer force of will. After so many years being subject to the whims of others as a young woman, she wished to rule herself entirely.

Returning to parliament on January 2, 1567, Elizabeth reasserted her authority.

"Who is so simple that they doubt whether a prince that is head of all the body may not command the feet not to stray when they would slip?" she asked loudly.

If the members of the parliament disliked her November speech, they would surely hate this one even more.

"Whether I live to see the like assembly or not, or whosoever it be, yet beware however you prove your prince's patience, as you have now done mine. And now to conclude, all this notwithstanding, the most part may assure you to depart in your prince's grace."

With that she turned to Sir Nicholas Bacon, lord keeper of the Great Seal, and said, "My lord, you will do as I bade you."

Bowing to his queen, he said aloud, "The queen's Majesty has agreed to dissolve this parliament, therefore every man may take his ease and depart at his pleasure."[14]

Parliament now dissolved, she was bound to no will other than her own. It was as clear as ever that the queen would not even entertain the idea of marriage—at least not now, and certainly not when compelled to do so by ordinary men.

★

In the meantime, the situation in Scotland had worsened, and Darnley's attitude toward Mary became almost if not completely unbearable. As early as December 1565, Thomas Randolph—the English ambassador who had been accredited to the Scottish court in 1563—noted the subtle changes at Mary's court.

"While there was nothing but 'King and Queen, his Majesty and hers,' now the 'queen's husband' is most common," he said. "His name no longer comes first in all writings and is now placed second. Certain pieces of money which have been recently coined with both their faces are now called in and others are framed as replacement."[15]

Mary's infatuation with Darnley had most definitely come to an end.

In March 1566, Mary's secretary David Rizzio—who many believed also to be Darnley's lover—became the target of a plan by the Scottish Lords to push back on Mary's recent orders to restore Catholicism in Scotland. With the birth of her son and the new election of Pope Pius V, she had never felt more powerful. Being an agent of the pope himself, Rizzio was blamed for Mary's recent lack of tolerance for Protestantism. He was also blamed for coming between the royal couple, as he was believed to have had relationships with both monarchs—though, of course, rumors were not necessarily true, and could be spread by parties who wanted to see the bond between the Scottish royal couple weakened. Regardless of the veracity of these claims, the plot certainly thickened when it was finally decided what must be done about Rizzio: he was to be murdered.

The fatal incident took place one cold winter night. Darnley, an accomplice to the plot, allowed the Scottish Lords—led by Lord Ruthven—to pass through his private apartment to reach Mary's. When they entered, they told her they were there as Rizzio "hath offended your honour which I dare not be so bold to speak of. As to the king your husband's honour, he hath hindered him of the crown matrimonial, which your Grace promised him…And as to the nobility, he hath caused your Majesty to banish a great part of them, and to forfeit them at this present parliament."[16]

Mary tried to defend Rizzio but she must have known that, with such an accusation leveled against him, his execution was a foregone conclusion. For her, the evil deed was the last straw; after this she would never again reconcile with Darnley. Furthermore, after Rizzio's death, the king's dagger was found in the body of the victim, leaving his wife in little doubt of his involvement in the plot. Guzman de Silva, the Spanish ambassador at the English court at the time, allegedly reported that there was no doubt that "the displeasure of the queen of Scotland with her husband is carried so far, that she was approached by some who wanted to induce her to allow a plot to be formed against him, which she refused, but she nevertheless shows him no affection."[17]

She might not have actively plotted against her husband, but it was clear that they were now estranged. As Mary started being seen out in public with James Hepburn, Earl of Bothwell, yet more rumors circulated: that Bothwell now had the queen's favor.

On Sunday, February 9, 1567, it was announced to the Scottish court that the king would return to Holyrood the next day. Then, in the very early hours of the following morning, the unthinkable happened. The good people of Edinburgh were awoken by the rattling sound of a massive explosion.

Mary awoke and demanded to know what was causing such noise. She was told that "the house at Kirk o' Field had been destroyed by the force of powder so completely that hardly one stone was left standing," and that "the dead body of the king had been found lying in the garden some sixty paces away."[18] Was it possible that Mary had

ordered his death? Could she be responsible, or at the very least somehow involved?

Rumors, of course, spread to all of Europe that Mary, along with
her closest advisor and alleged lover, Bothwell, were responsible for
the demise of Darnley.

Elizabeth reacted promptly to the news, her first instinct—rather
surprisingly—being to counsel and protect her cousin, telling her to
be mindful of Bothwell's potential involvement. She wrote to her: "I
beseech you to take this thing so much to heart that you will not fear
to touch even him whom you have nearest to you [Bothwell] if the
thing touches him, and that no persuasion will prevent you from
making an example out of this to the world: that you are both a noble
princess and a loyal wife."[19] She understood the importance of the
images women must project to the world.

The situation was complex for Mary, who was now very vulnerable. The little princess who was raised under the protection of
Henry II, king of France, and who had been shielded by her Guise
uncles, was now entirely alone in a realm torn apart by different noble
factions. Having been publicly insulted by Knox, who compared her
to one of the worst Roman tyrants, Nero, she knew that she now had
more enemies than ever—all of whom wanted her either gone or,
worse, dead.

As for Bothwell, whose name was now closely associated with
Darnley's demise, he saw the opportunity to strengthen his forces.
With this in mind he made several shrewd alliances—particularly
with George Gordon, Earl of Huntly—which allowed him to become
the most powerful man at the Scottish court, and his ambitions were
growing exponentially. Soon he officially started courting Mary, who
was completely shattered by the recent events and who consequently
had a difficult time discerning her friends from her foes.

Bothwell convinced Mary that she was no longer strong enough to
contain the divisions in her country. Indeed, at the time she said,
"Being divided in factions as it is, [it] cannot be contained in order
unless our authority be assisted and set forth by the fortifications of a
man."[20] She hadn't yet accepted his hand, but she was clearly under

his influence. Soon, however, Bothwell realized that he needed more than mere influence to convince Mary to marry him. He needed to control her physically, so he abducted her, taking her to his castle in Dunbar. This is where a campaign of manipulation and psychological abuse began, an ordeal that left Mary deeply scarred. Bothwell swore his love for her, telling her that through his own authority and therefore through their union he would eventually restore hers over all the Scottish Lords, and—desperate for this sort of protection—Mary reluctantly agreed.

In May 1567, they entered Edinburgh together and she publicly pardoned Bothwell for what everyone saw—including probably Mary herself—as her own abduction. On May 14, the marriage contract between Mary and Bothwell was signed. What Mary hoped would be the end of her ordeal was, however, only the beginning of her own terrible tragedy.

*

In England, Elizabeth was dismayed at news of the match, and wrote to Mary to tell her as much:

> How could a worse choice be made for your honour than in such haste to marry such a subject, who besides other and notorious lacks, public fame hath charged with the murder of your late husband… we beseech you to be careful how your son, the prince, may be preserved, for the comfort of yours and your realm, which two things we have from the beginning always taken to heart.[21]

Catherine de Medici's response to the news was less ferocious but no less decisive. In seeking to help Mary, Catherine sent to Scotland one of her closest secretaries, the dashing Nicolas de Neufville, Sieur de Villeroy, to offer her former daughter-in-law advice. On his way to Scotland, Catherine also asked him to contact Elizabeth, and ask her to express her support of the vulnerable Mary.

For her part, the Tudor queen assured him that she "was saddened by what happened to my good sister, the queen of Scotland. I am committed to ensure that she is liberated and accept to give you, Villeroy, a safe-conduct to reach Scotland."[22]

In reality, neither queen put much effort into rescuing Mary from her fateful errors. Unsurprisingly, Villeroy came back to the French court without achieving his goal (though his failure did not prevent his appointment as secretary of state later that year) and Elizabeth was determined to show no public support to Mary's cause as a result of the ongoing tensions—leaving Catherine with no other option but to focus her attention on domestic matters. It also provided her with another opportunity to connect with Elizabeth. In a letter, she reiterated her true wish to "confirm and continue our good deeds toward one another for the common, sincere, and perfect friendship that exists between the two of us."[23]

Mary's fate, meanwhile, seemed to be sealed. Her third marriage did not appease the tensions existing at her court, and soon the situation became unsustainable for the young queen. She was forced to abdicate and, although she escaped imprisonment, felt she was left with no choice but to flee if she were to protect her own life.

But where could she go?

★

In May 1568, news reached London that Mary had been seen crossing the northern borders. She had set foot in England to demand an audience with Elizabeth.

"I entreat you to send to fetch me as soon as you possibly can, for I am in a pitiable condition, not only for a queen, but for a gentlewoman."[24]

The situation was too hazardous for Elizabeth to risk bringing Mary to court. After all, the tensions that existed between them—most notably regarding the disputed title of the queen of England—remained an issue for the Tudor queen who knew that her cousin still posed a threat, even if she sympathized with her marital plight. The decision was made that Mary would remain in the north of England at different locations. From May to July 1568, she was in captivity at Carlisle Castle and was then moved to Bolton Castle until February 1569. There, she was allowed to go hunting and enjoy the countryside. But when she allegedly tried to escape, she was then moved to Tutbury Castle, where she would stay until April 1569. She loathed this residence and complained a great deal about the dampness and gloominess of the place.

Catherine pledged herself to Mary in a letter to Elizabeth, hoping that the Scottish queen "will receive the aid, favour, shelter, and friendship that she has the right to expect from you [Elizabeth] as a distressed princess."[25] While Catherine publicly showed her support, however, it was noticeable that she did not offer financial aid to her former daughter-in-law. Instead, during this time she multiplied her tokens of affection toward Elizabeth. And her campaign seemed to be successful, as the English queen was softening toward her French counterpart.

In July of that year, Catherine was suffering with a bad cold. It was nothing too alarming, but when Elizabeth was informed of it by her resident ambassador, Sir Henry Norris, she immediately sent a letter to him to personally deliver to Catherine, saying she "had true concerns about your recent health and I hope you will recover rather sooner than later."

The queen mother was touched by Elizabeth's good wishes and, in return, assured her that the Tudor queen "will never meet anyone who loves you or longs for your wellbeing as much as I do."[26]

By now, Charles was eighteen, but his mother still remained in charge of their domestic and foreign politics, and she saw yet another opportunity to strengthen her bond with Elizabeth. In October, they decided to send a new resident ambassador to the English court, one they knew would be charming and mellow, but also attentive to the actions taken by Elizabeth and her ministers. That man was Bertrand de Salignac, Sieur de la Mothe Fénélon.

His mission was simple: to ensure peace between Elizabeth and Catherine and perhaps even to conclude a marital union between the single queen of Europe and one of the sons of the queen mother of

France. Little did he know the difficulty of the task, however, or how fond he himself would become of Elizabeth.

His attempt to offer Charles to Elizabeth did not quite go as expected. In the midst of summer 1569, she granted La Mothe Fénélon an audience with her in her private garden. After more than half a year in his company by that time, his companionship seemed to have grown on her. As usual, the French ambassador came prepared; he knew the Tudor queen was preoccupied with other matters, most notably the situation in the north with Mary, who had been enjoying a stay in Wingfield Manor. Following the start of the Northern Rebellion, which aimed to replace Elizabeth with Mary, the Scottish queen had then been brought back to the castle she most despised, Tutbury. "Everyone is astonished by the great qualities that God has invested in you—your beauty, your knowledge, your virtue, and the greatness of your state," La Mothe Fénélon told her.

Elizabeth was still fond of flattery, but she also still knew that with flattery came requests—and, more often than not, unpleasant ones.

Smiling, he continued, "With all these qualities, it would be so tragic not to see a rightful successor to preserve your posterity."

Elizabeth remained silent as she listened.

La Mothe Fénélon felt he had her full attention, and made his move. "Any prince would be the happiest man on Earth if you were to choose him and there would be nothing more desirable in all Christendom to see a union between you, your Majesty, and one of the three princes of France, sons of King Henry II, especially the actual king of France, worthy of his father's legacy."

Elizabeth interrupted him. "The king could not possibly want me, as he would be ashamed to enter Paris with a queen for his wife who looks as old as I do."

Then, when La Mothe Fénélon tried to speak again, she interjected. "I am not at an age when I can leave my country, as the queen of Scotland did when she arrived so young in France. I have a country to rule, Sieur La Mothe Fénélon, and I intend to do so in person, not by proxy."

He nodded, a sign of submission but, under instruction from

Catherine, he could not simply leave the matter there. "Of course, your Majesty, I understand. But if such a union were ever to happen, it would be the most illustrious royal line to have ever existed, the combination of the two most noble and ancient Christian crowns."

He paused, carefully choosing his next words. He had her attention, certainly, but he did not have her approval. "As for your age, your Majesty, it is of little concern given that your beauty remains absolutely intact."

Elizabeth couldn't help but smile. She decided, for just a moment, to slightly entertain the idea of a potential union. After all, he amused her.

"And the queen mother, wouldn't she want someone younger for her son and as a daughter?" she asked him.

"The queen mother is the kindest soul with the most gracious conversation, and I have no doubt that if you two were ever to meet, you would never leave each other's side as you would get on so perfectly."[27]

Elizabeth smiled in response, but she had quickly grown bored of the courting game; with her right hand she simply dismissed La Mothe Fénélon, who was very confused by the sudden end to his audience.

Had his attempts been successful? Was Elizabeth finally considering Charles's hand? Much to his great dismay, courtiers continued to whisper that "the queen will never marry"—not the French king nor anyone else. When these words reached Catherine, she was undeterred. If Charles was not the right man for her, she had other sons who would perhaps stand a chance.

As for Charles, he found another match, though he didn't himself have much say in the negotiations. On November 26, 1570, he finally married Elisabeth of Austria, the second daughter of Holy Roman Emperor Maximilian II.

La Mothe Fénélon was willing to try again, and next time, he thought, he would try harder. In all honesty, he simply enjoyed the queen's company—something that became increasingly apparent during his seven-year embassy.

10

Henry: Overshadowed, 1570–1571

In the late summer of 1570, Bertrand de Salignac, La Mothe Fénélon—
who had by then been serving as French ambassador at the English
court for two years—was desperate to be granted an audience with
Elizabeth immediately.

Their relationship had begun cordially, but she had been avoiding
him for quite some time. He had been told on various occasions that
the queen of England would eventually meet with him but that at the
moment she was "in a house called Wyck in the woods, forty miles
away from London."[1] Nevertheless, if he was in a hurry to have an
audience with her and did not mind the lack of protocol, he was
more than welcome to join her there. Elizabeth also suggested that if
it did not concern "pressing matters," she would be able to receive
him in a more appropriate venue, such as at "Mr. Norris's house in
Oxford," in a few days' time.[2]

On that occasion, and contrary to his usual nature, La Mothe
Fénélon did not show any patience. He had a mission, and therefore
was determined to speak to Elizabeth as soon as possible—and doing
so in private, away from court, would be even better. After all, he had
delicate matters to discuss. It was a decision he would go on to regret.

Finally, Elizabeth "sent three gentlemen" to bring him to her, though
as it turned out, she could not be found at Wyck house; instead, she
was deep in the woods where she was hunting "fallow deer with
crossbow."[3] She was rather fond of hunting, and cut an imposing
figure as she indulged her pastime. Hunting fallow deer—or "drive

147

hunting"—was an art that prepared rulers for war; nobles, gentlemen, and kings all enjoyed using the activity to display their strength and stamina. A group of men would ride on horseback for hours before catching their prey. Hunting also allowed a display of wealth, given how expensive the attire was, with participants having to invest in leather boots, a black or dark green coat, dark grey breeches, and a riding cap.[4] To ride and hunt with a reigning monarch was therefore the ultimate status symbol.

Elizabeth loved horse riding—and excelled at it. In the contemporary depictions of the queen hunting, she can be seen wearing long dresses, gloves, a riding cap, a top hat, and leather boots. The fact that she was wearing a dress did not seem to slow her down; she was more than capable of hunting strong beasts, such as fallow deer, and she was particularly renowned for being fast when riding, as Catherine had been as a young woman, no matter what she wore.[5] Elizabeth spent countless hours on the back of her horse—a pleasure she undoubtedly inherited from her father, who was a hunting champion himself.

As early as 1557, when she was a princess of just twenty-four, Elizabeth went hunting in the forest, where she was met by "fifty archers in scarlet boots and yellow caps, armed with gilded bows; one of whom presented her a silver-headed arrow, winged with peacock's feathers." The princess ended that session by "cutting the throat of a buck,"[6] a ritual she would continue in hunts when she became queen. Her skills were as good as—if not better than—any of the men who joined her. On that afternoon in 1570 La Mothe Fénélon witnessed the queen's passion for this sport firsthand.

After killing six fallow deer, Elizabeth was finally ready to meet the ambassador, and at first sight she seemed "pleased to see him," though she asked him rather bluntly why he had come to visit her. What could possibly be so urgent that the matter could not wait until her return to Hampton Court, or at least until her few days in Oxford, where she had invited him? She did not appreciate being interrupted during her leisure time.

Reluctantly but firmly, the French ambassador took his courage in both hands and mentioned that "another ambassador, who he didn't know the identity of" had advised the French king that Elizabeth "was resolved in declaring war" and that his master was now concerned the accusation might be true—despite having no real evidence of its veracity.

Elizabeth was "dumbfounded," and immediately assured La Mothe Fénélon that her main goal was indeed the exact opposite—to avoid war and indeed to maintain "good relations" with France.[7] If the French ambassador and his king believed this "infamy," then they should be ashamed of themselves. La Mothe Fénélon did not want to risk angering Elizabeth—especially after seeing her hunting so ferociously—so he took the opportunity to excuse himself, asking if he could leave her presence. She granted his wish without hesitation.

He reported back to his masters, Charles IX of France and his mother, Catherine. While all the details of the audience can be found in La Mothe Fénélon's dispatch to the king, Charles shared the information with the queen mother, who was unimpressed with Elizabeth's behavior, both in this matter and in Elizabeth's dealings with Mary Stuart, who remained imprisoned in the north of England after her brief escape in May 1568. The French rulers were adamant: Mary had to be freed. After all, not only was she an anointed queen, but she had also been the queen of France and her poor treatment and condition were therefore not just an insult to her but an insult to all of them.

Catherine's other goal was to end the threat of a potential open war with England: she did not believe Elizabeth's assurances, and knew she could not afford to go to war, particularly as she was struggling to maintain peace inside the borders of her own realm.

"I am keeping my eyes open, as usual. Some of my informants have warned me that warships have been loaded on the English coast," Catherine revealed to La Mothe Fénélon. "Make sure that the English are not showing any kind of animosity."[8]

The French monarchs were not duped, and there was no doubt that Elizabeth had plans that could compromise them—the warships being spotted on the English coast were military support that Elizabeth was ready to give the Huguenots. It was a belligerent act and

Catherine was determined to put an end to it—either by force or by a marital alliance that would neutralize Elizabeth's power. And, for that, she was ready to rely on an old enemy of hers.

During the second war of religion that had ravaged France from 1567 to March 1568, Catherine had felt powerless. One of her worst nightmares had played itself out: the Huguenot leaders, Louis de Condé and Gaspard de Coligny, had invaded Paris, meaning that both her safety and that of her son, the king, were at stake.

On November 10, 1567, during the battle of Saint-Denis and fearing that Paris would be lost to the Huguenots' forces, Catherine named the faithful and great warrior Anne of Montmorency as head of the royal army. Unfortunately, during that battle, the Constable de Montmorency—who, at the age of seventy-four, had served the crown for decades—was shot in the back, dying two days later. Nevertheless, his men managed to win the battle.

While the conflict raged on for months after the battle, the Huguenot army was eventually forced to flee. Odet de Coligny—Gaspard's older brother and one of the most influential Huguenot figures—fled to England, where he sought asylum with Elizabeth.

The French royal family negotiated the Peace of Longjumeau on March 23, 1568, but that peace was fragile; all trust between Condé and the crown was gone. Months later, the third war of religion erupted in the Loire region, while Odet de Coligny was a refugee in England. Odet, who since 1534 had also been known as the Cardinal of Châtillon, was a tall and regal man of fifty years. His pale blue eyes seemed cold and imperious, yet it was said they exhibited a sense of duty—a duty to his brothers, but also to his country and faith. He wore impeccable military or religious attire and had the recognizable features of all the Colignys: a perfect Greek nose and a penetrating gaze. Though devoted to the Protestant cause since his conversion in 1561, Châtillon also seemed determined to find a compromise with the royal family.

During his years in exile, Châtillon wrote several letters to the French monarchs, maintaining that the Huguenots had nothing but a "desire to give full obedience, subjection and faithful servitude to the king" and the queen mother.[9] Châtillon was a zealous Protestant but he remained at heart a Frenchman, who was undoubtedly missing his homeland. Catherine saw an opportunity to continue a correspondence as a means of spying on Elizabeth; as a refugee and an important Huguenot figure, he had access to courtiers who were close to Elizabeth. He was therefore charged with informing Catherine of the English queen's supposedly real intentions regarding France—and, in his view, Elizabeth could be persuaded to negotiate a potential marriage to Catherine's second remaining son, Henri, Duke of Anjou.

In October 1570, Catherine remained mindful of a potential marriage between "the queen of England and my son," but revealed to La Mothe Fénélon that she had asked Châtillon's opinion on the matter. He confirmed that "this could happen easily, if we wish so,"[10] and also confided to Catherine that Elizabeth was in fact "under pressure to marry a great prince and that she had to comply."[11]

Catherine nevertheless felt cautious. If Châtillon was so open to discussing a potential alliance between Elizabeth and her son, it surely meant that it would also benefit the Huguenots in France, and Catherine feared this meant it would benefit their interests more than her own. Would she now be bringing an enemy into the family?

Having reservations, therefore, about this potential union, the French queen mother explained to La Mothe Fénélon that she had come up with a great alternative. By this point Elizabeth had been on the throne of England for more than a decade, repeatedly refusing suitors. Catherine now doubted that Elizabeth was "in search of an husband" and suggested "if there was a woman or a girl to be married who belonged to her [Elizabeth] and that she was willing to make her next heir to the crown after her, this would be more suitable" for the French family and for her son.

She insisted that this alternative "would bring the said queen all the joys and contentment that she could hope for" as she could see Henry, Duke of Anjou, as "her own son, as he is of such a good nature, that if she gave him that chance, he would serve and honour her with affection."[12]

This idea, however, was not well received. Elizabeth was shrewd enough not to have any such woman in her entourage; she wanted to remain the center of attention, and nor did she want any interlopers complicating her life. Catherine's suggestion, therefore, was cast aside almost immediately. And perhaps it even spurred Elizabeth into reconsidering her approach.

A month later, during a frosty morning at Hampton Court, La Mothe Fénélon was feeling anxious about meeting with the queen. Soon, he was met by Robert Dudley, who himself accompanied him to Elizabeth's privy chamber, where he found "her better dressed than usual."

He was surprised to find that Elizabeth was expecting him to discuss marriage negotiations, which had so far been dangerous territory. For years the French ambassador had been well aware of Elizabeth's position when it came to marriage, yet his new goal as an official ambassador, following the failure of Catherine's previous suggestion, was to interest Elizabeth in marrying Henry, Duke of Anjou.

Henry, Catherine thought, might have more of a chance than Charles. He was without a doubt one of the most handsome men in France. Tall, well built, and with dark, intense eyes, the young prince was already said to be a womanizer, pursuing quite a few relationships with various ladies at the French court. He had just turned nineteen and was his mother's favorite child. Nothing was too much for her prodigy. She had great plans for him.

Tactfully, the French ambassador began the conversation. "I remember well that you had assured us that it was not that you did not wish to marry," he started, "but that instead you had had the greatest regret not to have thought enough about your posterity and that you would never find a better party than this royal house, which is so much suitable to your quality."

She watched him for a moment, and then she smiled.

"I have great esteem for Monsieur Henry, Duke of Anjou, as he is from a family of excellent quality." She paused. "However, I fear that the young duke is more eager to marry the realm than he is to marry the queen herself, as it happens so often between great rulers who marry one another other without seeing each other first, and it is common knowledge that those of the French house have had the reputation of being good husbands who give honour to their wives, but do not love them."[13] This comment was barbed, perhaps even an insult aimed at Catherine's marriage to Henry II, as the late king had spent his whole life loving another instead of his loving, devoted wife and queen.

The audience ended abruptly after these words, but another month later, La Mothe Fénélon was ready to deploy another tactic, launching a counterattack by wondering whether the duke might be too young for the queen after all. This was a reason she offered her courtiers many times, but Elizabeth did not like to hear her words coming from another person's mouth. She rebuked the ambassador. "How could I not satisfy him?"

He was now in a thorny position. He stated that he was simply concerned by the wishes of her people, and her ministers. But the Tudor queen set the record straight.

"I am queen regnant, who does not depend on the members of her Council."[14] The one who had to be seduced and convinced was Elizabeth herself—no one else—and now the queen had another concern in mind. "I will not marry a man who will only honour me as a queen and not love me as a woman."

Nevertheless, the intervention seemed to have moved her to a serious consideration of a union, and steps were taken to set in motion a potential marriage. Henry would formally court Elizabeth, and both parties sent special envoys to court to ensure a happy outcome.

For her part, Catherine was relying on her informants in England: the Cardinal of Châtillon, of course, but also an influential Anglo-Florentine tradesman who had vowed his fidelity for years, Guido Cavalcanti. As for Elizabeth, she trusted Francis Walsingham, her resident ambassador at the French court, to pursue the negotiations on her behalf and to raise her personal concerns on the potential union, especially when it came to the question of religion. In early 1571 she also sent in Thomas Sackville, Baron Buckhurst, a cousin from her mother's side, so he could congratulate Charles on his marriage to Elisabeth of Austria (daughter of Holy Roman Emperor

Maximilian II), but more importantly so he could support Walsingham in the marriage negotiations with the French duke.

Guido Cavalcanti was the son of Giovanni, a Florentine merchant who had arrived in England in 1510 and gone into business with his brother, Estriota, exporting goods from England. He was the perfect agent: he was English enough to be trusted at court, and Florentine enough to be trusted by Catherine. He also had several business and diplomatic connections all over Europe. In other words, he had influence.

Cavalcanti served La Mothe Fénélon in his endeavors; when the French ambassador was sick in bed, Cavalcanti came to visit him, keeping him posted on the developments at court. Guido had met with Cecil and informed the French ambassador that he was on his way to Hampton Court for a few days. He was determined to prove himself worthy of Catherine's and La Mothe Fénélon's trust.

As the French queen mother trusted him, she ordered La Mothe Fénélon to send Cavalcanti for a private audience with Elizabeth, where he would undertake verbal negotiations. Catherine was adamant that an Anglo-Italian man who knew the English customs so well would be able to find a solution to the issue that left them all at an impasse: religion.

Henry was a fervent Catholic who had just won a decisive battle at Jarnac in 1569, defeating the Huguenots and their leader. He was cheered, and hailed as a Catholic hero all over France, with pamphlets praising his exploits printed in Lyon and Paris and circulated feverishly around the country. It was common knowledge that Elizabeth had supported the Huguenots in this conflict, and everyone from the reformed religion saw her as a Protestant savior. Would their religious differences derail the match?

In both courts, ambassadors, special envoys, and rulers all debated this, and wondered how an alliance between Elizabeth and Henry would affect their personal faith. Then, on the morning of February 23, Sackville, accompanied by Walsingham, arrived at court for an audience with the king and his two brothers, Henry and Francis, Duke of Alençon. (Catherine had two sons called Francis, as her youngest son

Hercule took on that first name following the early death of his brother, Francis II.) Sackville was the bearer of Elizabeth's letters, and had the mission of assuring them of Elizabeth's determination to remain a close ally to France in spite of their religious differences.[15]

Elizabeth spent months ordering Walsingham to come to some kind of resolution on this issue. "Monsieur has to comply with me,"[16] she said. From her perspective, there was simply no other option: Henry would need to bend to her will. But Henry, and the French royal family, were also somewhat perturbed by the idea of marrying a Protestant ruler who would not even grant him freedom of conscience. Elizabeth was once more doing what she did best: confusing her suitor by not giving clear indication of what she truly wanted. Was there to be a marriage or not?

It was time for Elizabeth and Catherine to start exchanging direct letters, tackling the conflict of interest. Bluntly, Elizabeth set out her stance: "My conscience will not allow me to comply with the demands made by the queen mother."[17]

After consulting Henry, Catherine decided to send another special envoy to the English court to make a case for her son: Nicolas de Grimonville, Seigneur de Larchant, who was Henry's Captain of the Guards. However, upon his return in midsummer of 1571, Larchant bore nothing but bad news: Elizabeth still did not wish to sign off on the articles relating to the question of religion.

Upon hearing this, Catherine took matters into her own hands and wrote directly to the English queen. "I assure you that a potential union between our two houses was only increasing my affection towards you. I beg you to continue the discussion with Henry himself. We all want to find solutions to the difficulties we are all facing."[18]

Elizabeth remained stubborn. If the marriage was to proceed, she would not grant him freedom of conscience at her court. "The matter has chiefly depended on the cause of religion; they [the French monarchs and ambassador] require toleration, and I deny the same." She made her point clear.

"I cannot permit him to have the use of any private Mass at his coming."[19] After all, if Henry wanted to be the king of a Protestant country, wouldn't he want to convert for his wife and queen—and for his new homeland?

The second matter—which was highly controversial at the time—was that Elizabeth fervently insisted, as she had before, that she would not marry someone she had never yet met. And so, yet again, both parties were facing a deadlock.

The French duke refused point-blank to make the trip until there was a written promise from Elizabeth that she would marry him, to which the queen retorted, "I will not promise myself to any party, without seeing the one who is supposed to be my husband."[20] Elizabeth would not budge on this point.

Catherine knew what was at stake. An alliance through marriage between France and England was what the French rulers needed to ensure Elizabeth would not declare war on them, to protect the Huguenots, and to ensure that Mary Stuart was shortly freed and reinstated as queen of Scotland. They needed her more than ever.

As the situation continued to unfold, La Mothe Fénélon seemed to have been developing a special relationship with the Tudor queen. He had always been something of an admirer of Elizabeth. In the summer of 1570, he recalled that she had invited him to court for a public audience with some of her courtiers, and that she had "decorated her court being herself well dressed and looking as a wonder."[21] La Mothe Fénélon noted each time Elizabeth made an effort in her appearance when seeing him; maybe he thought she did it for him, and maybe she did, but what is certain is that Elizabeth kept receiving the ambassador in public and in private, discussing more than just mere practicalities and political matters. She clearly enjoyed his company, and this was strongly reciprocated.

In January 1571, La Mothe Fénélon spent a great deal of time with Elizabeth and relayed her plans. "Those of this City of London have shown much happiness regarding the arrival of their queen, who, because of plague, had not been able to stay in the city for two years." During this absence, Elizabeth had remained in her castles all around London—including Richmond Palace, Greenwich Palace, and Hampton Court—but indeed had spent no time at all in the city itself. "She is going today to see a new building erected, huge and with a beautiful architecture, in order to give it a name, which until now has been called provisionally 'La Bource,' The Royal Exchange. There is to be a feast in the house of Master Gresham."[22]

Thomas Gresham was an English merchant and financier who had been a loyal servant to Tudor monarchs ever since Edward VI's reign. He was also the founder of the Royal Exchange, a building whose fame would last a lifetime—several lifetimes, in fact. This was an exceptional event, as Elizabeth was awarding the building its royal title as well as granting a licence to sell alcohol and valuable goods.[23]

La Mothe Fénélon reported that Elizabeth sought his company at this prestigious event. "I have been invited to accompany the queen of England to the feast of the Bource, which has been almost as solemn a celebration in London as her coronation, because she was received with crowds, the streets were thronged with people, and everyone in order, in his rank, as if it had been her first entry in the city, and I witnessed that it gave her great pleasure," he wrote. He did not leave her side for the whole celebration. "She wanted to leave around eight at night, the people in the streets did not tire, some in ranks, others forming crowds, with bright torches, to give her joyful honour."

And, in the middle of the crowd, the two shared private moments— moments when Elizabeth dropped her queenly mask. She wanted to get to know him.

"Do these festivities remind you of the ones held in Paris?" she asked.

"In many ways they are more impressive," he replied. She smiled.

"I must confess that it gives me great joy in my heart to see myself so loved and desired by my subjects," she confided quietly.

"Your Majesty, I can definitely see your greatness, which should always be praised."

Even after the celebrations had concluded, Elizabeth decided to continue the evening in La Mothe Fénélon's company and talked to him "for a long time" throughout the night.[24] The French ambassador divulged that they discussed several topics, "including her resolution to get married, not because she cannot do without it (as she had managed without a husband for some time) but to satisfy her subjects."

But in the midst of their conversation, the queen made another personal confession to La Mothe Fénélon.

"I greatly fear not to be loved enough by the man who will marry me. That would truly pain me."

He responded kindly. "I have no doubt that you will be greatly honoured and extremely loved."[25] She appreciated his kind words and thanked him for them.

They probably bonded that night as Elizabeth revealed the woman behind the queen: the woman who feared not being loved for who she was, giving La Mothe Fénélon the opportunity to reassure her. Behind her royal façade she was also a person, and had her own vulnerabilities. Perhaps this is why she valued her time with La Mothe Fénélon, and they remained close as the marriage negotiations between Henry and Elizabeth progressed, sharing several more private moments. La Mothe Fénélon exceeded his assigned duties and gained the trust—and maybe even the friendship—of one of the most powerful monarchs in Europe.

But as for the marriage negotiations, they had failed miserably: Elizabeth decided she would not marry Henry. But Catherine was a resourceful woman, and she had not had her last word on the matter. She had yet another son, one who was far more compliant and more tolerant when it came to the new religion. And, for that task, it became clear to Catherine that she had in her service the right negotiator, especially as he had already managed to acquire the favor of Elizabeth with his wit and agreeable company: La Mothe Fénélon himself.

II

Tears and Fury:
Francis, Elizabeth's "Frog,"
1572–1578

It was March 1572 and the weather in France was still dreadful, leaving Sir Thomas Smith suffering. He had been sent as a special envoy to assist Sir Francis Walsingham, resident ambassador at the French court, in important negotiations. It was not only the cold that bothered him, but also the constant rain, which seemed to seep into his bones.

Nevertheless, these matters required resolution, and an alliance between France and England against Spain needed to be confirmed. Philip II's power had continued to grow in recent years, threatening the two queens, but now the Spanish Netherlands faced terrible rebellions from the Protestant Dutch led by William I, Prince of Orange, an ally to Elizabeth I and the Huguenot leaders, Coligny, Jeanne d'Albret, queen of Navarre, and Henry, heir to the Navarrese throne. Catherine was reluctant to be at open war with Spain, but Charles convinced her to support the Dutch in secret, counterbalancing Spain's power in Europe.

Catherine knew that, if such a scheme was to work, she would need Elizabeth's help—with or without a marriage between the two crowns, though the possibility of dynastic alliance continued to occupy her. In this respect, her son Francis was now her last chance.

Catherine received Smith to discuss the possible arrangements for a secret alliance between the two crowns. She explained that the king, her son, was too unwell—suffering from a cold—to undertake the negotiations, so she would be at the helm. In reality, none of them could afford to have a Catholic king make an alliance with a Protestant queen against another Catholic king. After all, they had to keep up appearances.

On March 31, 1572, Smith successfully obtained an audience with Catherine for himself and Walsingham. She received them both early in the morning in her chamber.

Knowing that Catherine's time was precious, Smith cut to the chase. "We have asked for an audience with you to discuss the importance of securing a league between your son, the king, yourself and our mistress, the queen of England."

"I could not agree with you more," Catherine replied simply.

"When do you think your son will have his courier sent to finalise the treaty of peace between our two countries?" Smith asked.

"Soon enough," came the blunt response. Catherine seemed dismissive, as if she was uncomfortable discussing such matters further.

Smith, however, was determined to get an answer. "My mistress wishes the resolution of this treaty was more straightforward. We take the time lost with the courier very seriously. Some evil suspicion may be conceived, but I obviously do trust that the amity is already so established between the two realms that there shall be no suspicion. Am I right?"

Clearly, Smith was testing Catherine. He did understand the unnecessary delays: they suggested that the French had gotten cold feet. For the queen mother, the decision to side formally with England against Spain, even if the treaty was to remain a secret, meant jeopardizing France's relations with their Catholic neighbors. This could undermine her own personal relations with her granddaughters born of Elisabeth of Valois, Isabel Clara Eugenia and Catalina Micaela. But for Charles, who was now a grown man eager to make the important decisions, it was the right choice to make, and Catherine knew that she had to honor his choice.

Yet the question still remained: could Elizabeth ever truly be trusted?

"We greatly value our friendship and goodwill with your mistress, the queen of England," Catherine continued. "As you know, we are even offering our youngest son to her. What more proof do you need of our good faith?"

Walsingham remained silent, carefully observing Catherine's reactions. He had always been a good judge of character, great at seeing through people. Clearly, a tension existed between the queen mother and Charles on this matter. Catherine was not inclined, as she swore she was, to challenge Philip II's authority. He perceived that very well.

Walsingham was a fervent Protestant who was devoted to both Elizabeth and England. He did not hide his religious beliefs, even in the very Catholic city of Paris. As usual, he wore his black gown adorned with a white collar. Charismatic, with piercing blue eyes, Walsingham made an impression wherever he went.

Standing in the corner of the chamber, he was now staring at Catherine.

She felt the intensity of his gaze, and asked, "Is there anything you want to add, Sir Francis?"

As he stepped out of the shadows, he replied, "We are here to talk to you as plainly as possible, your Majesty."

Catherine knew he was suspicious of her hesitation.

"The league between France and England needs to be resolved soon," Walsingham paused before finally adding, "For all our sakes."

"And it will be. Fear not. Tomorrow you shall have an answer from my son, the king, and myself," Catherine replied.

Just as Walsingham was about to say something in return, she stopped him. "As you know, we desire nothing more than a very close bond with your mistress. It is now time to take your leave. We will talk about it again."

As they left the room, Walsingham turned and said, "And we do also desire the same, Madame."[1]

Catherine feigned a smile in response, but she couldn't hide her discomfort.

*

Two days later, Smith and Walsingham—who had both been sick during the night, probably due to consuming bad meat—were visited by

Sébastien de l'Aubespine, Bishop of Limoges, and Paul de Foix, who was now acting as a privy councillor to the French rulers.

They came with good news. Charles and Catherine had finally agreed to sign the secret league treaty with England—as long as Elizabeth did not get involved in Scottish matters and agreed to find a solution regarding Mary's imprisonment. More negotiations were underway, but both English diplomats—who were happy, overall, with the terms of the treaty—encouraged Elizabeth to ratify it.

Walsingham thanked the French commissioners and assured them "this bond between our two realms is desired in hearts, words, and deeds, and it should go forward for the benefit of all the three realms, including Scotland."

Eventually, the Treaty of Blois was signed. It entailed a free trade agreement between England and France, which was supposedly meant to compensate for England's trade loss with Flanders.

Whatever her true feelings on the matter, Catherine wrote directly to Elizabeth to express her contentment. "I cannot tell you how happy I am that the resolution of this new alliance, treaty, and confederation between our two realms has been agreed, and assure you of my great desire and affection to see it fortified and maintained."[2]

However, Catherine was sure that this new alliance was still not enough to secure Elizabeth's permanent support. She continued to believe that marriage was the only way to achieve this ultimate goal, the preservation of her dynasty.

Catherine also had her eye on another significant dynastic alliance. This time she was determined to make peace with Navarre, hoping to put an end to the religious division in France and to the animosity that existed between herself and Jeanne d'Albret, queen of Navarre and fierce Protestant leader of the Huguenots in France.

The very Catholic Catherine de Medici was now courting two Protestant queens—and promising both apparently unbreakable bonds. To Jeanne she offered her youngest daughter, the indomitable and enigmatic Marguerite of Valois. To Elizabeth she now offered her youngest son, the malleable Francis, Duke of Alençon, who would eventually become Duke of Anjou—a more prestigious title—in 1576.

Francis had always been an advocate for Protestantism in France and had even joined the side of the Huguenots in 1576 after a disagreement with his brother, Henry III. This made him popular in unexpected places. In 1579, William the Silent had invited Francis to become the next hereditary sovereign of the United Provinces in the Netherlands—which was seen as a true affront to Spain—and, in 1580, Francis, Duke of Anjou, was named "Protector of the Liberty of the Netherlands." In other words, no one showed more religious tolerance than he did, and a match with him could ensure peace with both Catholic and Protestant countries and territories.

★

In late 1571, Jeanne d'Albret agreed to start negotiations on the marriage of her heir, Henry of Navarre, to Catherine's young daughter Marguerite of Valois. In the midst of winter 1572, she finally arrived at Blois to be told that Catherine would receive her at Chenonceau, twenty-five miles away.

Jeanne was accompanied by her thirteen-year-old daughter, Catherine of Bourbon. They both had light brown hair, which probably lightened easily in the sun, pale blue eyes, and the same Greek nose and thin lips. As they stepped down off their coach they were received by Catherine, in her usual black dress representing her widowhood, and Marguerite, in a more flamboyant golden dress. At first, the two queens did not say a word. They simply embraced each other's daughters while looking tentatively at each other. The long-standing tension between them was still palpable. Was this meeting really a good idea?

Once they had all walked into the castle and had entered the dining room, Jeanne finally broke the uncomfortable silence. "I am starving," she declared.

In response, Catherine ordered that Jeanne be served first.

The dinner was brief and, shortly after it had concluded, Catherine invited Jeanne into one of her private rooms. "I believe we have things to discuss," she told her.

Jeanne followed without a word.

They spent hours locked away, while those outside waited expectantly. When they finally emerged, a radiant-looking Jeanne delivered the news happily: "The marriage between my son and Marguerite is agreed!"[3]

There was jubilation from all quarters.

Of course, certain matters still needed to be addressed. The next day Jeanne asked to see the English ambassadors, Smith and Walsingham, wishing to seek their advice on the situation. For Walsingham, the approach was a step toward the unity of France as well as a step even closer to an enduring alliance with England.

"I am holding the wolf by the ears," Jeanne said to Walsingham and Smith. "There are many dangers in concluding or not concluding this marriage. The king and the queen mother have expressed their desire that my son remain at court after the wedding, but refused to let him exercise his religion." She continued, with a nervous tone, "The worst is that they expect Marguerite to exercise hers when she comes to Béarn. I know that if I allow this, the Papists will see an occasion to take up arms against us once more."[4]

On that day, neither Walsingham nor Smith managed to find the right words to counsel Jeanne; they simply reminded the queen of the importance of promoting peace.

Walsingham assured Secretary of State William Cecil, Lord Burghley, that, "though it looks like the marriage won't happen, I think otherwise. They have too many reasons on both sides to see it through."[5] He was right.

On April 11, Jeanne finally signed the marriage contract, and she seemed relieved and happy about the resolution. She confessed to Elizabeth in a letter, "God in his goodwill has counselled the hearts of both sides to make this unbreakable resolution of the marriage of Madame Marguerite with my son happen. I want to thank you for your ambassadors' support and counsel in that matter."[6]

In many ways, it seemed God had decided to show Jeanne mercy; as it turned out, she would not witness the horrible events to come in summer 1572 herself. She had been quite unwell for some months, and in June she developed a fever, complaining that her whole body was aching. On June 9, she died.

Legend says that Catherine de Medici had offered perfumed gloves to Jeanne, having ensured that they'd been skillfully poisoned by her reputable perfumer, René Bianchi, another Florentine. There has never been any evidence that this was true. That the two women despised one another was common knowledge. That Catherine would poison the queen of Navarre—risking the vital marriage failing if anyone discovered her actions—is very unlikely. But it was perhaps a blessing in disguise for Jeanne that she avoided the events that were to come.

Now that the alliance with Navarre was settled, Catherine turned all her efforts toward ensuring another alliance with another Protestant queen: Elizabeth.

*

Catherine did not hide the fact that she was the driving force behind the proposal of a potential match between her youngest son and Elizabeth. This time, she was more determined than ever to see it through. And this time, Elizabeth would say yes to her son.

In early June, Catherine began courting Elizabeth on behalf of Francis.

"I am so thrilled to see that our friendship is so confirmed and renewed. I can assure you that my son, the king, and myself, have a strong desire to make it immortal." Catherine had reason to feel hopeful; she thought that agreeing to a Protestant marriage for her youngest daughter would demonstrate to Elizabeth her tolerance of the reformed religion, which would appease any suspicions regarding Catherine's religious motivations.

"I have nothing dearer to me than my son, the duke of Alençon, and it is with pure joy that we, my son, the king, and myself, offer him to you to marry. As you know, I have always desired to have the honour to love you like a mother loves her daughter, and with this alliance I could finally call myself your mother."[7]

Catherine did not wait for Elizabeth's reply before sending another letter expressing, yet again, her enthusiasm: "I have great esteem for you and I have the same affection for you that I have for my own daughter and I hope you will accept that I call you as such."[8]

Elizabeth must have been surprised by such an open expression of Catherine's desire to call herself her mother. She never commented on the turn of phrase, but one can imagine that it might have amused her. To put some distance between herself and the proposal—and, more importantly, Catherine—Elizabeth decided not to reply directly to the French queen mother and instead used her ambassador as her mouthpiece. This way, she would not have to respond directly to the bombardment of affection. In these answers, she remained diplomatic and distant.

This did not stop Catherine, nor did it slow her down even a little. She ordered her special envoys, Francis, Duke of Montmorency, and Paul de Foix—who had been sent to negotiate the treaty between England and France—to further discuss the potential marriage between Alençon and Elizabeth.

The Tudor queen, meanwhile, sent a letter to Walsingham to pass on to the French rulers. She swore to Charles and Catherine that she had no other intention but to maintain "and continue the amity that exists between us, as the last signed treaty proves. I am determined to increase this good alliance between us but because of the great difference of age between Monsieur of Alençon and myself, such a marriage cannot take place. Unfortunately this is not something I can change."[9]

But while Elizabeth initially seemed adamant in her refusal, three days later—in another letter she sent to Walsingham to pass on to Charles and Catherine—she gave the slightest hope to the French rulers. This time, she stated that she could be inclined to accept "an offer of marriage with the duke of Alençon" but that the difference of age was indeed what preoccupied her the most.

"I am so earnestly grateful to both your Majesties for the offer and I have such great desire to have the bond between us continued," she wrote. "I am sorry that I find such great difficulties in this matter but

I assure you it is no lack of desire in me to continue, and increase, the alliance between us."

Then, shrewdly, she left the door open for more negotiations: "Seeing and meeting one another in person might change my mind. I was told of his scars left by the smallpox and I confess I have the same blemishing on my face, so it won't play a role in my potential misliking."[10]

Looks had always been important to Elizabeth. All her courtiers were dashing, and she never hid the fact that she liked to be surrounded by handsome men. But she knew there were other attributes she should take into consideration—especially when it came to choosing a husband, or at least seeming to do so.

On July 25, Elizabeth invited Francis to visit her in England, though the invitation was rather blunt. "If we end up not liking one another, we will break off the match and blame it on religion."[11]

Within five days, Elizabeth sent Walsingham three letters for the French rulers. It was possible that Elizabeth was, finally, considering a potential husband. However, given her previous statements, it is quite unlikely that her claims were genuine. Instead, entertaining the match was probably a means of maintaining her good relations with France, and to have them within her control when the time came to discuss Mary Stuart's situation in the north of England. Indeed, Charles and Catherine could hardly defend Mary Stuart's interests while also courting Elizabeth—something Elizabeth knew, and was using to her advantage.

On August 21, 1572, Catherine seriously considered organizing a meeting with Elizabeth herself in the hope that she would finally be able to progress things. "Maybe during a calm and beautiful day we could meet between Boulogne, Calais, and Dover, and we could discuss the match," Catherine thought. Indeed, she wished "to see her in person as if she was my own daughter."[12] She truly believed that dynastic alliances with Protestant crowns would bring peace and prosperity to France. Finally, it would put an end to the religious divisions, as well as promoting tolerance across Europe.

Fate, however, had other plans.

Blood and fire were about to ravage first Paris and then the rest of France, seriously damaging the peace with England in the process.

*

Paris was Europe's first metropolis and, in the sixteenth century, it was home to 300,000 souls, 39 parishes, and 104 churches and monasteries. Paris was Catholic first and foremost.

At fifty-five years old, Admiral Gaspard de Coligny was a war hero and was now the most well-known Huguenot leader. Louis, Prince de Condé, had been killed during the 1569 Battle of Jarnac where the Catholic forces, led by Henry—Duke of Anjou, Charles IX's brother— confronted the Protestant armies. Louis's son, another Henry, succeeded him. Rather inexperienced, he more or less followed Coligny's orders and line of conduct. In other words, Coligny was essentially the face of French Protestantism.

He was now a privy councillor, attending several governmental meetings, and he had come to believe that Catherine wished to amend and unify the country. Indeed, with the wedding of Henry of Navarre and Marguerite of Valois, as well as the potential match between Elizabeth and Francis of Alençon, there was hope that better days were ahead.

But conspiracy was never too far away in sixteenth-century France, and this was truer than ever during the reigns of the last Valois kings.

Over the summer, Protestants arrived in great numbers in the capital, flooding inns and taverns. They were here to celebrate the royal wedding, and the peace that beckoned.

At first, Catholic Parisians seemed to tolerate their presence but, little by little, there was an increase in hate-filled preaching, in which Protestants were described as potential traitors to the crown and to France. The atmosphere grew tense in the streets, with fights between the factions erupting in inns and taverns. The peace suddenly seemed very fragile indeed. On Monday, August 18, 1572, the long-awaited wedding of Henry, recently crowned king of Navarre, and Marguerite of

Valois took place at the magnificent Cathedral of Notre-Dame. Thousands of Huguenots and Catholics attended the royal event.

While Henry was not particularly handsome, he was certainly charismatic and quite able to seduce women, and in fact he had become something of a womanizer. Marguerite was eighteen years old at the time and her dark hair and eyes, contrasting with her pale skin, made her a true Renaissance beauty.

On that special day she was dressed in a sublime "robe, sparkling with gems, a glittering crown trimmed with ermine on her head, and wearing a blue coat with a thirty-foot train carried by three princesses."[13] Charles IX and Henry, Duke of Anjou, were by her side, giving her away to become the queen of Navarre. While this was definitely not a love match but a strategic one, Marguerite—also known as Margot—had gone all out. She looked truly resplendent.

After the wedding, Henry of Navarre and Coligny left during the Mass. They rejoined the celebrations afterward and, while the attendees initially seemed to be joyful, tensions continued to grow between the two halves of the wedding party, throughout the evening, with the Guises glaring at Coligny and his fellow men.

Clearly, the celebrations wouldn't last long.

★

Friday, August 22, broke on a warm, pleasant morning. Gaspard had just left Le Louvre after a council meeting and seemed absorbed by the papers he held in his right hand, which probably detailed important state matters, given his increased influence at court and in government.

Then, as he turned the corner into the Rue des Poulies, a single shot was fired by Charles de Louviers, Sieur de Maurevert, a fervent Catholic who had strong ties with the Guises.

Coligny turned suddenly at the sound, so that the shot missed his vital organs, but instead "fractur[ed] his left forearm and [took] off an index finger."[14]

Fortunately, he survived the attack.

At the news of the incident, Charles IX, Catherine, and Henry, Duke of Anjou, attended the injured Coligny. Charles ordered that Ambroise Paré himself should treat the patient. Despite the shock, and the pain, Charles was sure that Coligny would survive.

As he looked into his eyes, Charles made a promise, "Whoever did this to you will be punished. Justice will be done. I swear on my honour."[15]

It was to mark the beginning of a nightmare. The true identity of whoever ordered the attack—which was part of an ordered massacre of hundreds, if not thousands, of lives of Huguenots—is still unknown. One thing is certain, however: Catherine de Medici, who took the blame for centuries, surely could not have been so reckless as to do so, not when she was doing everything in her power to ensure dynastic marriages with Protestant leaders, including Elizabeth herself. She would surely not have risked jeopardizing the secret Treaty of Blois that had been signed with England in April of the same year.

The Guises were the ones with the most obvious motive, who had the most to gain from such an attack. After all, Coligny and the Huguenots were influencing the French royal family, persuading them that reconciliation and unity were what France needed. For the Guises, what France needed most was to protect and maintain Catholicism at all costs. There was no place for heresy, nor, now, for tolerance.

During the night of August 23 to 24, the violence began to intensify, though no one knew exactly who was driving it, leaving ordinary people turning on one another, with Catholics entering Protestant homes in order to murder the inhabitants. All through the streets of Paris, hordes of people could be heard screaming that heresy should be exterminated in France. Blood spilled into the gutters as corpses lay in the streets or, in some cases, were hung from balconies. Among the chaos, others started fires, which engulfed neighborhoods and left people screaming for their lives.

Soon, Paris was the graveyard of many innocent souls, many murdered simply because of the wedding that they had attended—a wedding that was meant to mark the alliance of a Protestant leader with a Catholic princess.

Coligny didn't escape that bloody night. He was stabbed in his bed by a Catholic fanatic, Charles Danowitz—also called Besme—another accomplice of the Guises. Once the deed was done, Besme threw Coligny's body through the window so that the mob could grab it and drag it along the streets. They hung him by his feet at the Gibbet of Montfaucon, the main gallows and gibbet of the kings of France. This was traditionally the site of criminal executions, where those convicted were executed and hanged in public, marking a tragic end for a French nobleman. Coligny knew no pity in his death, nor honor—and it was the same for thousands of other Huguenots.

Upon witnessing the horror of the bloodbath in the city, a shocked Walsingham was grateful to be taken under the protection of Charles IX and Catherine. They opened their doors to any Huguenots who came knocking, hiding them away. Walsingham himself showed appreciation as he thanked "the king of France and the queen mother for the particular care they took of me and of all the English, during the last massacre."[16] If Charles and Catherine had known that a plot was forming against Coligny, they surely would neither have expected nor ordered the killing of thousands of their people.

But the murderous mood had started to spread beyond Paris, as killings eventually spilled into the French countryside, where Protestant towns, villages, and cities were all targeted.

Charles and Catherine ordered the end of the massacres but their protestations went unheard and, until October 1572, France continued to be subjected to fire and sword. The division between Protestants and Catholics had never been greater—indeed, it was now almost irreconcilable.

And equally troubling for the French court was that Charles IX and Catherine de Medici's reputations were tarnished by the events now known as the St. Bartholomew's Day massacre. Afterward, when discussing Charles and Catherine, people would even speak of two distinct eras: before the massacre and after it. In the aftermath, it seemed as though they had totally lost their ability to command their nation.

Elizabeth, watching closely, was horrified that such an event could occur in a neighboring country, but she knew her official reaction had to be carefully considered. She could not let it completely ruin her relationship with the French royal family—not with Spain gaining in power and strength.

★

While Walsingham was grateful to the French royal family for saving his life, Elizabeth was greatly distressed at the news of the event, hearing that "women, children, maids, young infants and sucking babes were at the same time murdered and cast into the river."[17] No one had been spared by the violent Catholic mob as it surged through Paris during that fateful night.

Two weeks after the massacre in Paris, Elizabeth received La Mothe Fénélon in her private chamber. This time she invited her privy councillors and ladies-in-waiting to attend too, and she didn't show her usual affection for the ambassador. Clearly, she was upset.

As he stepped in, La Mothe Fénélon immediately realized the gravity of the situation. Elizabeth's dark mood spilled out into her court, which was "in complete silence" now and, though he did not mention it in his letter, there were reports circulating that everyone present was "clothed in mourning attire."[18] It was a very different mood to the one he was used to encountering when he met Elizabeth.

Appearing sad and stern, Elizabeth walked a dozen steps toward Fénélon, pulling him by the arm over to the next window. She needed answers.

"I'm sorry it took me some time to receive you," she muttered, looking away, through the window. "Tell me the truth and only the truth, did it truly happen? Is Charles IX, whom I love and honour dearly and have trusted more than any other prince of Europe, responsible for the atrocities in France?"

"Your Majesty, I assure you that what happened in France was an accident, and that there's no one else on Earth who is more saddened and horrified by it than Charles and his mother, Catherine."

"Then explain to me what exactly happened."

Portrait of Lorenzo II de Medici, Duke of Urbino (1492–1519), circa 1518.
Private Collection. Photo by Fine Art Images/Heritage Images/Getty Images.

Francis I, King of France, circa 1520–1525 by an unknown artist. Francis (1494–1547) ruled France from 1515 and is regarded as France's first Renaissance monarch.

A late sixteenth century portrait of Anne Boleyn (1500–1536) by an unknown artist on display at the National Portrait Gallery in London, England.

Mary of Guise (1515–1560), 1537. Found in the collection of the National Gallery of Scotland, Edinburgh. Photo by Fine Art Images/Heritage Images/Getty Images.

Mary Stuart, Queen of Scots (1542–1587), 1559, by Jean Clouet.

Catherine de Medici (1519–1589), Queen of Henry II of France.
Undated lithograph. Photo by Bettmann/Getty Images.

Undated portrait of King Henry II of France, found
in the Collection of State Hermitage, St. Petersburg.
Photo by Fine Art Images/Heritage Images/Getty Images.

Diane de Poitiers, the favorite of King Henry II.
Portrait by an unknown artist, in the castle of Anet.

Ambroise Paré is shown treating a wounded soldier in a tent. Undated gravure after a painting by Ed Haman.

This photograph taken on July 16, 2017, shows an aerial view of Château Chenonceau on the River Cher, some 30 kilometers east of Tours. Built in 1513 by Katherine Briconnet, it was enriched by Diane de Poitiers and enlarged under Catherine de Medici. It became a place of meditation for the white queen Louise of Lorraine, then it was saved by Louise Dupin during the French Revolution and, finally, transformed again by Madame Pelouze. Thus it is nicknamed the castle of the Ladies. Photo by Guillaume Souvant/AFP via Getty Images.

Sieve Portrait of Queen Elizabeth I, 1583. Painting by Quinten
Metsys II. Siena, Pinacoteca Nazionale, Buonsignori Palace.

Jeanne d'Albret, Queen of Navarre (1528–1572), circa 1570 by
François Cloue. Found in the Collection of the Musée Condé, Chantilly.

Double portrait of Henri III, King of Navarre, the future King Henry IV of France (1553–1610), and Margaret of France (Marguerite de Valois) (1553–1615), known as the Queen Margot. Miniature from the Book of Hours of Catherine de Medici, sixteenth century. BN, Paris, France. Photo by Leemage/Corbis via Getty Images.

St. Bartholomew's Day Massacre, by François Dubois. Dubois (1529–1584) was a French Huguenot painter. His only surviving work is the best known depiction of the Saint Bartholomew's Day massacre of 1572.
Photo by Universal History Archive/Universal Images Group via Getty Images.

Portrait of Henry III of France on horseback. Painting by a French school.
Chantilly, Château, Musée Condé. Photo by DeAgostini/Getty Images.

Elizabeth I's signature, circa 1560. Photo by Hulton Archive/Getty Images.

Michel de Castelnau (1517–1592), seigneur de La Mauvissière, 1731.
Private Collection. Photo by Fine Art Images/Heritage Images/Getty Images.

Portrait of Henry I, Duke of Guise (1550–1588), by an unknown artist, circa 1585. Found in the collection of Musée Carnavalet, Paris. Photo by Fine Art Images/ Heritage Images via Getty Images.

Portrait of Catherine de Medici by an unknown artist, found in the Collection of State Hermitage, St. Petersburg. Photo by Fine Art Images/ Heritage Images/Getty Images.

Procession Portrait of Queen Elizabeth, circa 1600–1603, by an unknown artist. Found in the collection of Sherborne Castle, Dorset. Photo by Fine Art Images/Heritage Images/Getty Images.

As he leaned forward, La Mothe Fénélon whispered, "There was a plot to assassinate Admiral Coligny. While we are not certain of who ordered it, there are very strong ties with the Guises, as I'm sure you're not surprised to hear. The truth? Other plots targeting the French royal family have been discovered. This is when everything got out of hand and the violence started. The French rulers are determined to bring justice to those who participated in the killings."

Elizabeth continued to look out the window, seeming pensive. "This is just absolutely horrible. So many Protestant lives were lost." She paused, then looked straight at La Mothe Fénélon, who didn't dare meet her gaze. "I am grateful that my ambassador and dear councillor, Sir Francis Walsingham, was protected during that night but I am also very concerned about the consequences of it all, especially when it comes to the edict of peace of Saint-Germain, signed in 1570, finally putting an end to the bloody wars in France. Are Charles and Catherine still willing to see it implemented?"

"I have no doubt that they are, your Majesty," La Mothe Fénélon replied.

"What exactly happened and who is responsible for it needs to be Charles's priority. I will continue my friendship and alliance with him and the queen mother as long as they honour the edict of peace and restore their reputation by bringing justice," Elizabeth stated.

La Mothe Fénélon bowed and thanked her for being so virtuous toward France. Then he added, "Be assured that there is nothing more important to the French rulers, my masters, than fortifying and maintaining good relations with you, your Majesty."[19]

While Elizabeth had revealed her great discontentment, the Anglo-French alliance had not been too severely undermined by recent events.

*

In the following months, Charles and Catherine redoubled their efforts to consolidate their relations with Elizabeth. They sent even more letters illustrating their affection and expressing their desire to see a dynastic alliance established between them.

By now Charles and his young wife, Elisabeth of Austria, were expecting their first child. The family decided to ask Elizabeth to be the second godmother. She couldn't be the first, as she didn't share the same religion as the French royal family. So, Elisabeth of Austria's mother, Maria of Austria, would take that role.

On October 27, Charles's spouse gave birth to a healthy baby girl— a disappointment for many who had hoped for a male heir, but a joy nonetheless for the royal couple. After all, they believed she would be the first child of many. She was to be named after her two godmothers— Marie-Elisabeth—but Elizabeth had not yet accepted their offer, which had been relayed by La Mothe Fénélon.

Eventually, she agreed, though with one caveat: "I willingly accept but only if the French rulers do me the honour of asking directly."[20]

★

Upon hearing this news, Charles and his wife both sent formal letters to the queen, begging her "to accept our offer to become one of the godmothers of our daughter and to send who you think would be appropriate for the christening, which will fortify this true and perfect amity that exists between us."[21]

A few days after receiving their letters, Elizabeth gladly confirmed her acceptance to La Mothe Fénélon, "Though I imagine that Charles had hoped for a dauphin, I can assure him that the little princess is welcome in this world and I pray that God will make her as happy as I am to be descended from a good lineage, and like myself, she will be beautiful and virtuous."[22]

However, this apparent reconciliation was hiding other motives. The massacre had provided the perfect opportunity for Elizabeth to take the upper hand in the partnership with Charles and Catherine.

Elizabeth granted La Mothe Fénélon an audience in late November 1572, during which they returned to old themes, and the French ambassador tried once more to explain the events in France. She interrupted him by saying, "It is, even for princes, unlawful to kill or to order the killings, aside from in just two cases: one in times of legitimate war and the other for the execution of justice to punish crimes." As the French rulers were desperate to see the alliance forti-fied, Elizabeth could afford to make some snide comments regarding Charles's royal authority without any reprimand.

La Mothe Fénélon defended his masters' reputations. "Of all the princesses of Europe, you know how difficult a situation can be when it comes to religious disorder. You experienced one yourself not that long ago."

His reference to the 1569 Northern Rebellion, where English noble-men had tried to replace Elizabeth with Mary Stuart, was a step too far for the English queen.

In a stern tone, Elizabeth replied, "I am willing to excuse what hap-pened in Paris but I can see no excuse for what followed in Rouen and other cities. This shows a lack of control from your king and his mother." Once again, she took the moral high ground rather than answering any questions about Mary, who was still imprisoned.

She could afford to do so. Indeed, in the current situation, France could not afford to lose Elizabeth.

*

Now in the midst of the fourth religious civil war, which the mas-sacre in Paris had started, Catherine continued to push for success in the ongoing marriage negotiations. Elizabeth certainly seemed inter-ested: in recent correspondence, she showed great interest in Francis's physical appearance and continued to be adamant that they should meet in person.

Catherine wrote to praise her son's good looks, knowing that Eliz-abeth sought assurances of this. She hoped this would be sufficient to overcome the need for a meeting.[23]

"Francis has no deformity," she wrote. "On the contrary he is of a good, dignified height, from the same house and issue as his own father and mother, has a very good heart and hearing too, and there is nothing to say about his face aside from it happened by accident when he caught the smallpox. Otherwise, he is like my son, Henry, Duke of Anjou, whom the queen of England has loved so much."

Elizabeth maintained they should meet. It had been a common refrain: how could she marry someone she had never met before?

Catherine, finally, had no choice but to agree. "My son, the duke of Alençon, is very eager to come and see you in England and has asked me and his brother to take his leave from us to be able to join you, knowing your determination not to marry anyone without having seen him."[24]

Elizabeth replied that she was "more than happy to grant him a safe-conduct for his voyage to England." She also, however, reminded Catherine that despite Francis's willingness to meet her in person, she could not "promise to accept him as a husband," even after seeing him.[25] In other words, Catherine's son might be rejected, even after making the effort to travel to England. It was a risk he needed to be willing to take.

But timing would not allow it. Francis was needed in France: the religious war currently ravaging the country continued to intensify. He could not risk leaving to go to England. This further delayed the negotiations, though they were never completely halted. Catherine was determined to see her son, one day, become king of England.

The political upheavals did, however, put the marriage negotiations on the back burner. For one thing, there was Charles.

Charles IX had a fragile immune system, and in spring 1574, his condition worsened. He began coughing up blood, having reported feeling more and more unwell. Catherine was convinced he would feel better soon, however, and therefore didn't worry too much: he was a sickly man, but he always recovered.

But this time, Charles did not recover and, on May 30, the French king died at his Château in Vincennes, probably of tuberculosis. He was just twenty-three.

His death came as a huge blow to Catherine. Henry, Duke of Anjou and heir to the throne, had been elected king of Poland in 1573—after the death of the Polish ruler Sigsimund II Augustus on

July 7, 1572. The French had sent their envoy, Jean de Monluc, to negotiate the election of Henry to the now vacant Polish throne. His
election required months of negotiations but in September 1573, it
had been decided: Henry would become the next king of Poland.
When the news of his brother's death broke, Henry was therefore
not present to take his rightful crown. So, Catherine had to serve
once more as regent, waiting anxiously for the return of her favorite
son. Of course, she was also greatly affected by the loss on a personal
level: it was another wound that would never fully heal, as she
expressed in the letter she sent to Henry via her special envoy, one of
her trusted officers, Monsieur de Chemerault.

> I beg the Almighty to send me death rather than see this again…
> Such was his [Charles's] love for me at the very end, not wishing to
> leave me and begging me to send for you without delay, he asked me
> to take charge of the kingdom until your arrival and to punish the
> prisoners whom he knew to be the cause of the troubles in the realm.
> After this he bade me farewell and asked me to kiss him, which almost
> broke my heart.[26]

Elizabeth was one of the first to offer her sincere condolences.
Catherine appreciated her sympathy, "which makes me all the more
desire to continue the friendship between us which I assure you my
son, the king, will extend upon his return to France."[27]

Charles's death marked a shift in Anglo-French relations. Henry,
Duke of Anjou and king of Poland, was no longer a child—and he
was no teenager either. A charismatic man of twenty-two, he had
gained both political and military experience over the years as Lieutenant General of the Realm and as a privy councillor to his brother.
He knew how fragile peace could be. A fervent Catholic and a former
war hero for his victory at the Battle of Jarnac against Louis, Prince
of Condé, Henry also knew the importance of unity in order for a
ruler to govern efficiently.

Henry had always been Catherine's favorite; she called him "my
everything." He was dashing, smart, and athletic, and had a bright

future ahead of him—or he would have, had it not been for the bloody religious civil wars and other health troubles, which threatened the prosperity of this powerful young man.[28]

A new reign had begun and, this time, despite his strong affection for his mother, Henry would be the one in charge. He was, of course, happy to receive Catherine's advice and wisdom, but his attitude toward ruling was very different to that of his brother, and as he grew older he ensured that his mother understood her place. She was still to receive ambassadorial reports—a favor granted by Henry— but he was to rule. Catherine wasn't yet ready to give up her power, and ensured that she was a close advisor to her son and still very much involved in European politics, especially concerning matters in England. But he was her favorite son, and she ultimately respected his authority.

On February 13, 1575, at Reims Cathedral, Henry III was crowned king of France and quickly married Louise of Lorraine-Vaudémont— a cousin of the Guises, who would sacrifice her family ties for the love of her husband the next day, by swearing her true and only allegiance to the Valois dynasty.

This was not only the year of Henry's coronation but also the year of La Mothe Fénélon's return to France—something that permanently affected the dynamics of the diplomatic relations between England and France. His replacement was Michel de Mauvissière, Seigneur de Castelnau, a devout Catholic closely allied to the Guises. He despised Elizabeth for imprisoning Mary Stuart and vowed to help secure Mary's freedom. He would certainly not enjoy the level of intimacy that La Mothe Fénélon had managed to achieve with the English queen.

While La Mothe Fénélon had repeatedly complained about the English weather and had often asked to return to his home country, he was nonetheless saddened by the idea of leaving Elizabeth, and their friendship had brought both parties pleasure. By spring 1575, he was nevertheless preparing for his return and was no longer requesting audiences with Elizabeth, which she took to heart. On May 26, he was invited to an audience at Greenwich Palace, which on this occasion he did attend.

As soon as he stepped into the room, Elizabeth began talking. She could not hide her disappointment. "It seems that you have forgotten all about me," she told him. "You must have had very pressing matters to not seek my company."

Elizabeth was not the type of woman who liked to be ignored.

"I beg for your forgiveness, your Majesty. I have been busy, but it is with immense joy that I am now with you again,"[29] Fénélon replied.

After that the atmosphere eased a little, and they continued their conversation with the familiarity they were used to. La Mothe Fénélon remained in Elizabeth's good graces, and he knew how lucky he was to stay in that position.

In July 1575, as he was preparing to leave—which he eventually did in September of that year—Elizabeth decided to receive him for a final time in more informal surroundings. She was hunting near Woodstock and invited La Mothe Fénélon to join her. After her hunting session she asked the French ambassador, "I hope you will agree to join me for dinner?"

"It will be my pleasure, your Majesty," he replied.

After a dinner that La Mothe Fénélon found "sumptuous," Elizabeth took him aside, and he brought up a sensitive matter that had been raised by Henry and Catherine.

"My masters, the king and the queen mother of France, have heard rumours that you are supporting the Protestants in Flanders and German countries but also in France. Henry, king of France, values your friendship and only wants to see it strengthened, but this support will eventually undermine your alliance with France."

"I am not doing anything that would prejudice to the king of France," came the reply. "What they have heard is all lies. I would not dare to jeopardise my alliance with your masters."

While she seemed sincere, Elizabeth had of course always been a fervent supporter of the European Protestants, mingling in any affairs that concerned them; any such situation also concerned herself and the question of religion in England. She couldn't, however, openly admit to this. As a result, it is difficult to know her true feelings about the French royal family at this moment. It's true that she did show them high regard, and took the rare step of addressing them as her equals, but she also participated in their demise when supporting the Huguenots. It was a way for her to protect her own power and authority: for a queen, the only true loyalty could be to oneself.

"I am more determined than ever to see the alliance between our two countries strengthened. We should pursue further the marriage negotiations with the king's brother, Francis."[30] Elizabeth smiled, in an attempt to conclude to conversation.

Promising a dynastic alliance was the Tudor queen's favorite card to play to avoid discussing delicate political matters.

La Mothe Fénélon believed her interest was genuine and in his last dispatch, dated September 20, he gladly reported that this time Elizabeth "would give her final answer regarding the marriage proposal to Francis in the next four or five days."[31]

This was, of course, a promise she never kept.

★

In the midst of the sixth and seventh religious civil wars, the negotiations regarding the marriage between Alençon (who became Duke of Anjou in 1576) and Elizabeth continued to take a back seat. The French rulers were becoming increasingly concerned by Elizabeth's funding of the Huguenots, and tensions between the two crowns were starting to grow. Catherine now wanted more from Elizabeth: she wanted her to publicly take the side of the French rulers. She also wanted Elizabeth to answer for an apparent expression of conflict, the rumor "that England has sent three big vessels boarding 1,200 soldiers with more war vessels to follow."[32] The exact number and exactly when she sent support to the Huguenots is unknown, but it was indeed true that Elizabeth did provide military aid to her fellow Protestants in France.

Elizabeth wanted to enjoy the best of both worlds: to continue to support her religion across Europe, but also to maintain a cordial relationship with the French, particularly Catherine, who she did truly respect. If she was to continue as a double agent, Elizabeth had no choice but to make the French monarchs believe she was *entirely* on their side. She was finally willing to agree to a match with Francis of Anjou. Catherine's relentless pursuit of Elizabeth's hand was about to see a breakthrough.

Never had she been so close to becoming Elizabeth's mother-in-law. And never had Elizabeth been so close to agreeing to a marriage proposal.

12

Last Chance at Marriage
and a Lost Mother, 1579–1584

When Catherine offered one of her sons to Elizabeth, the person she was really offering was herself. As both women grew up motherless, they knew the importance of having a maternal figure in one's life, and Catherine believed that she could fulfill that role for Elizabeth. While it was true that the alliance was also politically convenient, Catherine's letters to Elizabeth also expressed a desire for a greater intimacy. Written in her very own hand, she claimed as early as 1572 that: "I love you as a mother does her daughter and I hope for a happy day when I might name myself as such [...] I pray God that you know the friendship and affection in which I hold you."[1]

By 1579 the ongoing marriage negotiations, which had continued to ebb and flow, were rekindled yet again. Now, it wasn't just Catherine behind the scheme: Anjou himself threw all his energy into it. He knew that such an opportunity might not arise again.

In late 1578, he sent to the English court one of his most trusted officers, Jean de Simier, Earl of Saint-Marc. Upon Simier's arrival in England in early January 1579, Francis vouched for his man's loyalty to him and for his desire to pursue the marriage negotiations further. Francis also begged Elizabeth to "take my affection as it is, faithful in my soul." He ended his letter with praise and swore that he was mesmerized by her as "the most perfect goddess in the heavens, I will humbly kiss your hands."[2]

Simier was the perfect representative to make Francis's case. He was cheerful, a romantic at heart, and knew well the games played at a royal court. As a token of affection to Francis—and perhaps as a playful belittling of the new courtier at court—Elizabeth made a play on his name, calling him her "singe" (monkey). He was to be based at Syon House in Middlesex, which had been prepared for this arrival. First, however, he stayed with the French ambassador Mauvissière at his residence at Salisbury Court, located between Fleet Street and the river. He found the arrangement most pleasing, and expressed gratitude to Elizabeth:

"I don't know where to start to express my most sincere gratitude, after receiving so many honours from you," he began. As he continued, he adopted an almost flirtatious tone. "I swear on my soul that you have no one more loyal and faithful to you than myself and I want to spend the rest of my life proving it to you. I am your monkey and happily obliged to answer all your orders, and to ensure that you continue to hear from your frog who has never been in better health and who is longing to see you in person."[3] It was as though he were pledging his own self to her.

Syon House was in a particularly convenient location, situated not too far from the Palace of Richmond, where Elizabeth was residing for the winter. If she was to be courted successfully, proximity was key. The house conveyed grandeur and prestige, and it had a history to match. In 1553 Lady Jane Grey and her husband, Guildford Dudley, had lived there. Later, during Elizabeth's reign, the house was acquired by Henry Percy, Earl of Northumberland, and had remained in his family since. The choice of this venue for Anjou's representative is revealing; it was a house that had clear royal connections, and it must have been believed that a successful union was close. Simier brought with him "ten or twelve thousand crowns' worth of jewels" to offer to the queen and her favorite courtiers, and to charm Elizabeth further.[4]

At the end of January 1579, Elizabeth left Richmond Palace to return to Whitehall Palace in London. Again, Simier followed. Moving with the court, he stayed at Mauvissière's household to ensure regular audiences with the queen.

The queen's arrival in London was much welcomed by the people of the city. Riding a Spanish horse, Elizabeth was dressed like the sun, glorious in a beautiful golden dress. The people knelt before her as she passed as though she were a goddess, calling out their thousands of blessings. Mauvissière and Simier were impressed by the outpouring of love for the queen: they were more used to witnessing bloody and violent civil wars in their home country.

At the end of February, Catherine—with Francis's approval—sent her own special envoy, Monsieur de Roquetaillade, to Elizabeth's court. He was one of her secretaries, and now he had the duty of handing Catherine's letters to Elizabeth. Wherever Francis was courting, Catherine was close behind, and Elizabeth was flattered by the attention, as she told Catherine:

"I assure you that I remain in my heart not insensible to the honour you do me; but estimating the fruits of your affection at the price of the opinion I have always had of them, I am constrained to love and honour you yet more."[5]

Roquetaillade had been well received at court, though he did not enjoy the same privileges as Simier. Indeed, during his stay Simier was granted audiences with the queen three to four times a week, a sure sign, the French believed, that marriage negotiations were going well.

In early April, Simier was invited to the intimate Christian ritual of the washing of the feet, which the queen always performed herself. It was an honor to be invited to such a private moment. After the ceremony, Elizabeth asked Simier to follow her—she had a surprise for Francis that she wanted Simier to approve. A few miles from Whitehall, south of the river where the court was currently residing, Elizabeth had ordered the construction of some tennis courts.

As she turned to Simier, her gaze full of pride and joy, she exclaimed: "They are for Francis. Mauvissière has told me that he was a real athlete and liked this type of sport. I hope he'll be as delighted as I am when he sees them next month."

"I have no doubt of his delight at the sight of them," Simier responded, bowing.

They continued their conversation in the gardens nearby before returning to Whitehall, where the French special envoy had been invited for dinner.[6] Simier confessed to a fellow diplomat in attendance—Roch de Sorbiers des Pruneaux, from the Netherlands—that he was "spending most of my time with the queen and she has agreed to look at the different articles of the marriage proposal. I have every good hope that this time the marriage will be concluded but I will wait until the curtain is drawn, the candle is out, and Monsieur is in her bed."[7]

As their time spent together increased, rumors spread that Francis's visit to England was imminent. People even gossiped that his mother would accompany him—after all, Catherine had really been the one pursuing Elizabeth with all her sons, for over a decade.

*

The rumors were partly correct. A meeting was certainly in the works.

In May 1579, the queen had asked her privy councillors to give her their individual opinions about the potential marriage with Francis. Once she'd received their papers, she rode to Wanstead Manor House—Robert Dudley, Earl of Leicester's main residence—and stayed there a few days as she examined their responses—which were conflicting. Dudley was her favorite for good reason; she trusted him to help her make the right decision, not only for herself as a woman, but for England and the unity of the country.

Upon her return to Whitehall, she summoned the whole Council for a number of sessions over the course of several days; they started at around two o'clock in the afternoon and finished at two o'clock in the morning. They discussed the pros—preserving a strong alliance with France against Spain—and the cons—having a Catholic king by the queen's side—of such a match. Elizabeth had never asked her Council to take a marriage proposal quite so seriously before.

Privately, Leicester was fuming—and consumed by jealousy. He did not favor such a match and did not like the attention Elizabeth was giving Simier, nor the multiple letters she wrote to Francis. The

French prince was a real threat to his own close relationship with the queen. He was outraged that Elizabeth and Francis had never met and yet she already seemed quite fond of him.

One evening after dinner, a melancholic Elizabeth—who was disappointed at the reticence her court had expressed about the potential marriage—invited Simier to her private chamber. To him she confessed, "I am deeply saddened that my councillors disapprove this marriage, which I desire so much."

Simier tried to reassure her: "Your Majesty, nothing is decided yet. We will convince them to change their mind."[8]

Simier could not be certain of his success, but he could certainly try. Both he and Francis knew that they had to win the councillors over, including Leicester, if they were ever to see this enterprise succeed. Nothing was worth more than Francis becoming Elizabeth's husband and king, especially as it was a position, and title, he had now been waiting to obtain for over eight years.

Francis set out to make peace with Leicester. He offered him two Spanish horses—the best and most desired racehorses in the world. Simier also organized two extravagant banquets for the councillors, in the hopes that lavish gifts and French generosity would win them over. Some were swayed but others, notably Leicester, remained inflexible, swearing on his life that he could not support the match. Perhaps he should have chosen his words more carefully.

In 1578 Leicester had married Lettice Knollys—Anne Boleyn's grandniece and Elizabeth's cousin—in secret. They feared Elizabeth's reaction if she were to discover the marriage, and were right to do so. Francis and Simier had eyes and ears everywhere, and were well aware of the situation. With Leicester's continued reluctance, which they felt was an affront to French authority, the French special envoy saw no other option but to reveal the awful betrayal in the earl's presence.

Elizabeth was horrified. Upon hearing the news, Elizabeth pointed at Leicester and screamed, "Take him to the tower of Greenwich! Get him out of my sight!"

Some said he was lucky that Elizabeth didn't send him to the Tower of London, while some said it was thanks to Thomas Radcliffe, Earl of Sussex, that Leicester avoided worse punishment. Despite having been Leicester's rival for decades and being the one to reveal the marriage to the French ambassador and envoys, Radcliffe pleaded his rival's case to the queen. He explained that no man should be punished for a lawful marriage—and he also probably felt that his treachery had gone a step too far if Leicester was being imprisoned.

Now that Leicester was out of the way, Francis felt the obstacles between him and the English queen were dissipating, and he was more determined than ever to plan his journey to England and conquer Elizabeth's heart. By June 1579, talk of a visit was high on the agenda. Roquetaillade was sent back to France with the passport for Francis: their first face-to-face meeting seemed inevitable, though the date had not been confirmed.

"I am burning with impatience,"[9] Elizabeth said, referring to him in a letter as "my dearest."[10]

During the next month, July, Simier became Elizabeth's shadow. He followed her everywhere: she spent all her time with him in Greenwich and gave orders for him to be accommodated at the palace alongside her. Her favorites—especially Christopher Hatton—burned with jealousy at Simier's bond with the queen.

Unfortunately, in early August 1579 plans were derailed by an offensive pamphlet that was circulated at court. Written by Puritan lawyer John Stubbs, it was a real affront to the queen and insulted the Anjou match. Stubbs did not hold back when he wrote *The discoverie of a gaping gulf whereinto England is like to be swallowed*. He warned the English people that "the French have sent us hither, not Satan in the body of a serpent, but the old serpent in the shape of a man, whose sting is in his mouth, and who doth his endeavour to seduce our Eve, that she and we may lose the English paradise."[11]

At first news of the pamphlet did not reach Elizabeth's ears—and for good reason. She was busy preparing for Francis's arrival, sure that it was imminent. The French prince was bringing his royal household with him and, to ensure the secrecy of his visit, he took the code name of Seigneur du Pont de Sé. After leaving Paris on

August 3, Francis landed in England fourteen days later. He was only days away from what he had been desiring for nearly a decade. To avoid being recognized by the court gossips, Francis exchanged cloaks with Simier.

Bursting with longing to finally see her match, Elizabeth ordered him to be brought to her at Greenwich Palace immediately. And so it was that on a warm summer afternoon, the moment finally came.

Francis was received by the English queen in a private room. When he entered, he found her standing with just one lady-in-waiting by her side. While at first they were both timid, Francis asked for permission to embrace her, explaining that it was customary to do so in France.

She gladly granted the request.

As they hugged and kissed on the cheeks several times, Elizabeth could not hide her excitement.

Neither could Francis. "I have been waiting for this moment for so long, your Majesty," he told her. "It is a true honour to be in your presence." As he bowed, he sneaked something from his pocket and, when he rose again, he was holding a beautiful and precious diamond ring—one allegedly worth 10,000 crowns.

"May I?" he asked, reaching out for her hand. She nodded and he placed the diamond ring upon her finger, vowing his "eternal devotion to you."

Delighted, Elizabeth turned to her lady-in-waiting and made a sign. In response, she brought her a slightly bigger box, which Elizabeth handed over to Francis with great pride.

As he opened the present he was visibly delighted. "What a wonderful jewelled arquebus!"[12] Elizabeth also gave Francis a golden key that could apparently open all the doors in the palace—even those most private ones.

Elizabeth continued to publicly deny that Francis had arrived, to allow her space to consider her next steps. In her view, this was the best way to conceal her thoughts, and to delay revealing her final answer to the public. However, she could not hide from the sharp eyes of the court. The many spies working for the Spanish, Venetian, and other European royal households of Europe reported the same thing: Elizabeth and Francis were definitely together. In fact, it seemed as though they could not spend a minute apart. It was even said that they were frequently alone together from morning until night, with only one of Elizabeth's ladies-in-waiting attending, whose identity remained undisclosed. They seemed absolutely inseparable.

Some of Elizabeth's closest allies had also been told of Francis's presence. On Friday, August 28, William Brooke—Lord Cobham—organized a dinner at Cobham Hall in Kent, to which Francis and the queen were invited. It was the last dinner of the French prince's trip and Elizabeth wanted them to spend some time together away from the court, where she knew gossip was raging.

As they stepped aside from the party, Elizabeth confessed, "I am so pleased that we have met in person. I admire you more than any man I know."

"The feeling is very mutual, your Majesty, and my admiration for you knows no bounds," he replied.[13]

The next day, just before he was due to return to France, it was Elizabeth's turn to give Francis something, "a most beautiful diamond ring in the shape of a heart."

As she stood before him, moved by his imminent departure, she said: "Now the world will see whether I, as was pretended, have made you prisoner, or whether you have not rather made me a prison and yours ever most obliged."[14]

It was undeniable that their first meeting had been a great success, and while the French prince left without a formal response to his proposal, he now believed it was now only a matter of months before he became king of England.

Francis wrote to Elizabeth the next day, on the journey back to France, claiming to long for her and swearing his undying allegiance: "I am your most faithful and affectionate slave that has ever existed."[15]

But all was not well. Discontent and opposition to the match continued to grow in England, stirred up by Stubbs's pamphlet. He was condemned for it, and his right hand cut off as punishment. But that did not suppress the negative sentiment. Even at court, favorites and councillors alike were now openly challenging Elizabeth, expressing concern at what the union would mean for France's power over the country. Sir Philip Sidney, the poet and courtier, wrote an open letter to the queen setting out the reasons why he thought such a match would be a disaster for both Elizabeth and England.

Despite these concerns, Elizabeth "kept dwelling upon the duke's good qualities and praising the queen mother."[16] She was extremely fond of him. But was that enough for her to renounce her full royal authority as queen of England?

*

Simier had remained in England with Elizabeth but, in November 1579, he was sent back to France by the English queen with the goal of concluding at last the treaty for the queen's marriage with the Duke of Anjou.

A few days after his dispatch Simier wrote to her, signing his letter, "Your very humble, very obedient, very faithful servant, your Majesty's monkey." Just as La Mothe Fénélon seemed to have charmed the queen years before, and had enjoyed a close relationship as a result, Simier had also created a special bond with Elizabeth. In doing so, he had also made his French masters proud.

Just before his departure, Elizabeth gave Simier a gift of this own: "jewels and pearls valued at 8,000 crowns."[17] After a long and perilous voyage, Simier only arrived in Paris in April 1580—creating yet another delay to the marriage negotiations. Nevertheless, during this time Elizabeth and Francis continued exchanging letters, now showing their affection toward one another. "My dearest" was now Elizabeth's favorite nickname for her "frog."[18] Catherine was also maintaining her own channel of communication with Elizabeth and, in February 1580, she had insisted once more that all she had ever wanted "was to see the good resolution of the marriage between you and my son."

The question of religion still stood, of course, but Catherine begged Elizabeth not "to let this be a reason why this marriage should not happen."[19]

Catherine was also meeting regularly with Elizabeth's resident ambassador, Henry Cobham. At around ten o'clock on Monday, February 15, Cobham arrived at Catherine's residence in Paris. The house was made of stone and had three beautifully proportioned stories. In one of the further corners of the courtyard, one could climb the stairs leading up a turret of thirty fathoms high—built entirely of stone— and admire the view over most parts of the city.

Monsieur Gondi, one of Catherine's secretaries, received Cobham at the entrance.

The meal he'd been invited to seemed rather unofficial, and Catherine took advantage of the informality to immediately cut to the chase. "Sir Henry, I imagine that you know why I have invited you here, into one of my most intimate houses," she started. He nodded. "You won't be surprised if I tell you how much I desire to see the marriage between your queen and my son, the duke."

Cobham smiled. All of Europe knew how much Catherine wanted to marry off one of her sons to Elizabeth. People even said that she was Elizabeth's most determined and relentless suitor.

"You see, Sir Henry," she continued, "I'm no longer fair and young and my true desire now is to see my son blessed with children. Such an alliance would be the best thing that could ever happen to France and England."

The English ambassador wasn't sure how to respond, apart from giving his usual reassurance that his "mistress, Elizabeth, has never more favoured and adored a royal house than yours."[20]

This was a simple answer, but it pleased Catherine, who then invited him to the next room where other ambassadors and people of the court were awaiting them. It was not a private dinner, after all.

While Elizabeth continued her affectionate correspondence with the duke, there was still no definitive response on the marriage question.

Mauvissière, the French resident ambassador in England, conveyed the French rulers' and Francis's impatience and irritation. "Your Majesty, you must make a decision. Will you or will you not marry the duke of Anjou?"

Elizabeth did not like his tone. "This is not a matter that should be concluded in such a hurry," she bluntly replied. "I have to take into consideration not only my own desire but also my Council's and my people's."

Mauvissière had never been an admirer of Elizabeth. Her constant delays and apparent dissimulations irritated him. "In that case, your Majesty," he rebuked, "you should not be surprised when the duke is forced to publish the letters he has received from you to exonerate himself from having come to England." Mauvissière had no idea if the duke would ever agree to do so, but perhaps it was worth threatening the queen, forcing her to make up her mind.

Elizabeth jumped out of her seat and looked Mauvissière squarely in the eye, raging. She was also quite embarrassed. "He would not dare!" she shouted.

"Yes, he would,"[21] Mauvissière replied, defying the queen, and then asked to take his leave.

She granted this promptly; the sight of him was starting to make her feel uncomfortable.

After his departure, Elizabeth was left alone with Cecil and Edwin Sandys, Archbishop of York, who were both in attendance. "My Lords," she told them, "here I am between Scylla and Charybdis. Anjou has agreed to all the terms I sent him, and he is asking me to tell him when I wish him to come and marry me. If I do not marry him, I don't know if he will remain friendly with me; and if I do, I shall not be able to govern the country with the freedom and security that I have hitherto enjoyed. What shall I do?"

Cecil moved closer to her and, with his usual paternal gaze, simply answered, "If it is your wish to marry you should do so, but if you don't intend to marry you ought to undeceive Anjou at once."

"That is not the opinion of the rest of the Council, who think that I should keep him in correspondence,"[22] Elizabeth pointed out.

Cecil nodded. "Those who trick princes trick themselves."

Elizabeth had nothing to say to that, and she knew that the present situation could not be sustained. She had to make a decision. The French royal family, particularly Catherine and Anjou, were getting more and more impatient by the day.

In another letter sent in August, in which she pleaded for the resolution of the match, Catherine reminded Elizabeth of her undying eagerness for "the time I can finally call myself what I desire most that I yet do not dare to write down." She was impatient to be able to sign her letters "your mother."[23]

Elizabeth had never been the most straightforward of women, but at this moment she had never shown so much inconsistency in her life. She was waiting for a sign, something that might tell her which choice to make.

On September 17, Elizabeth went to John Dee's house. She had gone to the astrologer's home before, but she only made the journey on rare and grave occasions. Catherine also believed in astrology and its predictions—another thing they had in common. Not much is known of Elizabeth's visit, other than that she spent a great deal of time thinking in Dee's garden, and that they discussed several matters privately. One of them, surely the most significant, must certainly have been the Anjou match.[24]

In many ways, Elizabeth felt trapped. Whatever her answer, she would have to face the consequences of either alienating the French and hurting Francis, whom she genuinely cared for, or alienating her own people and some of her councillors. She had to choose between affection—or, as some speculated, love—and power and security.

Elizabeth still showed favor to the French ambassador, whom she invited to accompany her to Eton and Windsor for feasting and to celebrate Accession Day on November 17. The French continued to remain hopeful—if impatient. A month later, Catherine's impatience had become too much, and she finally decided to be more blunt with Elizabeth. While she had always made her desires very clear, her tone took on a new intimacy:

"I cannot express how much I want to see the good resolution of this marriage and to see the friendship between us reaffirmed and increased," the letter began,

> I would be so devastated if I were to die before seeing this union happen and finally being able to call you daughter rather than sister.

There's another great desire of mine that I can no longer keep to myself. I would like to see you become the mother of a beautiful son as it is the most joy and happiness that one can know in this world.[25]

Catherine could insist all she wanted but, despite her touching words, Elizabeth still remained unsure. The queen mother and Francis were convinced that they simply had to try harder.

He had to see her again. He had seduced her once; he could seduce her even more with a second journey to England.

*

In February 1581, Francis sent another special envoy, Marchaumont, to Elizabeth, as Jean Simier had temporarily fallen out of favor, having been caught accepting Spanish bribes to provide information on the match. Elizabeth was pleased with the new envoy, and they met almost daily.

He was there to discuss Francis's arrival later in the year. This time, the duke desired to stay in England permanently, and be married to the queen.

La Mothe Fénélon had accompanied Marchaumont as a means to please Elizabeth all the more. However, this time things were different. While they had enjoyed a special friendship in the early 1570s, she now seemed less fond of him and granted him fewer favors. Despite this, on August 30, they were invited to dine with Walsingham and Burghley at Cecil House on the Strand. The conversation, however, didn't quite go as expected.

"My lords," started Walsingham, "you need to understand that the situation is very complicated for our mistress, the queen. The pope keeps sending Jesuit priests to England and Spanish troops are sent to Ireland." He paused, embarrassed by the intense gaze he was receiving from Marchaumont from across the table. Walsingham cleared his throat and continued, "This marriage project has raised the hopes of English Catholics, which therefore threatens our queen's life."

"Nonsense!" Marchaumont objected. "The marriage with our master, duke of Anjou, will appease the tensions as the Catholics will have to accept the union and Elizabeth's authority."

Burghley remained quiet. He allowed Walsingham to continue digging his own grave as the French commissioner's irritation became palpable.

"That is one way to look at this, and it is not what my informants all over Europe are reporting." Before he could be interrupted again, he continued, "Another problem, you see, gentlemen, is that the queen risks great danger giving birth at her age and the duke's position in the Netherlands also means that England could be dragged into a war."

Before Marchaumont could say anything in response, La Mothe Fénélon interjected: "This is quite astonishing for us to hear. We consider the marriage as settled. This is why we are here."

Walsingham and Burghley looked at each other knowingly. It was far from being the case.

This time it was Burghley who intervened. "I'm afraid, my lords, that nothing is settled until the marriage is signed and consummated. Surely, as experienced diplomats, you should know that."[26]

This was an outrage. Feeling insulted, the two French commissioners immediately took their leave. It was to mark another period of indecision, as Elizabeth continued to agonize.

In May 1581, in a private audience that she had granted La Mothe Fénélon in her garden, she confessed, "The marriage is in the hands of God."

Even La Mothe Fénélon could no longer hide his frustration. "It is in yours, your Majesty. You just have to say yes and Francis will be here marrying you the next day."[27]

To make things even more complicated, Elizabeth had added several new requests to the negotiations, this time regarding religion and the alliance with France. This time they were sent to Henry III, Francis's brother; perhaps this was Elizabeth's way of putting some distance between herself and Francis.

However, the French king was now determined to support his brother's match. He replied to Elizabeth that he would consider all her new requests diligently as she was "the princess of this world whom we see as the dearest."[28]

Further preparations were made for Francis's arrival, and nothing seemed likely to stop his intended journey. Elizabeth was feeling the pressure. She knew she could not withhold an answer for much longer.

Francis finally arrived in England with a small group of companions—including Jean Bodin, the French philosopher and reformer—on October 31. The Sheen House and The Red Lion near Richmond had been prepared for them. In the latter lodgings, a garden had been established with bay, eglantine, jasmine, and rosemary.

On November 2, Francis arrived at Richmond Palace. Later on, he was seen leaving the castle with the queen for a hunting party in the nearby countryside. Yet again, rumors were rife: now, there were only two outcomes. The duke would either marry Elizabeth or would be shattered for good, his efforts to win her over all for nothing.

But the signs seemed positive. The court could not help but notice that Elizabeth and Francis were spending all their time together, from morning right through to supper. It was clear she held a candle for him. Francis revealed to the queen that, this time, he was here "to win over the English people."[29] For a queen devoted to the service of her subjects, it must have been music to her ears. She invited him to all public celebrations and tournaments, and while in attendance he was always to be found at the queen's side. There was surely no doubt in his mind: he would, he believed, become king.

On November 22, Elizabeth made an announcement before Leicester, Walsingham, the French commissioners, and Francis too. "You may write to the king that the duke of Anjou shall be my husband."[30] She then turned to Francis and kissed him on the lips, drawing a ring from her own hand and giving it to him as a pledge of her sincerity. He gave her one of his own rings in return. Upon hearing the news, the French courtiers in attendance were filled with joy. After a decade, their French prince would become king of England. The euphoria was palpable.

While the French were celebrating, however, the English felt embarrassed and ill at ease. They believed that Elizabeth had been overcome by the moment, and didn't truly mean her spontaneous declaration.

They were right.

The next day, she repudiated her promise to marry Francis, stating that she needed to hear first from the king that he would meet her final demands. She had likely been subject to pressure from her advisors, having previously expressed her desires so clearly. Francis was devastated. But still the French pressed on.

In late November, Secretary Pinart—a close advisor to both Henry and Catherine—arrived at court with a clear mission: to agree to all the conditions Elizabeth might insist upon before she could marry Francis.

Elizabeth returned to old grievances. She boldly asked that "Calais be restored" and for assurances that an "alliance against the queen of Scotland and her son" would be made. These were terms that she surely knew the French would never accept—*could* never accept. It was another stalemate, however much Francis flattered or expressed his fondness for her.

By December, discussions of the duke's departure had begun. Jean Simier had just arrived from France, pardoned by Henry for his indiscretions, having been entrusted with the mission to finalize the flagging negotiations.

In a private audience on a cold late December morning, Francis— who was truly losing patience now—told Elizabeth that the situation was becoming insufferable. "You are mine and I can prove it with the letters and words you have written to me, confirmed by the gift of the ring. If I cannot get you for my wife by fair means and affection I must do so by force, for I will not leave this country without you."

Elizabeth was perturbed by his words. "The ring was only a pledge of my perpetual friendship," she explained. "Also, you shouldn't make such threats to a friend who helps you financially in your enterprises in the Netherlands. You are in no position to make threats or to force anyone here," she added, raising her voice.

Upon leaving the room, she found Simier and complained to him, "Anjou is pressing me too closely."

"You should stand firm on the conditions you are demanding from the king of France, your Majesty. The marriage should be on your terms as they are the ones wooing you,"[31] Simier replied. It may have been that he was employed by a third party—possibly the Spanish—to sabotage the negotiations.

Francis apologized for his outburst and was restored to Elizabeth's good favor. He stayed for New Year's Eve and lavished her with sumptuous gifts, including a flower made of gold, garnished all over with sparkling rubies and diamonds, and a hind sitting upon it, with two small pearl pendants.

All his gifts, flowers, and affectionate words, however, were in vain. His second trip proved to be as unfruitful as the first.

He left in February 1582 with a broken heart and a bruised ego.

He was the fool who, for over a decade, had thought he could tame Elizabeth I of England.

*

The bigger fool, however, was his mother, Catherine, who had been pursuing Elizabeth since 1564. In December 1583, two years after the talks had officially ended and Francis had left England, Catherine accepted that her attempts had come to nothing. In a letter, she confessed that all she had ever wanted was to "call you my daughter, having offered to you all my sons, one after the other, but God has not wished to give me that contentment, a regret that I will have for the rest of my life."[32]

Soon enough, fate would strike, eliminating the last bit of hope she might have had.

On June 10, 1584, Francis, Duke of Anjou, died of malaria. His death was to trigger chaos in the years to come, as the next heir to the throne was now Henry, king of Navarre, leader of the Huguenots.

The news devastated Elizabeth, who had always had genuine feelings for the young man. In July, she wrote to Catherine, stating that she wished she could "have visited you in the company that I make with you in your sorrow, which I am sure cannot be greater than my own. For inasmuch as you are his mother, so it is that there remain to you several other children. But for me, I find no consolation except death, which I hope will soon reunite us. Madame, if you were able to see the image of my heart, you would see the portrait of a body without a soul."

Marriage might no longer be a possibility, Elizabeth added, but "you will find me the most faithful daughter and sister that ever princes had" and signed "as if I were your daughter born."[33] Perhaps these were empty words, for Elizabeth had turned down many proposals. But her kind words seemed to show real fondness.

Without a potential suitor—without a son to marry—how would Elizabeth and Catherine deal with one another now? The future of their friendship was far from certain. Indeed, without the prospect of a marital union, they no longer had any reason to hold back their true feelings for one another, whether good or bad.

Against the backdrop of their loss, the situation in Europe worsened—in France with another bloody religious civil war, in England with incessant plots from rebels who sought to replace Elizabeth with Mary.

The future was looking unclear, but one thing was certain: a storm was coming, and only one of them would be victorious.

PART 4

Warrior Queens

1585–1589

13

A Protestant Champion and
a Catholic Hammer, 1585

The death of Francis, Duke of Anjou, had cataclysmic repercussions in France. Foremost were the consequences for the Catholic League, which had been founded in 1576 and which was led by the Guises, Mary Stuart's cousins: Henry I, Duke of Guise; Charles, Duke of Mayenne; and Louis, Cardinal of Guise. The power of the Guises had dwindled in recent years, and any potential conflict had lain dormant, but after Francis's death it was fully revived, and now had one single goal: to prevent the Huguenot leader and king, Henry of Navarre, from taking the French throne. Instead, the Guise brothers supported Charles, Cardinal of Bourbon, Henry de Navarre's uncle, who had vowed to spend his life eradicating Protestantism and who was a prince of blood, giving him his own claim to the throne. It was clear that the conflict between Catholics and Protestants would continue to rage, even more so at the dawn of a new era.

In 1585, the Cardinal of Bourbon made this clear, declaring that the League would "never suffer the reign of a heretic nor would we suffer the domination of a non-Catholic prince." He also reminded everyone of the special link between the French rulers and the Roman Catholic Church: "The first oath that our kings take when they are crowned is to maintain the Catholic Apostolic and Roman religion."[1]

If they failed to do so, he implied, it was the French Catholics' duty to fight them.

Catherine aligned herself with them; Elizabeth, on the other hand, continued to support Henry of Navarre and the Huguenots instead.

As a result, by 1585 no reconciliation was possible between the two women. It was hard to believe that they had once almost been mother and daughter.

★

In February 1585, the apparent mastermind behind another plot attempting to murder Elizabeth and replace her with Mary Stuart had been apprehended. His name was William Parry and, four months earlier, he had been elected as an MP for Queenborough. He had become known for denouncing the harsh treatments of Catholics in England but also had been working for Cecil. His betrayal came as a surprise.

When Parry was interrogated by Walsingham, he confessed to knowing about several possible conspiracies against the queen—before retracting his words. Though there is no evidence that Parry was tortured, it is fair to assume that he was at least threatened, which may have made his testimony less reliable or forced the retraction. His self-contradictions increased suspicions of him and he was tried for treason in Westminster Hall on February 25. It was believed he had been recruited by the English Catholics in Reims, such as William Allen, who "had been one of the moving spirits behind the setting up of English seminaries on the continent."[2]

He was found guilty of the charges.

On March 2, as he stood before the crowd in Westminster Palace Yard, Parry spoke his final words. "I am not come hither to preach nor to make you any oration, I am come hither to die. And here I protest unto you all, I am clean of that I am condemned to die for: I did never intend to lay violent hands on her most sacred Majesty."

The crowd attending his execution witnessed what they would later report as a particularly painful and violent death, hearing him "groan as his bowels were cut out."[3]

His demise marked a turning point, galvanizing the government into passing a law, named 27, Eliz. 1, c. 1, that further ensured the queen's safety by declaring that a tribunal of at least twenty-four peers and privy councillors were permitted to investigate any threat of invasion or rebellion in England. It also meant, inevitably, that the persecution of the Catholics in the realm would increase.

Yet Parry's death did not solve all of the Elizabethan state's problems.

During his tortured confession, Parry named another traitor who had worked as a double agent for years, pretending to work for Walsingham when his true allegiance was to Mary Stuart: Thomas Morgan.

Morgan was a Roman Catholic whose activities came to light in 1572, during the aftermath of the Ridolfi plot. At that point he had been arrested and sent to the Tower for ten months, before being released. He later traveled to France several times to conspire against the English crown—in many ways his time in the Tower had radicalized him further. Then, in the 1580s, he became acquainted with William Parry, who confessed to him that he was ready to kill people at the very top of the English government in order to honor his religion. To this, Morgan famously replied, "Why not the queen herself?"[4]

By 1585, Morgan had escaped to France. So, when he was once again named as a traitor and conspirator, Elizabeth was furious. She would not allow him to escape justice again. She ordered the immediate extradition of Morgan—though her current estrangement from Catherine meant she wrote directly to Henry III, her son, instead:

> It has been discovered a few days ago that one of our subjects intended to make an attempt upon our life. He has confessed that another of our subjects, who is now a fugitive in your realm, explicitly incited him thereto; an act so detestable and of such dangerous consequence for all princes. We hope you will agree to put into our hands the author of such an unhappy enterprise.[5]

This request put Henry in a difficult position. Facing potential divisions among his people and another bloody religious civil war, he could not afford to appear to be the strong ally of a Protestant queen. He could also barely afford to antagonize Elizabeth, who he knew was still sending aid to the Huguenots while also supporting the Dutch Protestants against Spanish rule. Should he force France to make a choice between religious and purely political alliances in order to counterbalance Spanish power in Europe and beyond?

He chose not to reply to her directly. Instead, he wrote to his ambassador, Mauvissière, "You will tell the queen that I cannot accede to her demand of handing over the refugee but that she should be reassured that he will face the required punishment in France."[6]

Catherine had her own view, and her advice to her son was clear: he could not send Morgan back to England. If he did he would appear to be a weak Protestant sympathizer, and this would only encourage the Catholic League to take up arms against the crown. But she knew Elizabeth was dangerous, and so she was prepared to play lying games with the English ambassadors—whom they had already received and entertained multiple times at court—to appease the tensions between them and Elizabeth.

On February 23, the special envoys sent by Elizabeth—Ambrose Dudley, Earl of Warwick, brother to Elizabeth's favorite Robert Dudley, and Henry Stanley, Earl of Derby—came to the French court with two missions: bring Morgan back to England for justice, and ensure that the French would remain allies with the Netherlands.

As soon as the ambassadors arrived, the French rulers made sure that they were particularly well treated, lodging them next to the Louvre in the Anjou residence. At their first audience with the king, they offered him on behalf of Elizabeth the necklace of the Order of the Garter—the highest and most prestigious rank in England, "hoping that your Majesty will continue to protect the oppressed in the Netherlands."[7]

A week later, again in honor of the English ambassadors, Henry organized festivities in the bishop's magnificent Palace of Paris, located just to the south of the Cathedral of Notre-Dame de Paris, overlooking the river. The ambassadors were in awe of the magnificent view. All the most beautiful noblewomen of the court received invitations to the gathering and, after dinner, all attendees donned masks and danced until three o'clock in the morning.

Keeping the ambassadors content was of paramount importance, but, in spite of this rather grand welcome, they would strongly dislike Henry's responses to their requests. They already had their suspicions, given that their official audience had been continually delayed.

Finally, on the Sunday, Henry received them. This time he chose to do so in his cabinet, which was a more intimate place than his chamber of estate, where he usually received resident ambassadors. He dismissed all of his ministers except Pomponne de Bellièvre, one of his very close advisors, and his secretary, Pinard.

The atmosphere was more relaxed in the cabinet but, as they all sat down, the king started with a warning. "I have to thank you, my lords, for your and your Majesty's good will towards me but, as you know, the situation in France has never been more complicated and I have to act accordingly."

"We do appreciate it, but a solution must be found on two important matters to our mistress, the queen," Warwick said, before pausing briefly. "The first one being your decision to continue your protection of the Netherlands—as a tribute to your late brother, who was their Lord Protector—and the second, the extradition of the fugitive and conspirator, Thomas Morgan."

"You have my word, my lord, that I will continue to be a good neighbour," the king responded calmly. "The last thing I want is to give anyone an excuse for open war. You will remind your mistress, the queen, that our people benefit from the maintenance of a good alliance between our two countries." Henry intensified his gaze. "Unfortunately, since the death of my dear brother, France has faced great difficulties and I am afraid that, with his death, delays for negotiations in the Netherlands continue to be a worry."

"But something needs to be done," Warwick interrupted. "Spain's power is growing and, without the protection of France and England, the Netherlands will fall under its complete control."

Pensive, Henry responded, "If I were to intervene abroad, that would only cause greater trouble here in France. It would put myself in jeopardy by trying to win, I would end up losing myself. I do support the enterprises of your mistress, the queen, in the Netherlands, but I cannot spare forces to support her efforts until the situation inside the borders of my own realm is more stable."

This time it was Derby who spoke: "Can France really afford to have Spain's power growing? The best thing to do is to join England in a more secure alliance than ever before, and then jointly together to oppose the king of Spain's domination over Europe."

"All I have done since the beginning of my reign," the king informed them, "is to maintain good relations with my good sister and cousin—your mistress, the queen of England—and I hope these good relations will continue, but an intervention of French troops in the Netherlands is, at this time, simply impossible."

When Derby, Warwick, and Sir Edward Stafford, the resident ambassador in France, later inquired about Morgan, the king's answer was the same as he had previously communicated through his ambassadors: "The traitor will be judged and imprisoned here in France at the Bastille. For this you will have my word that justice will be done."[8]

The ambassadors had no chance to express their disagreement as, upon finishing his speech, Henry dismissed them at once.

Thomas Morgan was imprisoned in France for two years, after which he was released.

After their conversation, Stafford—who found it strange that the queen mother was absent from such a gathering—went to meet with Catherine separately. He needed to understand her silence on the matter. He found her in her cabinet room with other ministers.

She looked very worried and anxious, and was not particularly pleased to see him. After all, she knew that he had come to persuade her once more to change her son's mind.

To preempt his plea, she greeted him and immediately assured him, "I have done all I can to convince my son, the king."

"You must use your authority if you still wish to maintain good relations with your English neighbour," Stafford warned.

"I have tried, my lord," Catherine replied, sighing and looking serious. "Every day my son, the king, is reminded of the importance of maintaining the relationship with England, but he seems distracted.

He occupies himself with other business, which will no doubt endanger his estate."

"You know what you have done and wished for. Like a kind mother who sees no remedy, you are making excuses for your children's faults,"[9] Stafford said before taking his leave.

Stafford was both right and wrong. Catherine did know what she had done—she always did. However, in truth she was not making any excuse for her son's decision: this time, she was behind him completely. France could not afford to lose its military forces in the Netherlands, and nor could they afford to send a Catholic to his death in England. She despised Elizabeth for even daring to demand such a request, and her contempt would only grow over the coming years.

Once Elizabeth had received her ambassadorial reports, and understood that she would not get what she desired, rage consumed her. How dare the French rulers come between her and one of her subjects?

In response she wrote directly to them both, clearly doubting Catherine's alleged remorse regarding her son's behavior. Elizabeth was well aware that Catherine's influence at court had not ceased because of yet another religious civil war; Henry still confided in his mother and listened to her counsel, even if her public presence had lessened.

"The letters before the last sent to me by my ambassadors confirmed me in my love and honour for you, informing me of your great care of my life by giving order for the apprehension of him who has often attacked it in divers ways, being the greatest traitor to ever live in a prince's realm," she started, "but this pleasure [liesse] is like a fire made of straw, which flames up more than it endures, for now I have a packet of lies which has made me very angry, hearing that not only was he not delivered into my hands, but that my ambassadors have not been permitted to see his ciphers and writings."

The actions of the French had been a total affront to her own authority—an abhorrent thought for Elizabeth, who had spent so much time entertaining a match with them. She must surely have been thankful, in that moment, that she had not agreed to a union. She did not try to conceal her anger as she continued her note to Henry in forceful and expressive style.

"My God, what necromancer has blinded your eyes, that you cannot see your own danger, to whom God has not granted such sincere and adoring subjects that you may not have the balance of their fidelity shaken!" she exclaimed. "Even amongst barbarians, such iniquity would be punished in exemplary fashion before all the world. Certainly it would be expected from the most Christian king."

Nevertheless, she still sought their help, so Elizabeth concluded as she usually did—with some slightly more tactful closing remarks.

> My good brother, you will excuse this roundness, which is only from my love to your renown throughout all lands, which I hold so dear that I desire to have no just cause to abate the affection I have vowed to you; coming not from deceitful lips (from which may God guard you) that under cloak of piety have little care for your greatness.[10]

In her letter to Catherine, her tone was slightly different. She wanted to show the queen mother that she had not been duped into thinking Catherine had played no role in the decision made by Henry. She knew the truth:

> I excuse you, my good sister, by the adage *chi fa quell que puo non e tenuto a fare piu* [whoever does what he can is not obliged to do more]. Otherwise I would grieve that a princess whom I have loved so dearly has permitted the king so to forget his office as not only to refuse to deliver up the traitor but, which is worse, not to allow his papers, letters and ciphers to be searched, as if he made more account of a villain than of a prince.

She then warned Catherine of the potential repercussions of such political decisions: "The time may come when those who have hindered so just an act may give him more pain."

She ended her letter by simply reminding Catherine that for years, particularly with her late son, the Duke of Anjou, Anglo-French relations had been at their strongest:

> Her Majesty is wise, so I will say no more but only that if the dead were living, he would not permit such an insult, and one which happened at a bad time, for never was I more devoted to any prince than to the king both in heart and will, as my own acts have proven and as God knows.[11]

Neither Henry nor Catherine replied to these letters.

In truth, there was very little they could say in response, as in their hearts they knew they would have to deal with the consequences. It was clear now that their relations with Elizabeth were even more compromised and that her efforts to protect the Netherlands and the Huguenots would only be redoubled.

*

To ensure her success in supporting the European Protestants, Elizabeth relied heavily on her privateers—or what they called in Spain and France her pirates. The most famous—and the one most feared by Catholic powers—was Sir Francis Drake, who had been knighted by Elizabeth in 1581 for his achievements against Spain. Despite this great honor, it is worth noting that Drake's countless achievements were rooted in his personal involvement in the slave trade along with his cousin, John Hawkins, who would attack Portuguese slave ships and sell the slaves off to local plantations in the Caribbean islands. Seen as an English hero by many, for others he was the ultimate villain, looting cities and towns and contributing to the spread of slavery.

In 1585, Elizabeth used Drake's services to attack Spanish fleets and cargo, not only in Europe but in the New World too. In May that year, Henry III was watching Drake's activities closely, especially his voyage to the West and East Indies with eighteen great vessels and 3,000 Englishmen. The French king was in awe of Drake's exploits in the New World, and always inquired about his achievements. However, he soon realized that the English superiority at sea was causing a real problem for French fleets. Elizabeth had ordered her privateers to attack any Spanish or French fleets they came across, ensuring that the cargo she sent to the Netherlands and France—with soldiers, weapons, and money—would arrive safely at their destination.

The crisis between France and England intensified in July 1585 when, under pressure from the League, who continued to win the support of major French cities and towns, Henry made the decision to ally with them and to fight openly against the Huguenots and their leader, the rightful heir to the French crown, Henry, king of Navarre.

On June 20, the Guises and Lorraines sat down with the king to discuss the terms of a new treaty between them.

"The only thing that matters is the protection and maintenance of the Catholic Roman Apostolic religion, everywhere in the realm," said Charles, Cardinal of Bourbon.

"I agree, Uncle, it is," Henry III solemnly replied.

"All edicts that say otherwise must be revoked at once,"[12] Henry of Guise insisted.

The French king nodded in response.

On July 7, Catherine signed the Treaty of Nemours, on behalf of her son, with the Catholic League. Henry of Navarre was removed from the line of succession and both parties agreed to fight alongside each other against the Huguenots and the Protestants in the Netherlands—causing much trouble for the Catholic powers, especially Spain.

Five days later, Henry went to his mother's castle in Saint-Maur to discuss the details of the treaty and its implications. Catherine was now a fervent supporter of the alliance with the Guises, as well as the edict he was about to draft, which would cause great distress to the Huguenots. Her abhorrence and contempt for them—but now mostly for Elizabeth—was growing day by day.

On July 18, Henry III signed an edict that annulled all previous decrees granting religious freedom. On his way to ratify the document, he stopped and turned to his uncle, Charles, Cardinal of Bourbon, to explain himself.

"My uncle, in the past I have ratified edicts that granted religious freedom to the reformers of my country. I did it willingly but against my conscience. I did it in the hope that it would bring peace to France. Today I am here to ratify the edict that puts an end to this religious freedom and I do it in accord with my conscience. I also know that this will bring further wars and might ruin my state and people."

After signing the paper, the king left the palace as Catholic Leaguers cheered him on:

"Vive le roi! Long live the king!"[13]

*

Meanwhile, the English ambassadors continued to be batted away, systematically refused an audience with the king and the queen mother. On August 4, Elizabeth did not shy away from speaking her mind to Henry III:

> Monsieur, my good brother, I have found so strange the recent news coming from your realm which truly stains your honour and that of France. I am even more astonished to hear that my representatives in your country are no longer given audiences with you, when they could express to you my opinions and intentions.

Elizabeth did not wish to be involved in an open war with France, but she also knew she needed to offer her protection and support to any European Protestants who requested it—and that included Henry, the king of Navarre.

She warned the French king: "I pray to God that he will inspire you to open your eyes and see clearly your detractors, among whom I will be in the last place. Your abused good sister, Elizabeth."

Having received no response from him—apart from his mundane dispatches to his newly arrived ambassador, Guillaume de l'Aubespine, Sieur of Chasteauneuf, a Guisard to his core—Elizabeth prepared England for war, determined to protect the Protestants of Europe, particularly those in the Netherlands who were under siege from Spanish forces.

On September 4, Elizabeth signed the Nonsuch Supplementary Treaty, which ordered a shipment of 5,000 footmen and 1,000 horses "to support the Netherlands" affairs in the present dangerous state."[14] The treaty was ratified twenty days later by the Dutch. The ship was then delayed until the end of October, when it finally sailed for the Netherlands.

Elizabeth also ordered her privateers to attack any Spanish or French fleets that stood in her way. As for Drake, he was given a more delicate task: to raid Galicia and ravage important Spanish ports in the New World. And while he was not entirely successful in this quest, Drake did indeed manage to inflict serious damage on the Spanish—ensuring the safe transport of English troops throughout the Netherlands.

Of course, Drake's activities at sea soon started affecting French affairs and, on December 21, 1585, Henry complained directly of this to Elizabeth:

> Drake, general of your army, met at sea near Cape Finister a vessel named "La Magdeleine" which was new and sailing her first voyage with a cargo of salt from Portugal belonging to Jacques Procheau, a marine trader from Sables d'Ollone. Your general seized the said vessel with its crew and goods. We demand justice for such a hostile enterprise.[15]

The king also ordered his ambassador to demand reparation from Elizabeth during a diplomatic audience, yet reparation and justice would never be granted. Attacking merchants and traders was a vital part of Elizabeth's military tactics. She knew no pity and showed no mercy when it came to defending her faith and the borders of her realm. For too long, she felt, she had been underestimated by the Spanish and French kings.

Elizabeth's power continued to grow in Europe as a result of events at sea. Catherine watched developments with interest, and became determined to have a private audience with Stafford, the English resident ambassador in France.

On December 28, Stafford accepted the invitation and found Catherine in her private cabinet, where she exclaimed, "My lord, I am so very pleased to see you!"

Stafford could detect the sarcasm in Catherine's voice, and rightly feared that this conversation was going to be unpleasant for him—and even more unpleasant to report back to Elizabeth.

As Catherine showed him where to sit, she cut to the chase.

"You see, my lord, I have asked you to come here to discuss the affairs of your mistress, the queen of England, in the Netherlands." She was now looking straight into his eyes. The tension was palpable and, somehow, Stafford knew that his best defense was to remain silent.

"You have to tell your queen that, in over twenty years, she has never given me more joy than she has now by being at open war with Spain over the Netherlands."

Catherine was waiting for a reaction, but Stafford remained stoic. She decided to continue:

"She now has so many irons in the fire that she will be soon forced to open her purse but to quench one fire at once and that, my lord, means that she is leaving herself open to many unpleasant events." By now Catherine was smiling. She had Stafford exactly where she wanted him: uneasy with such unfamiliarity.

She ended the short audience with a piece of advice: "You should warn your queen that she cannot win on all fronts and that she should think carefully about her next steps when it comes to her involvement in French affairs."[16]

By the end of 1585, Catherine was filled with animosity toward Elizabeth. She no longer made claims of a potential friendship—as if, all this time, she had only been pretending to seek a union with the English queen. Or perhaps it was quite the opposite: that she had endured so much rejection from Elizabeth, on behalf of both herself and her sons, that she felt she had nothing to lose by finally becoming an enemy of the English queen.

Anjou's death, Elizabeth's increasing boldness, and the struggle for power in Europe meant there was no longer any chance for reconciliation between the two women.

Yet again, they were at odds—but, as in 1562, would Catherine triumph once more? Only time would tell.

14

The Rose and the Thistle, 1586

Peace between England and France once again seemed unattainable, with Elizabeth mastering the seas like no other European ruler. Drake, Raleigh, and other lesser-known privateers—pirates—were working relentlessly to ensure England's safety from a foreign invasion. Spanish and French ships were now constantly and ruthlessly under attack, much to the outrage of their courts.

In March 1586, another complaint reached the French king, and this was to be the straw that broke the camel's back. Henry had received reports about Elizabeth's treatment of his merchants, and they left him exasperated. Estienne Dasmeguettes—a merchant from Saint-Jean-de-Luz, who was trading in the Channel near the Isle of Wight—had found himself completely powerless when English sailors attacked his ship, plundering his goods.

Henry III demanded reparations for the unacceptable treatment of one of his subjects: "She must order that the sea is purged of so many pirates. Her subjects are ruining our commerce,"[1] he said of Elizabeth.

When his complaints reached her, she ignored the French king's demands. After all, the goods or gold confiscated from her enemies only made England wealthier and more powerful; besides, riches notwithstanding, the stability of her religion was at stake. For these reasons she had no interest in stopping her subjects doing whatever was required to make her country safe. In any case, it was her continuing belief that Henry should have supported her in the Netherlands when she had asked him to do so.

Henry was furious at what he perceived to be Elizabeth's sense of entitlement. After all, she was only a woman, and he found her tone insulting.

In April and May he tried to reason with her again, but his efforts were, as usual, in vain. Catherine shared his frustration, but this time she refused to get involved in the matter. She could not stand hearing of Elizabeth. Instead, she focused on her new priority: consolidating the relationship between France and Spain.

Her granddaughter, Catalina Micaela—second daughter of Elisabeth of Valois, who had died in 1568, and Philip II of Spain—had given birth to a healthy son. Sensing an opportunity to show her allegiance to Spain, Catherine wrote to Philip directly:

"I am blessed by God as before dying, I can see the birth of a son who is the descendant of the daughter that I have loved so much." She explained that her greatest wish was to see "the intensification of the alliance and amity that exists between our two crowns that I only want to see continue and endure."[2] It was exactly the same kind of declaration that she had made to Elizabeth years earlier.

Henry could not keep ignoring the persistent attacks from the English, nor Elizabeth's slights. By now merchants from all over France—Paris, Toulouse, Troyes, Rouen, and Calais—had also had their cargo ransacked or stolen by the English.

"This goes against the treaties between our crowns and the liberty of commerce between our subjects,"[3] Henry insisted.

But Elizabeth was too busy bleeding dry the French crown's trade in the Channel, weakening its position and its ability to fund military forces against the Huguenots. She sensed victory was close.

Henry knew this all too well, and on April 7, he revealed his exasperation. Henry sent orders to Chasteauneuf.

"You have to tell the queen of England that I can no longer bear the support that she is giving to the king of Navarre and my rebel subjects, who have taken up arms against me and my crown."[4] He knew, ultimately, that Elizabeth was a keen supporter of Henry of Navarre and his claim to the throne, and this posed even more of a threat than the attacks at sea.

In June, after much consideration, Henry III tried a new strategy. Neither pleading nor persuasion had worked. So this time he decided to threaten Elizabeth.

"Let the said lady queen, my sister and cousin, know that because of the piracy at sea, I am arming vessels in Normandy and Brittany to counter-attack the English vessels' piracy."[5]

Chasteauneuf, a resident ambassador in England, made sure that his master's reprimands were heard by the queen. In response, she said simply that the English piracy was not within her control.

"I have condemned my subjects' actions of attacking French vessels."[6]

The French did not believe her, and on July 19, 1586, Henry repeated his threat.

However, arming his vessels had not quite worked as well as he had imagined. In truth Henry had very little leverage, as the religious civil war currently ravaging his country did not allow him the necessary funds to protect French commerce in the Channel.

He knew it. Elizabeth did too.

*

Elizabeth did not rely entirely on piracy to maintain her dominance in Europe. As always, she knew the importance of forging important and secure alliances.

Philip II was now her greatest enemy on account of the religious situation, but she tried not to antagonize him publicly. At this moment in her reign, Henry III was—at least in her eyes—a weak king who had far greater problems to face within the borders of his own realm to be a real threat to her; in contrast, Philip II posed a bigger problem, and Elizabeth was interested in fortifying herself further against it. It was in this spirit that she appealed to her Scottish counterpart King James VI of Scotland, her godson and the son of her nemesis, Mary Stuart, who had been imprisoned in the north of England since 1568. She was offering both an offensive and defensive alliance, binding the two monarchs to defend the Protestant religion in each kingdom, but also—and more importantly—to protect each other from invasion.

The recent Catholic plots against Elizabeth had forced her to take draconian measures when it came to religious freedom in her own realm, and English Catholics had by now experienced two decades of persecution. Laws such as the anti-Catholic proclamation of 1591 would enable the persecutions until the end of her reign.

In March 1586, thanks to a Scottish sailor just arrived from Spain, Elizabeth discovered that a great naval force was being prepared against her in Europe.

"From what I have seen with my own eyes, there were twenty-seven galleons in the port of Lisbon, which were not ships but floating fortresses," the sailor reported to the queen.

"Do you know the reported purpose of this armament?" Elizabeth asked him.

"It is said it was for La Rochelle, but others told me it was meant for Flanders and others for England, your Majesty,"[7] the Scot told her.

Elizabeth turned to Sir Francis Walsingham, who was attending the audience with her, and mumbled a few words to him that he did not seem to understand. Frustrated, she threw a slipper at him, hitting him square in the face.

Elizabeth was right to fear for the worst and to seek James's support; while her reputation as a Protestant savior continued to grow, her list of allies was diminishing.

Elizabeth had pursued her alliance with James VI of Scotland for several months, yet some of the practicalities remained undecided, including how much money James would receive. In a richly allusive letter on April 26, she made it clear to her Scottish counterpart that she knew well what was at stake concerning their friendship. She also wanted to ensure that he would sign the peace treaty, so she added, "I dare thus boldly affirm that you shall have the better part in this bargain."[8] Indeed, she finally agreed to grant him £4,000 a year, unless he broke the terms of the treaty—which he never did.

Although James had tried to negotiate for more, it was a great deal better than nothing, and he showed gratitude to Elizabeth, promising to remain her greatest ally.

"I am and will always remain your most steadfast and devoted friend."[9]

It had taken a few months and some bold negotiations over financial subsidy but in the end the Tudor queen was pleased with the conclusion of this alliance with James. "My trial of your sincere affection, my dear brother," she told him, "in the concluding of our league has been both pleasing to mine expectation and necessary for your government."

To this James replied, "I commit you, Madam and dearest sister, to God's holy protection."

The resulting Treaty of Berwick was signed on July 6, 1586. James's mother, Mary, was not mentioned. In many ways, this was not at all surprising given that James had never really known his mother; she had left him behind in Scotland when he was only a toddler. He was a pragmatic man, who was well aware of the importance of remaining in Elizabeth's good books if he ever wanted to be officially named as her successor.

*

On the same day, a man named Anthony Babington was busy changing the course of history with a letter he wrote to Mary Stuart, whom he addressed as "most mighty, most excellent, my dread sovereign lady and queen, unto whom I owe all fidelity and obedience."

In this letter, he explained that he had laid plans to break Mary free from her prison. In great detail he set out the invasion plans for "the deliverance of your Majesty. Myself, with ten gentlemen of quality, and a hundred of followers, will undertake the delivery of your person from the hands of your enemies; and for the dispatch of the usurper."[10]

Unfortunately for Babington, he misjudged and underestimated Walsingham's network of spies and their influence: they were everywhere—and they were intercepting any and all letters sent from or to Mary Stuart.

Babington had been born in October 1561 at Dethick in Derbyshire to a family that had always been inclined toward Catholicism. He briefly met Mary Stuart around 1579 when he was serving as a page in the household of Sir George Talbot, Earl of Shrewsbury, fourth and last husband to the wealthiest woman in England, Bess of Hardwick. Talbot had been in charge of Mary Stuart, and when Babington saw how she was being treated, and held against her will in the household, he immediately felt great sympathy for her.

In 1580 Babington left for Paris, where he met Thomas Morgan and James Beaton, Archbishop of Glasgow, who was acting as Mary's representative in France. During that time, it is very likely that the men lamented the treatment of Mary Stuart, while also asserting their belief that she was the rightful queen of England.

At some point during 1583 or 1584, Babington came back to England, and—thanks to his network of conspirators located in the north of England—he was able to carry some letters to Mary from Morgan. Clearly, his devotion to the prisoner knew no bounds.

In May 1586, the Catholic priest John Ballard contacted Babington about a potential plot against Elizabeth, the aim of which was to liberate Mary. He had started planning this conspiracy in Rome back in 1584, and had also been in touch with Bernardino de Mendoza, the Spanish ambassador, who was now serving his master, Philip II, at the French court.

Mendoza was determined to rescue the Scottish queen and, in June 1586, he begged Philip II for "40 crowns a month to Morgan, to be paid here, as he is the person who is most in the queen of Scotland's confidence, and with very good reason, as he is extremely faithful and intelligent."[11] The request was granted by the Spanish king.

Morgan, the traitor who was still imprisoned by the French authorities, was in fact allowed to continue pursuing his conspiracy against Elizabeth while detained, and even received favorable treatment, being permitted a private channel to continue his secret correspondence with Mary's sympathizers. Mary Stuart held him in high regard; she was extremely grateful for his service to her. It is not known who supported Morgan but one can imagine that it must have been an important figure at court—probably a Guisard.

Meanwhile, Elizabeth continued to arm English ships, mindful of a possible invasion coming from Spain. Drake was ordered to take a fleet and set sail for Spain to delay their preparations.

Both the Spanish and the French were convinced that Philip's own naval forces would crush the fleet without too much effort. Mendoza reported to Philip that "The king of France and the queen mother are quite convinced that the queen of England will come to terms with your Majesty, giving up anything your Majesty may like to demand, as she is not powerful enough to continue the war for any length of time."[12]

Elizabeth continued to show her confidence in public but, in reality, she was extremely anxious about the outcome of the war against Spain. Throughout her reign, she had tried to avoid such a moment by using a combination of her diplomacy and her privateers as shields against the Spanish Empire.

By now, support was strong for Mary Stuart across Europe. Her cousin, Henry, Duke of Guise—who was in constant correspondence with Mendoza and Philip—was determined to free his cousin and put her on the English throne, ridding Europe of the threat of Elizabeth. The religious conflict in France had turned him into something of a war hero, and his initially frivolous ambition—to one day become king of France himself—now started to seem like a possibility. He was, after all, one of the most powerful men in France, if not the most powerful, given his popularity. As for Catherine, she was now a fervent supporter of her former daughter-in-law; how times had changed. There was little doubt in Catherine's mind that the end of Mary could somehow constitute the end of the French royal family; their inability to rescue her revealed their weakness to all of Europe.

*

By August 1586, several others had joined Babington and Ballard in their cause to murder the Tudor queen. They included John Savage, who had served in the army of Alexander Farnese, Duke of Parma and nephew of Philip II; Thomas Salisbury, who had met Babington a few years prior; and other notable fellow Catholics. Parma was a strong and respected military man who had captured over thirty towns in the south of the Netherlands so that he could return them to the control of Catholic Spain. Ruthless, ambitious, and determined, he was making his uncle, Philip, proud.

Gradually, Babington had become the leader of the plot, given his connections to Mary. On July 17, 1586, Mary finally responded to his plan. She was delighted, and keen to make sure it was a well-planned mission, writing back that

> to ensure that we are successful in our enterprise, you need to carefully think about how many people, on foot and on horseback, will you be able to raise and how many captains in each county will lead them, if we cannot have one leader. Make a list of cities and ports that our allies can safely arrive to, in the north but also in the west and south of this realm, to receive the necessary support from the Netherlands, France, and Spain. Think also about where we shall assemble all our forces.

She warned that if they failed and if Elizabeth "managed to win over our forces, I will never see again the daylight and all my supporters will be persecuted." She knew exactly what was at stake. She finished by signing, "your devoted good friend forever, do not fail in burning this letter."[13]

Unfortunately for Mary, all the letters were intercepted and the plotters quickly identified. Walsingham—the man behind the interception—had so far kept Elizabeth totally in the dark about the scheme, fearing the ferocity of her response.

> My only fear is that her Majesty will not use the matter with that secrecy that appertained, though it import it as greatly as ever anything did since she came to this crown, and surely, if the matter be well handled, it will break the neck of all dangerous practices during her Majesty's reign.[14]

Undoubtedly, however, Walsingham was determined that this plot would be the end of Mary Stuart. And as the investigation continued, it became clear he could not keep the conspiracy from Elizabeth. He revealed all to her. There is no record of her response, but she did comply with her privy councillors' requirements. The plotters needed to be arrested.

On Tuesday, August 2, 1586, a proclamation was published ordering the arrest of the Babington conspirators; citizens were encouraged to contact the authorities if they knew where any of them were hiding. To ensure success, portraits of the conspirators' faces were published all over the City of London, as well as being dispersed in several other locations throughout the realm. Elizabeth also had private copies of the portraits, so she would be able to recognize the perpetrators if any attempted to come to court. The next day, arrest warrants were issued all over the country.

John Ballard was the first to be apprehended; he was taken to prison on August 4.

Panicked, Babington rushed to Savage to break the news. "Ballard has been taken," he told him. "We will all be betrayed soon. What remedy now?"

"There is no longer a remedy but to kill the queen presently," Savage replied solemnly.

"Very well," Babington agreed after a moment of consideration, "then you go to the court tomorrow and execute the fact."

"Nay, I cannot go tomorrow," Savage said. "My apparel is not ready, and in this apparel I shall never be allowed to come near the queen."

Impatient and irritated, Babington burst out, "Go to find a new apparel! Here is my ring and all the money I have."[15]

As it turned out, neither Savage nor anyone else in the group ever made it to the court and, soon after, all of the conspirators were arrested before any attempt could be made on Elizabeth's life.

In the days that followed, celebrations all around the City of London took place to acknowledge the capture of the traitors. Church bells rang and bonfires were built in the streets as people feasted and toasted to Elizabeth's good health and continued safety.

Once again she had survived a plot made against her life. But she kept her feelings to herself. After all, showing even a little relief would be a sign of weakness. Yet she also knew that certain decisions had to be made; she could not continue living her life in fear of being murdered.

*

For days Mary remained unaware of the arrest of the plotters but when, on August 11, she was arrested while hunting in Sir Walter Aston's park, she must have known that the plan had gone awry.

Mary was held at Aston's house at Tixall in Staffordshire while all her possessions, letters, and ciphers at Chartley—where she had been imprisoned for a year—were thoroughly searched. There was clear evidence that Mary had been in contact with the plotters as well as other agents in France and Spain, including with the French ambassador, Chasteauneuf.

On August 18, Elizabeth wrote an official letter to the Mayor of London—and his citizens—from Windsor, which set out her thoughts. It was clear that the public support had moved her, she explained, using the royal "we":

"We did not so much rejoice at the escape of the intended attempt against our person," she wrote, "as to see the great joy of our most loving subjects at the apprehension of the contrivers thereof, which to make their love more apparent they have omitted no outward show that by any external means might witness to the world the inward love and dutiful affection they bear towards us."[16]

The next day she wrote to Sir Amias Paulet, Mary's keeper, who had played a important role in foiling the plot. Here her language was much less moderate, and her fury was strongly expressed:

Let your wicked murderess know how with hearty sorrow her vile deserts compel these orders; and bid her, from me, ask God forgiveness for her treacherous dealings towards the saver of her life many a year, to the intolerable peril of her own; and yet, not contented with so many forgivenesses, must fall again so horrible.[17]

The traitors were tried at Westminster on September 13, 14, and 15 and, being found guilty of high treason, they were all sentenced to death. The French rulers, including Catherine, denied any knowledge of the plot, despite having had one of its perpetrators within their walls, and ordered Chasteauneuf to maintain this stance with the English queen. A few days later, Chasteauneuf steeled himself when his presence was sought at an audience with the queen.

Elizabeth's gaze was stern as she greeted him. "Monsieur the Ambassador," she said before pausing for a moment, "we are aware that you have had great and secret communication with the queen of Scotland."

When he tried to deny it, she interrupted him. "Believe me when I say that I know everything that is done in my kingdom. Do not forget that I, myself, was a prisoner in the time of my sister; I know too well what devices prisoners employ to gain over servants and how to undertake secret communications."

The French ambassador tried to pledge his loyalty to Elizabeth—as well as insisting upon his ignorance regarding the plot against her life—but his protestations were in vain.

Elizabeth ended the short and unpleasant audience with a warning: "I will keep an eye on you."[18] This warning, he knew, was also aimed at Henry and Catherine.

Most of those involved in the plot had now been dealt with, yet the question still remained: what to do with Mary Stuart?

Mary had certainly encouraged the conspirators, and clearly she still had support, so therefore continuing to move her from place to place in the north of England was no longer an option. Elizabeth was adamant that she should be tried, so that a more permanent resolution might be reached, but where would such a trial take place? The Tower of London was the most obvious choice but William Cecil, Lord Burghley, bluntly refused. It was too risky to have her in the City of London, he insisted.

It was eventually agreed that the most appropriate venue for the imprisonment and trial of the queen of Scotland was the castle of Fotheringhay. A Norman motte-and-bailey castle dating from the High

Middle Ages, Fotheringhay was used as a state prison throughout Elizabeth's reign. It was the perfect secure location for this situation.

The commissioners in charge of the trial included Walsingham and Burghley, both of whom arrived at Fotheringhay in early October. Before their departure, however, Burghley's loyal secretary William Davison wrote briefly to them, having discovered another potential threat to the Tudor queen's life.

"I have just met with a Dutchman who just came from Paris and who is friends with the queen mother's jeweller," Davison wrote. "He told me that the jeweller warned him that the queen of England should be more circumspect of her person, and should avoid showing herself publicly."[19] On the continent, and particularly in Paris, rumors of another imminent attack on Elizabeth were circulating. This only increased the suspicion in which Catholics were held across the realm.

As the commissioners began arriving at Fotheringhay, Mary stated bluntly that she refused to stand trial. In her own mind, she was not an English subject and therefore was not subject to English laws: she was a Scottish queen.

Elizabeth, upon hearing of the news, wrote directly to Mary: "It is with great and inestimable grief that I understand that you are void of all remorse of conscience, and pretend with great protestations not to be in any sort privy or assent to any attempt against my state or person. We have found clear and evident proofs of the contrary and this will be verified and maintained against you. I am sending to you divers of the chief and most ancient noblemen, together with certain members of the Privy Council to judge that most horrible and unnatural attempt."

She then reminded her cousin of her position. "You have been living within my protection and thereby you are subject to the laws of my realm. I advise you to give credit to the commission in place," she said, commanding Mary to participate in the trial. Once again, Mary refused.[20]

But Mary's mind would be changed. Sir Christopher Hatton—another close favorite of Elizabeth's, vice-chamberlain to the queen, and commissioner of the trial—begged her to participate so that she might clear herself of all charges: "Believe me, the queen herself will be much affected with joy, who affirmed unto me at my coming from her, that never anything befell her more grievous, than that you were charged with such a crime."[21] His charisma and his conviction that she had a chance of winning Elizabeth round did the trick. The next day, Mary informed him that she would indeed stand trial.

However, like all those accused of high treason, Mary was denied counsel, which meant she was forced to defend herself with little knowledge of English law. Even if she had known the law, it was unlikely that she would have escaped the wrath of Elizabeth on this occasion. Nevertheless, still she sought to make her case.

On October 11, after the remaining English commissioners had arrived at Fotheringhay Castle on the banks of the River Nene, Mary made her plea in front of all of them. "It grieves me that the queen, my most dear sister, is misinformed of me; and that I, having been so many years straitly kept in prison, and grown lame of my limbs, have lain neglected, after I have offered so many reasonable conditions of my liberty."

She paused, allowing her words to settle for a moment, and then smoothly continued, "Though I have thoroughly forewarned her of many dangers, yet has not credit been given unto me, but I have been always contemned, though most nearly allied unto her in blood."

Mary was not exactly telling the truth; she never warned Elizabeth of any dangers.

She cleared her throat, seemingly overwhelmed with emotion as she continued:

The laws and statutes of England are to me most unknown; I am destitute of counsellors, and who shall be my peers I am utterly ignorant. My papers and notes have been taken away from me, and no man dares step forth to be my advocate. I am clear from all crime against the queen, I have excited no man against her, and I am not to be charged but by mine own word or writing, which cannot be produced against me. Yet can I not deny but I have commended myself and my cause to foreign princes.[22]

On the second day of the trial, Mary reasserted both her vulnerability and her determination:

"I came into England to crave aid, and ever since have been detained in prison, and therefore could not enjoy the protection or benefit of the laws of England." If she had not enjoyed the protection of English law herself, she said, how could she be expected to follow it?

The commissioners were unconvinced, and cited civil and canon law to Mary, dismissing her argument as invalid for reasons that to her were probably entirely unclear.

"I am no subject and I would rather die a thousand deaths than acknowledge myself as a subject," Mary exclaimed in response. "I am, however, ready to answer all things in a free and full parliament as I know all of you have been appointed against me. I would also like to remind you to look at your consciences, and to remember that the theatre of the whole world is much wider than the kingdom of England."[23]

Given that Mary continued to refuse to be subjected to the laws of England, there was now discussion on how best to try her.

"You are accused of having conspired in the destruction of our lady and queen anointed. You say you are a queen, so be it," said Hatton. "But in such a crime a royal dignity is not exempted from answering, neither by the civil nor canon law, nor by the law of nations, nor of nature. For if such kind of offences might be committed without punishment, all justice would stagger, yea, fall to the ground."

"I refuse not to answer in a full parliament before the estates of the realm lawfully assembled," Mary replied, "so as I may be declared the next to the succession; yea, before the queen and Council, so as my protestation may be admitted, and I may be acknowledged the next kin to the queen. To the judgement of mine adversaries, amongst whom I know all defence of mine innocence will be bared, flatly, I will not submit myself."[24]

But Mary had no real power against Elizabeth's desires. Eventually, she was left with no choice but to listen to the charges made against her, and informed that her participation was optional, and that if she chose not to defend herself, the commission would proceed without her.

So, on October 14, Mary was finally presented with the evidence against her, namely the letters and ciphers exchanged between her, Babington, and Mendoza.

"I know no Babington," she protested, "and I have never received any letters from him, nor wrote any to him. I have never plotted the destruction of the queen."

Her statement, however, was immediately repudiated: Babington had already confessed that they knew one another and had also admitted to recognizing the letters exchanged between them.

"Many letters have been exchanged between me and many men," Mary claimed in desperation. "These letters were written by one of my secretaries. I believe that the incriminating part of the letter has been added and I require that my own subscription, under my own hand, might be produced so the handwriting can be assessed against one another. Babington or someone else could have made up my involvement in the plot," she added.

Burghley ignored her pleas, instead reading aloud the letters that had been exchanged between Babington and Mary.

"I want to see the original copies," she ordered, refusing to acknowledge them. "My only crime is that I have done my best endeavour to recover my liberty, which nature itself allows, and have solicited my friends to deliver me; yet to some, whom I do not wish to name, when they offered me their help to deliver me, I answered not a word."[25]

She then continued to accuse the laws of the realm of persecuting Catholics, stating that she could not be judged for wanting to defend her faith against unjust treatment. Testimonies from her secretaries— notably Gilbert Curle and Claude Nau—were read aloud, setting out details of a conversation that took place between Mendoza and Ballard regarding Mary's escape from where she was imprisoned.

"It does not prove that I have consented to the destruction of the queen," she pointed out.

They continued to produce more letters and other writing that incriminated her, as well as accusing her of conspiring with the king of Spain to take over the English throne. She dismissed these.

"The circumstances may be proved but never the fact. My integrity depends on the credit and memory of my secretaries, who I know are honest and sincere men. Yet if they have confessed anything out of fear of torments or hope of reward and impunity, it was not to be admitted,"[26] Mary protested.

Her objections went unheard; Burghley charged her with past mistakes and, notably, her correspondence with Morgan—as well as her involvement in earlier plots.

"Ah," she said, "you are my adversary."

"Yes, I am adversary to Queen Elizabeth's adversaries," he rebuked, "but let us now proceed to proofs."

"I refuse to hear them!" she cried.

"Yet we will hear them!"

Once again, the letters to and from Mendoza, several French agents, and the conspirators to the Babington plot were read to the room.

By the end of these proceedings, Mary was in tears. "I want to be heard in full parliament or in person with the queen, who would have regard of a queen,"[27] she insisted.

This audience, of course, was never granted.

However, before the verdict could be delivered, Elizabeth recalled her commissioners to London. She wanted Mary Stuart's trial to be continued by Star Chamber at Westminster, where Mary would ultimately be found guilty on October 25, 1586. In the meantime, Mary was left without any answers or reassurances. Perhaps this way, Elizabeth was allowing herself more time to change her mind.

*

Over in France, Catherine was now very much preoccupied with domestic politics, and in particular a potential compromise with the king of Navarre to put an end to the bloodshed caused by the eighth religious civil war.

Catherine spent most of the first six months of the year in Paris working on this plan. With her son's consent, she made the decision to negotiate with her son-in-law, Henry of Navarre. Finally, in July, she went to Blois and then Chenonceau, sending one of her most faithful servants, the abbot of Gadaigne, to the king of Navarre to arrange a meeting. Catherine relied mostly on her powerful rhetoric, and trusted that a face-to-face meeting would lead to a reconciliation between the crown and her son-in-law.

Unfortunately, the Huguenot leader was not as receptive as she would have liked; he turned down her offer.

She continued to send other servants with the same aim, professing her care for him and her desire to bring peace and stability to the whole realm. While on the one hand she was professing her resolution to bring peace, on the other hand she was ordering her governors—in Brittany, Saumur, Bellegarde, and Orléans—to keep on fighting the Huguenot forces. As usual, she was playing the political games of the French court: to seek peace, you also needed to show that you were not afraid to continue the war. Knowing this, Henry of Navarre was worried that the meeting she was asking for was, in fact, a trap—but he also did not want to show any weakness by revealing his fears and refusing the meeting.

On November 23, 1586, the king of Navarre finally agreed to meet with Catherine, but he insisted that she come to Cognac, a Protestant town. Catherine agreed with these terms and, on December 3, left Saint-Maixent, where she had resided since the beginning of the autumn. She took up residence in an old castle, which belonged to Marguerite of Angoulême, sister of the late Francis I. Henry of Navarre asked for the meeting to take place in the castle of Saint-Brice, located only three miles away from Cognac.

Finally, on December 13, the two enemies met in person, Catherine embracing her son-in-law and kissing him on the cheeks. But the conversation was to be disastrous.

After the courteous empty greetings, Catherine got straight to the point.

"Do you wish to be the reason behind the ruin of this realm?"

Shocked by this provocative question, Henry of Navarre responded precisely. "I am not. However, the king of France, your son, is trying to ruin me."

"If my son had wanted to ruin you, he would have done so," Catherine continued. "Instead, I am here to make you understand that by opposing his orders and not laying down your arms, you are challenging his authority."

"I am only opposing the schemes of the League, nothing else."

By now, Catherine was losing her temper.

"That is enough, my son." Her tone was sharp and assertive. "The Leaguers are the sons of France and the best Catholic people in France. They do not wish to see the Huguenots take control of their Catholic realm." She calmed her voice a little, knowing that their conversation had taken a bad turn. "Tell me what your conditions are for surrender and I will convince my son to give them to you."

"I did not ask for this meeting. I am not asking you for anything, nor the king. If you have something to ask me, I am listening and will take it to my fellow Huguenot leaders. I cannot promise anything without consulting them first," Henry replied calmly but firmly.

Catherine knew that losing her temper once again would not be in her best interests.

"Fine," she said instead, "if this is how you want things to be. I just want you to know that my son and myself love and honour you, and we wish to be able to embrace and kiss you as a good brother again."

Henry was now the one who could not control his emotions, as he complained of how he had been treated by the king and herself.

"The king—who is like a father to me, as I am one of his subjects—instead of feeding me like one of his children, has declared war on me and attacked me like a wolf. And as for you, Madam, you have been attacking me like a lioness."

Catherine was outraged. "Lies! I have only treated you as a mother."

"Maybe when I was a child, yes," he admitted, "but you have changed and you are no longer like a mother to me."[28]

At first, Catherine was speechless, and probably hurt by these home truths. She could not deny that, over the years, she had made decisions that were not in her son-in-law's best interests. The conversation continued, with both of them trying to heap the blame on the other. She asked him to consider converting to Catholicism to put an end to this civil war. He refused. Once again, they had reached a stalemate.

While she was away demonstrating the strength of her commitment to the Catholic religion, Leaguers had started to spread rumors in Paris that Henry III himself had sent his mother to plot with the Huguenots. The French king found himself in an unenviable position, forced to defend Catherine's right to negotiate with the Huguenots on his behalf, emphasizing that he trusted her to find a solution that would not compromise the preservation of the Catholic religion in France.

As for Catherine, given her efforts on the home front, she was now happy to take a less active role in Anglo-French relations. However, this did not prevent her from keeping an anxious eye on the Tudor queen's actions across the Channel. A friend—a daughter—had become an enemy.

Meanwhile, in London, Elizabeth now faced incredible pressure from her parliament, who had long wanted to see Mary dead. But would she—or could she—bring herself to order the execution?

15

A Queen Must Die,
November 1586–March 1587

On November 3, 1586, just a few days after the opening of the sixth parliament of Elizabeth's reign, three vehement speeches were made against Mary, Queen of Scots.

Sir Christopher Hatton was the first one to make his case.

"At first she married into France, where she took upon the coat and arms of England," he began. "Next, her husband in France dying, she chose to marry a subject of England and of nobility, named the Earl of Lennox, in hope thereby to enter partly into the hearts of the people and come nearer the crown. Afterwards, she was banished from Scotland for the death of her husband and came to this realm, where she was protected by her Majesty. Yet, notwithstanding that favour, aspiring still after this crown, she plotted to marry the Duke of Norfolk and thereupon stirred a rebellion to come to the crown."

This was pretty damning testimony, but there was far worse to come. Hatton went on to emphasize Mary's ongoing treachery, focusing on her recent correspondence with Babington.

"She wrote to him," Hatton informed his audience, "commending him for his zeal in religion, wherein she professed to spend life, land, and goods. She advised him further that care must be taken when it came to looking at the aid that was coming from foreign forces and where to expect them, and where the succour given from the Netherlands, France, and Spain should assemble."

Hatton continued to name Mary's many connections to the

continent before explaining that surely she had been an active player in the recent plots aiming to murder Elizabeth.

Drawing his condemnations to a close, he simply concluded with what everyone in the Chamber already knew he would say: "All her actions were aimed at usurping the crown of England, murdering her Majesty, altering the religion of this realm and destroying all of us."[1]

Next came Sir Walter Mildmay, Chancellor of the Exchequer since 1566, who stood up to make his own short speech. He had been one of the commissioners at Fotheringhay and largely agreed with the verdicts of his peers.

"The Queen of Scots has been the cause of much blood, who remaining, her Majesty—whose safety we all ought to provide for—cannot be in safety."

Sir Ralph Sadler, a longtime Tudor courtier who had served as privy councillor to Henry VIII, agreed. "If the queen's Majesty does not provide justice, she will never be safe again."

"Hear, hear!"[2] the members of parliament called out with enthusiasm.

Over the following days, several other members of parliament continued to make their case against Mary. This led to a petition—signed by both lords and commoners—demanding the execution of the Queen of Scots, which was presented to the queen on November 12, 1586. Its warnings to Elizabeth were clear:

"We find that if the said lady shall now escape the due and deserved punishment of death for these, her most execrable treasons and offences, your highness's royal person shall be exposed to many more and those more secret and dangerous conspiracies than before."[3]

Elizabeth knew this was true. In fact, she had always known the risks she was exposed to. But she could not fathom that she might yet do the unthinkable, the unimaginable, the unacceptable: ordering the execution of not only her kinswoman but of another anointed queen, another daughter of a king. While there is no written record of her thoughts at this moment, it was clear from her ongoing indecision on the matter that Elizabeth had always struggled with the idea of agreeing to such an execution. So far, she had managed to avoid what now seemed inevitable.

Elizabeth addressed the parliament twice that month.

On November 12, she explained her dilemma, commencing her speech with the assertion that—even after the plots against her, and the evidence against her cousin—she continued to bear Mary no malice.

"If the case stood between her and myself only," she explained, "if it had pleased God to have made us both milkmaids with pails on our arms, so that the matter should have rested between us two; and that I knew she did and would seek my destruction still, yet could I not consent to her death."[4]

However, she and Mary were not just two women: Elizabeth was a queen, and as such a threat against her was the threat against the whole country, and all of its subjects. Such a situation required a different solution.

With this in mind, she continued,

To your petition I must pause and take respite before I give answer. Princes, you know, stand upon stages so that their actions are viewed and beheld of all men; and I am sure my doings will come to the scanning of many fine wits, not only within the realm, but in foreign countries. And we must look to persons as well abroad as at home. But this be you assured of: I will be most careful to consider and to do what which shall be best for the safety of my people and most for the good of the realm.[5]

The members of parliament were not satisfied with this answer, and they were even more displeased when, two days after making her speech, Elizabeth asked them to suggest an alternative to the execution. But they would not change their mind, and were once more unanimous: "Upon advice and great consultation we cannot find that there is any possible means to provide for your Majesty's safety but by the just and speedy execution of Mary, Queen of Scots."[6]

On November 17, they issued another proclamation expressing the same, this time entitled "considerations for the queen's safety."[7] In the face of such strident opinion, Elizabeth could no longer delay her decision. Therefore, on November 24, she addressed her parliament once more. As she did, it was clear that the decision weighed heavily on her.

> When I first came to the sceptre and crown of this realm I did think more of God who gave it to me than of the title. And, therefore, my care was to set in order those things which did concern the Church of God and this religion in which I was born, in which I was bred, and in which I trust to die.[8]

She continued, explaining that she had always placed her faith in God and that he had always protected her from her enemies. But she knew that she needed to say more to reassure the men who were standing in front of her.

> I must say and confess that there was never prince more bound to his people than I am to you all. I can but acknowledge your great love and exceeding care of me to be such as I shall be able to requite, having but one life, except I had as many lives as you all. But I will never forget it while I shall breathe.

But even then, at the end of her speech, having professed her love for her country and her people, Elizabeth did what she had always done—she continued to postpone her decision.

"But now for answer unto you, you must take an answer without answer at my hands."[9]

Of course, this was not a satisfactory response for the assembled men. Her privy councillors—including Robert Dudley, Earl of Leicester, who had briefly returned from the Netherlands—continued to pressure Elizabeth into agreeing to the execution. During their private audiences, Leicester must have shared his worry with the queen, and is likely to have appealed to her desire to maintain peace and stability in England. She had to protect her own life to protect that of her people.

They had worn her down. Finally, on Sunday, December 4, at Richmond Palace, Elizabeth proclaimed the sentence of Mary's death. She swore that she was left with no choice but to make the drastic decision to sign her cousin's death warrant, even if it was clear that she was still reluctant to do so.

When the French royal family heard of the parliament's petitions, they were outraged, sending one of their most trusted advisors and experienced diplomats, Pomponne de Bellièvre, to England. He arrived with personal letters from both Henry III and Catherine, begging Elizabeth to forgive Mary and ensure her release. As Elizabeth read these letters during her diplomatic audiences, their contents remain unknown, but the letters Catherine sent to other royal councillors and ambassadors give an indication of their content.

Catherine was desperate to find a way to save Mary's life.

"Send another letter to Bellièvre on my behalf," she instructed Villeroy, who was now secretary of state. "Order him to do all he can to save my daughter-in-law's life. He has to convince the queen of England to change her mind, imploring her to do so for the love she has for the king, my son." More importantly, Catherine gave further advice that, "Bellièvre has to warn the queen of England that such an action might create more trouble for her that will come from Spain and the pope."[10]

In another letter sent to Monsieur de Courcelles, French ambassador to Scotland, Catherine confided her sorrow.

> With the king, my son, we have sent Bellièvre to England in order to assist by all means the queen of Scotland, Madam my daughter-in-law. I am deeply hurt by what is happening to her as if she were my own daughter and I truly wish to do all I can in my power to help her. I have even sent a letter, written in my own hand, to the queen of England, that Bellièvre is ordered to deliver in person.[11]

Unfortunately, the letters sent by the French rulers did not seem to move the queen in the slightest. With her intelligence informing her of Chasteauneuf's own secret correspondence with Mary, she was persuaded that the French royal family were now her enemies too.

Even so, when the news broke, Bellièvre insisted he be received by the queen at once.

*

On December 8, Bellièvre and Chasteauneuf were received by Elizabeth in her Presence Chamber. This was a bigger and more formal venue than normal, used so that most of her nobles and courtiers could attend the meeting. The choice of room was a show of strength from Elizabeth, and a sign that she wanted no intimacy with France.

Bellièvre was in his late fifties, as his silver hair and beard could attest. His long hooked nose and hooded eyes made him instantly recognizable at court. As he stood in front of Elizabeth wearing his usual long, dark coat, which contrasted with his white collar, he bowed and began his address.

> Madam, his most Christian majesty, the French king, has been in extreme pain at the news of your proclamation sentencing the Queen of Scots to death. His pain is not only in respect to the said lady who is his kinswoman, his ally, and his sister-in-law, but also in respect to yourself, madam, whose friendship the said lord values, and desires all his life long to value. He begs you once more, madam, that you will take into your wise consideration the prayer which he made to you, which he deems full of justice and honour, and to be no less for your good than for that of the person in favour of whom he returns to entreat you not to refuse.[12]

Elizabeth dismissed her courtiers and councillors, expressing her desire to speak with the French ambassadors alone. Her audience obeyed, and when they had left she finally offered her response.

> Your master, the king of France, needs to understand that the queen of Scotland has always pursued me. It is, in fact, the third time that she has sought to make an attempt upon my life by an infinity of means, which I have borne too long with much patience, and that nothing has

ever touched my heart so keenly as this last accident, by reason whereof I have spent more sighs and tears than I have done on the occasion of the loss of all my other kinsfolk.

She paused, taking a moment to reflect.

You know I have read many books. Yet never have I found nor heard of such an act as the one that has been designed against me and pursued by my own kinswoman, whom the king, her brother-in-law, could not and ought not to support in her malice, but should rather aid me to bring her speedily justice as an example. I know what it is to be a subject and a sovereign and I have no doubt that the Queen of Scots's action was an act of treason with the aim to overthrow me. It is the most wretched and most inhuman practice that can be devised against a sovereign.

Elizabeth may initially have been unsure about the best course of action when it came to Mary, but now she seemed determined in her resolution.

Chasteauneuf remained silent, diverting attention to his counterpart who was now employing all his considerable diplomatic talents to save Mary. Bellièvre explained that while Henry wanted to preserve the life of his former sister-in-law, the queen of Scotland, he by no means wished to antagonize Elizabeth.

The said lord acknowledges you as a queen and sovereign princess, who has in this matter a common interest with other kings and sovereign princes, and a particular one, inasmuch as the said lady the queen of Scotland is also your nearest kinswoman. And as to the offence that your Majesty professes to have had done to yourself, your goodness has many times declared that you seek no vengeance thereof, and thus we believe it.

Bellièvre paused before continuing his compelling case, allowing Elizabeth to take in his skillful arguments.

But as to the doubt which remains to you, that in preserving the life of the queen of Scotland, your own may be in danger, for which alone you desire provision to be made, the king your good brother enters into this thought with your Majesty, as is very reasonable, and considering whence more evil and danger might befall you, or repose, safety, and contentment, as well in regard to your person as to your affairs, he judges that without any doubt the death of the queen of Scotland befalling thus as some counsel you, would be infinitely more prejudicial to you than her life can inconvenience you.[13]

Elizabeth did not seem convinced. Indeed, her gaze intensified and her tone sharpened as she made her fulsome response.

When the Queen of Scots came into this kingdom, she was not made a prisoner, but only arrested so that she might not leave it, and she lived in the estate and rank fitting to a queen, with her own train and household, in the houses of great lords, having the service and free recourse of all her servants whosoever they were. I even allowed her to have ambassadors. She then plotted first with the Duke of Norfolk, whom she attempted to marry. Even then, she continued to enjoy her former liberty, until there were again conspiracies which aimed at murdering me and in which she played a role. In her eighteen years in this country, she has constantly plotted against my life and my people.

Elizabeth continued by citing Cicero and several of the ancient laws, asserting how unnatural it was for Mary to be involved in such assassination plots. This, she said with finality, left her with no choice but to agree to the execution.

Bellièvre listened intently before offering his response. "The greatest precept for reigning well and happily is to abstain from bloodshed. One bloodshed leads to another, and such executions usually have a sequel." He gave examples from both history and scripture.

He explained that, in his view, Elizabeth's forgiveness in this matter would make her legendary, would see her praised by all Christian princes, particularly Henry. "The French king will be further bound to you and will continue to ensure that nothing is undertaken against your Majesty."

Elizabeth chuckled at this, for she knew it was beyond Bellièvre to promise such a thing. "The truth is your king will never be able to ordain that nothing be undertaken against me and that no such attempts be made. Let's not forget that two of the conspiracies against my person have been hatched in France, without the knowledge of the king, and by the goodness of God been discovered in England."[14]

Elizabeth was merciful enough to accept the lie he had just uttered, when he protested that Henry III knew nothing about any of these plots against her. She simply did not believe that was the case. But she also reminded Bellièvre that the Guises were extremely influential at court and that they too had been involved in the conspiracies against her, so how could she trust a king who trusted them?

Bellièvre found himself in a tight corner now, and could only repeat himself. "Your Majesty will live in greater safety if the queen of Scotland remains alive."

"Let's conclude this audience, shall we?" Elizabeth said abruptly. "My lords say that the judgement is rigorous and extraordinary while ambassadors who haven't participated in the commission nor seen the evidence against the queen of Scotland have harshly accused the nobility and lords of this realm of not having sufficient evidence."

But before he could be dismissed Bellièvre interrupted with one final missive. "His most Christian Majesty, the French king, just hopes that your goodness will reject a counsel so foreign to your sweet and benign nature which is given you against the queen of Scotland. But if you decide to proceed with your decision, my lord, the French king, has given us, his ambassadors, charge to tell you, Madam, that he cannot but resent it as a thing beyond the common interest of all kings which will greatly offend him in particular."

"By saying so, it is as if you desire to put myself and the realm in fear of such words, so bitter, proffered in the name of your king," said Elizabeth sharply, before dismissing both French ambassadors at once.

If Henry wanted her as an enemy, so be it. She was not afraid of him, nor of any other European princes.

★

The French interventions had failed and therefore, on December 10, Elizabeth drafted Mary's death warrant.

The news was reported back to Mary, who was awaiting the decision at Fotheringhay. When she heard the verdict, she was devastated; she had surely hoped that, once again, Elizabeth would turn a blind eye to her actions.

On December 19, Mary wrote an intimate letter to her cousin, hoping it would touch her heart.

> I know that you, more than any other, ought to be touched to the heart by the honour or dishonour of your race, and of a queen, the daughter of a king. Then, madam, by the honour of Jesus—under whose name all powers obey—I require you to permit, after my enemies shall have satisfied their desire for my innocent blood, that my poor desolate servants all together may carry away my body to be buried in holy ground, and with some of my predecessors who are in France, especially the late queen, my mother.

She continued with words that she hoped would resonate with Elizabeth. "Before God I give you no blame: but may God cause you to see the truth of all after my death."

Along with the letter, Mary returned a ring Elizabeth had sent her years ago as a token of affection. Concluding her note, she begged once more for her life. "I entreat you again, and require you in the name of Jesus Christ, out of respect for our consanguinity, and for the sake of King Henry the seventh, your ancestor and mine, and by the honour of the dignity which we have held and of the sex common between us, that my request may be granted to me."[15]

But her entreaties were in vain.

★

Days and then weeks passed, and still there was no news from London. Mary had expected her execution to be imminent and yet, once more, she was left waiting. The strain must have been enormous.

Meanwhile, Bellièvre had been ordered by the French king and the queen mother to continue in his efforts to rescue Mary. Catherine was furious. How dare Elizabeth make such a decision, and go against the will of her European counterparts? Such an action undermined her son, and she would not stand for it.

She was adamant. "Saving the queen of Scotland is of first importance for the service of the king," she told the ambassador. "It touches the king's and the realm's honour."[16]

In Paris, the Guises were much alarmed by the news, and they continued to raise their concerns with the king. His inability to rescue their cousin was, in their eyes, not only an act of great incompetence but also of treason because it undermined the Catholic cause.

Soon, rumors began to spread that Henry was conspiring with Elizabeth to see Mary gone, with people gossiping in the Parisian streets. "It is well known that the king despised the whole race from Lorraine," went one such rumor.[17]

While the Guises were certainly no longer great favorites of Henry III, he certainly understood the need to keep them happy: it is hard to imagine that the French king would not see the potential risk for his own life and reign if Mary Stuart was executed.

Catherine understood this too—and feared it above all. "Mary's execution will touch the king's authority and diminish the greatness of the name of this realm. It must be avoided at all costs," she warned.[18]

But Elizabeth, who had originally been hesitant in her decision, had recently learned of a new plot against her life, confirming in her mind that she must act decisively if she were to protect herself.

These new conspirators included William Stafford, younger brother to Edward Stafford, ambassador in France—whose own allegiance now started to be questioned—as well as Chasteauneuf's own servant, Leonard des Trappes, and Michael Moody.

Lord Burghley was losing patience. This time, there could be no excuses: Elizabeth must sign the drafted death warrant and Mary Stuart had to be executed at once, or else these acts of subterfuge would continue to threaten the queen's life.

As des Trappes tried to board a ship near Rochester, he was apprehended and questioned by the local authorities. Moody had also been caught promptly and swore that he had no idea about the plot. On January 9, however, after a longer interrogation that would probably have included some torture, Moody confessed: "Des Trappes, Chasteauneuf, and myself have discussed taking away the queen's life either by gunpowder or by poisoning her shoe, or some other Italian device."[19]

On January 11, it was William Stafford's turn to be interrogated, and eventually he confirmed that Chasteauneuf had approached him about plans to kill the queen. "Moody and myself were told that if we were to take the life of such a heretic we would be renowned throughout the world and would have pensions of 1,000 crowns from the pope himself."[20]

Chasteauneuf vehemently denied all charges, and complained to Henry III about the arrest of his servant and the confiscation of his papers and ciphers. Elizabeth had already warned him that she knew he was conducting private correspondence with Mary—which was hardly surprising given Chasteauneuf's personal connections with the Guises. Nevertheless, Henry continued to support his ambassador, instructing Bellièvre on his last days at the English court to defend Chasteauneuf.

Elizabeth was furious, left with no choice but to remind Henry of who he was dealing with.

"I was not born in so lowly a place," she wrote, "nor have I been ruling such little realms that in right and honour I will yield to a living prince who insults me and doubts that I am strong enough. My turn to give you some pieces of advice. I beg you to fortify our friendship rather than diminish it: living states do not allow too many enemies, and do not put bridles on startled horses for fear they will shake your saddle."[21]

To ensure her message was heard loud and clear, the Tudor queen sent a special envoy to the French king. On the morning of January 24, William Waad was received by Henry III in his cabinet.

"What are the causes of your dispatch, monsieur the ambassador?" Henry asked, with faux naivety.

"I have been sent by her Majesty, the queen of England, in regard to a new plot that has been discovered, which involves two of your subjects: the French ambassador, Guillaume de l'Aubespine, Seigneur de Chasteauneuf, and his servant, Leonard des Trappes," Waad replied.

Wide-eyed, Henry said, "Please, Monsieur Waad, take a seat. I want to declare that I had and have proceeded, and always will continue to proceed with all respect concerning her Majesty, avoiding all occasions to give her discontent. I remain her sincere friend and ally."

Waad seemed satisfied with the king's seemingly sincere shock at the news. Henry also had his own concerns—this time not so much for Elizabeth's life, but for his own honor.

It is strange to me that my ambassador, knowing his inclination to continue his work, should forget himself so much as to be in any way partaker of so bad a practice, which I hope, though suspicion might be conceived of him, should not cause any falling out. I hope that as the queen had a care to be informed in a matter that concerned her so near, so she would withal have regard to my honour, which be touched in the person of my ambassador.

"Her Majesty had conceived no doubt nor found any occasion for aught that had been brought to light in these last practices to suspect the sincerity of the good love and friendship you professed and, therefore, this incident troubled her so much,"[22] Waad told the king, reassuring him.

Henry asked to see any evidence Waad could provide of this, and he happily obliged and showed him private letters written in Elizabeth's own hand. Henry also asked for the return of des Trappes to France so that he could be appropriately judged within his realm.

In return, Elizabeth had her own request. "Her Majesty would like Morgan and Charles Paget to be returned to England," Waad reported. Paget had been an agent of Mary's in France for a long time, and had been implicated in many conspiracies against the queen since 1583.

"This is not the matter we are discussing," Henry snapped, interrupting the English envoy, who adjourned the meeting. However, the king knew the situation was not resolved, and sent his advisors—Bellièvre, who had just arrived back from London, and Brulard—to further discuss the matter with Waad.

"Our master, the king, is deeply perplexed regarding the accident with his ambassador, to be accused of so great and odious a matter as to promote the death of the queen of England, he being a minister of the king's, and knowing how his master does esteem the amity and friendship of her Majesty," Bellièvre stated.

"I can reassure you that her Majesty still wants to pursue her good intelligence with your master, but justice must be done,"[23] Waad responded.

Soon enough, the blame was shifted onto des Trappes and his connections to Spain; for Brulard and Bellièvre, it was clearly possible that he might have plotted something against Elizabeth without Chasteauneuf's knowledge.

Even if this was a possibility Waad did not mind entertaining in front of the French advisors, des Trappes would not be sent back to France for trial. Elizabeth decreed he would remain in custody in England unless an exchange of prisoners was made: Morgan and Paget for des Trappes.

This was an unacceptable compromise for the French king—they had reached a stalemate. In any case, the resolution of the matter would need to be postponed, as a more pressing issue was at hand: Mary Stuart's fate.

There were now false rumors circulating at court that Mary Stuart had escaped and that a foreign invasion of the realm was imminent. It was clear that action could be delayed no longer.

On February 1, Davison met with the queen to break the news of the rumors. He had in his hands the death warrant of the Queen of Scots, ready for her to sign.

Panicked and exhausted, Elizabeth finally exclaimed, "Bring me a pen and ink!"

She signed the warrant there and then, explaining to Davison as she did so why she had so long deferred it, and how difficult it was for her to make such a decision. "I wish there were another solution to guarantee the safety of my person and of the state. Do get the warrant and carry it to the Great Seal, and command the office of the Great Seal to dispatch it to the commissioners at Fotheringhay."

As Davison was about to leave to carry out his duties, she added, "Do not trouble me with this any further."[24]

Davison went directly to Lord Burghley's chamber, where he found him with the Earl of Leicester. They were delighted to see the signed death warrant at last.

The next day, however, Elizabeth asked to see Davison again.

"Has the warrant been sent to the Seal?" she asked him.

"Yes, your Majesty."

"What was the haste?" she inquired.

"You commanded me to do so, your Majesty," Davison said, bowing.

Elizabeth was agitated as she explained that she did not mean for him to do so right away. She was terribly conflicted and now doubted her decision. Once it was made, she knew it would be irreversible.

When she dismissed him, Davison went straight to Sir Christopher Hatton to discuss his meeting with Elizabeth.

"I fear the queen does not wish to carry this burden alone and might find any pretext, and though she has asked me to send the warrant to the commissioners, I am absolutely resolved not to meddle in it alone,"[25] Davison said firmly.

Hatton took him to Lord Burghley, who agreed that the Privy Council should support Davison and his mission. And so it was that, the next day, Lord Burghley wrote letters to the commissioners committing Mary to death, enclosing the signed warrant.

*

A few days later, Elizabeth asked for Davison to join her in her privy chamber.

"I had a bad dream last night," she told him somberly. "I dreamt that the Queen of Scots was executed. I swear a sword could have run through me."

"Your Majesty, do you think whether having proceeded thus far, you had not a meaning to go forward with the execution?" Davison asked with great earnestness.

"Yes," she vehemently replied, "but there has to be a better way, as this casts the whole burden upon myself."[26]

She dismissed him and he left her alone with her dark thoughts. Clearly, Elizabeth was already haunted by her decision.

On February 5, Robert Beale was dispatched by the Privy Council and arrived to deliver the death warrant to Sir Amias Paulet and Sir Dru Drury, who were in charge of Mary Stuart's imprisonment, and two days later the death warrant was read aloud to Mary Stuart by George Talbot—Earl of Shrewsbury and Mary's former keeper—and Henry Grey, Earl of Kent, who had both been dispatched for the execution.

Initially Mary showed little emotion. By now, she was surely resigned to her fate.

"I am prepared to die," she said eventually, before breaking into sobs and weeping bitterly. When her tears had been shed, she was silent.

On the same day, across the sea in France, Catherine had a moment of intuition. She wrote to her son that "as we have not convinced the queen of England to show mercy to the poor queen of Scotland, I am afraid that she will order her execution soon enough, given her responses to Bellièvre and Chasteauneuf."[27]

Catherine's instinct was right.

Her former daughter-in-law was about to face her death.

*

Early on the morning on February 8, Mary Stuart prepared for her execution. After over eighteen years spent as a prisoner in England, her involvement in many plots and conspiracies would finally come to an end.

Her defenders might say it was the years of imprisonment that had caused Mary to plot against Elizabeth, and that she had also been badly served by her mother-in-law Catherine, who might have been interested in her now but had rejected her years before. While this was certainly the case, it was also true that Mary's threat of religious rebellion had been constant. As early as 1568 Mary had pleaded to both Philip II and his wife—her childhood friend, Elisabeth of Valois—to be rescued so she could "re-establish the ancient and good faith throughout this whole island."[28] In truth, Mary had never recognized the legitimacy of Elizabeth's claim to the English crown and had always seen herself as the rightful queen of England. It was a title she pursued all her life. While Elizabeth had been reluctant to see her executed, it was almost certainly the case that, had Mary been allowed to survive, it could have been at the expense of Elizabeth's safety.

Mary was tall of stature, but imprisonment had taken its toll and by the end of her imprisonment she was quite corpulent, with a hunched back. Her face was now round and broad with a double chin—and the features that had been so praised during her youth had diminished. Her hazel eyes, however, which had attracted so many men to her cause, remained as striking as ever.

That morning, Mary wore a dress made of lawn, a fine linen fabric edged with bone lace, a pomander chain, and a small carved lamb around her neck, which was a reminder of Christ. She held a crucifix in her hand and wore a pair of beads at her girdle, with a golden cross at the end of each. Her gown was of black printed satin—the train and the sleeves dragging across the ground—with acorn buttons of jet, trimmed with pearl, and short sleeves of satin, lace cut, with a pair of sleeves of purple velvet underneath. She wore shoes made of Spanish leather.

Leaving her chamber, she approached the place of her execution, where the commissioners and other knights awaited her.

One of her servants, Melvin, kneeled in front of her, weeping. "Ah!" he cried. "Madam, unhappy me, what man on Earth was ever before the messenger of so important sorrow and heaviness as I shall be, when I shall report that my good and gracious queen and mistress is beheaded in England?"

"My good servant," Mary replied gently, "cease to lament, for you have cause rather to joy than to mourn, for now you shall see Mary Stuart's troubles receive their long expected end, and determination for knowing, good servant, that all the world is but vanity, and subject still to more sorrow, than a whole ocean of tears can bewail. But I pray you carry this message from here that I die a true woman of my religion, and like a true queen of Scotland and France."[29]

As she turned to the lords, she made some final requests: that her servants would be treated well after her execution and that they would be able to stay to witness her death.

These were all denied, her captors fearing that they would "put some superstitious trumpery in practice."

Before the commission of her execution was read aloud, Mary was granted a few additional words. Proud until the bitter end, she spoke as clearly as she could—despite the tremors in her voice—choosing to remind her enemies of her pedigree: "I am cousin to your queen, and descended from the blood royal of Henry VII, and a married queen of France, and an anointed queen of Scotland," she said, as if to high-light the remarkable nature of her plight.

Mary then stepped up to the scaffold, "being two foot high and twelve foot broad, with rails round about, hanged and covered in black, with a low stool and long fair cushion."[30] She lowered herself onto the stool.

Doctor Richard Fletcher—Dean of Peterborough, and a Church of England priest and bishop—tried to give Mary the Protestant prayer.

Four times Mary refused him. "Mr. Dean, trouble not yourself nor me, for knowing that I am settled in the ancient Catholic and Roman religion, and in defence thereof, by God's grace I mind to spend my blood."

He asked her to change her mind and repent. She refused.

While all the audience were repeating the dean's prayer, Mary wept, praying in Latin and kissing her crucifix.

Then, as her two executioners approached her for pardon, she gently said, "I forgive you with all my heart; for I hope this death shall give an end to all my troubles."

Two women helped disrobe her as she continued to pray in Latin; they burst into tears as Mary tried desperately to remain calm and appear serene. Their cries filled the otherwise silent room while the onlookers awaited the big moment.

As she finally laid herself upon the block, Mary shouted out in Latin: "Into your hands, oh God, I commend my spirit!"

One of the executioners held her straight. She did not struggle. As the assembled audience watched, the other executioner raised the axe in the air and gave two strokes before cutting off her head— though, it was noted, he "left a little gristle behind." As the deed was done, the executioners exclaimed, "God save the Queen."[31]

Finally, Mary Stuart was dead.

While this should have been a relief for the English queen, however, more troubles were brewing. For a start, Elizabeth now had to live with the repercussions of her decision.

★

As the news of Mary's execution spread, it seemed as though every bell in London rang out; joyous bonfires were lit, and banqueting and celebrations took place all around the city. But the queen could not be found anywhere in the city. Some might have speculated that she had been away hunting, but eventually the news reached its destination.

The next day, a seemingly dumbfounded Elizabeth reappeared,

and asked Davison the cause of the celebrations that had occurred
the day before. Wherever she had been, these had not escaped her
notice. When Elizabeth was told the news she was furious, stating
that she never truly meant for the death warrant to be sent to Fotheringhay. She targeted her rage solely at Davison himself. Was Elizabeth
that naive regarding Mary's fate? Hardly. But in truth, she probably
felt genuine remorse about the situation. She had committed the
unthinkable and, while perhaps her hand had been forced, she now
had to face the consequences of her actions.

Needing a scapegoat, she turned to Davison. He was sent to the
Tower shortly after, though he was freed a few months later.

The reactions were just as strong in France. Before the news had
even reached the French court, Catherine was increasingly antagonized by Elizabeth and her connections to the Huguenots, especially
now she needed Henry to make a decision on her alliance with the
king of Navarre. It was hard to believe that, not so very long ago, she
had been on the verge of a familial union with the English queen, and
her ill will was clear for all to see, especially Henry.

> My son, I urge you to show everyone that you have strong forces;
> given all the things happening, I fear we will need them greatly, espe-
> cially given the ill-will I see in the queen of England. I have always
> suspected her of helping our subjects of the reformed religion behind
> our backs, but now given the recent events, you have to strengthen all
> your ports and cities.[32]

Catherine no longer sought to contain her anger at the woman she
had once pursued for so long. Bluntly, she told Bellièvre her true
thoughts about the English queen: "By refusing all our requests and
pleas to save our daughter-in-law, Elizabeth has declared herself our
enemy."[33]

At that moment, little did Catherine know that not only had Elizabeth ordered the execution, but that it had already taken place. This
news dropped on the streets of Paris, and on the French royal family,
like a bomb. No detail was spared in the retelling of the death; from

what Mary was wearing and how her executioner had to strike her twice with the axe, gruesome tales were shared with the old and the young alike.

The whole French court went into mourning immediately, with Catherine leading by example, and the Guises were already on the rampage, blaming the French king for his failure to save their cousin. Another sign of his weakness, they believed.

The English ambassadors, Edward Stafford and William Waad, meanwhile, were refused an audience with the king, such was his displeasure, though this did not prevent them from witnessing the reactions at court.

"I must needs write unto your lordship the truth that I never saw a thing more hated by little, great, old, young, and all of the religions than the Queen of Scots' death, and especially the manner of it."[34]

On March 13, a memorial was established in Mary's honor in the Cathedral of Notre-Dame de Paris, with all Catholic Leaguers vehemently denouncing her death—they were united in their outrage that a French Catholic king could have let such an affront occur.

Over the following days several pamphlets were printed attacking Elizabeth, many of them posted on the door of the cathedral. Some of these also blamed Henry and Catherine for their inability to save Mary's life. This was a major blow to their royal authority, despite their efforts to show their grief to the public.

While Henry kept his troubles and emotions mostly hidden, Catherine did not even try to do so. She was outraged, and told Bellièvre: "Among so many issues I have been plunged into during this miserable time, the cruelty that has been used against the queen of Scotland, madam my daughter-in-law, has deeply saddened me."[35]

To Villeroy, secretary of state, she continued to pour out her woes: "I cannot hide the terrible pain I suffer due to the cruel death of this poor queen, and those who are of the same religion as the queen of England should still feel repulsed by such inhumanity."[36]

Elizabeth's actions made Catherine sick, and now no reconciliation between them would ever be possible. Yet Elizabeth did not seem troubled by this; she believed that the power in France had moved away from Catherine, and now all her letters to France were addressed to Henry only. With Mary out of the way, Elizabeth could focus her attention and efforts on Spain. Little did she know, however, that an unexpected alliance was about to emerge from the bloodshed.

16

Endgame, April 1587–August 1589

Mary Stuart might have been dead, but another threat to Elizabeth's life remained.

Philip II of Spain had steadily been building a vast naval force, and now he redoubled his efforts against his enemy. This time, Elizabeth would not be spared, and she would be made to regret her actions. This, at least, was what he hoped.

But Elizabeth had firepower of her own. On April 2, 1587, Elizabeth ordered Drake to leave Plymouth, where he was stationed, for Spain. He reached Cadiz on April 19, and his mission from the queen was simple: destroy Philip II's fleet.

What Drake and his crew witnessed when they finally reached their destination was worse than anything they could have imagined; the sight of many huge ships ready to be loaded with all kinds of weaponry, cannons, and firearms, all to be sent to England, made them shiver. They knew they had to act quickly.

They had prepared their attack carefully, and executed it deftly, burning thirty-two of the ships and carrying away four more, which would go on to sink to the ocean floor. They did not succeed in destroying all the vessels, but even so, their mission had been a success. "There was never heard of so great an invasion!" Drake exclaimed, speaking of the scale of the Spanish naval power he had witnessed. Yet he had managed to avert it, and damage the enemy considerably.

Drake might have shown his strategic might, but even he feared that there was worse to come, as he explained in a letter to Walsingham.

"I dare not almost write your honour of the great forces we hear the king of Spain has out in the Straits. Prepare in England strongly, and most by sea. Stop him now, and stop him ever. It is the Lord that gives victory."[1]

The time had come for Elizabeth to declare all-out war on one of her oldest enemies. And yet she would also discover that Mary's death could not entirely dispel the other plots against her.

*

On April 29, Elizabeth finally agreed to receive Chasteauneuf, the French ambassador. Relations had been strained since the news of Mary's execution. She met him in the forest near Croydon, where she had been enjoying the fresh air for four or five days, and invited him to meet with her after dinner at Croydon Palace. While she seemed pleased to receive him at first, she had an ulterior motive. She wanted to speak to him of the plot against her involving his servant, des Trappes.

"I am very desirous to discuss the death of the Queen of Scots with you, monsieur the ambassador," she told him, "but first let Sir Francis Walsingham walk to the Council Chamber."

Upon hearing his name, Walsingham entered the room.

Grabbing Chasteauneuf's arm, Elizabeth said, laughing, "Here is your man who wanted to have me killed." She looked at him, still smiling. "Something I have never believed, except when you refused to reveal anything to me, even though my life was in danger. But, after all, you were only speaking as an ambassador that it had been a trick of two knaves, one of whom—Moody—was wicked enough to commit any bad action for money, but that now I love and esteem you more than ever, Chasteauneuf, allowances ought to be made for the times, and the anger of sovereigns."

Chasteauneuf was wrongfooted, and had no idea how to respond. He knew that Elizabeth could show mercy when it suited her, and the fact remained: she had just had her nearest kinswoman executed.

Luckily for him, she continued speaking. "Des Trappes is now at liberty to go whenever he pleases," she said while holding Chas-teauneuf's hand and walking him to the corner of her apartment.

"You see, monsieur the ambassador, I have now experienced one of the greatest misfortunes and vexations that has ever befallen me, which is the death of my cousin—of which I vow to God, with many oaths, that I am innocent. Yes, I signed the death warrant but it was only to satisfy my subjects. It was never my intention to put her to death, unless—of course—I had seen a foreign army invade England or a great insurrection of my subjects in her favour... then perhaps I might have put her to death."

Getting closer to Chasteauneuf, she whispered, "The members of my Council have played a trick on me I could never forgive, and I swear to God that but for their long services, and also because what they have done has been out of consideration for the welfare and safety of my person and of the state, they should have lost their heads. I beg you to believe that I am not so wicked as to throw the blame upon a humble secretary if it was not true. This death will wring my heart as long as I live."[2]

When she had finally finished this lengthy discourse, she ordered Walsingham and Leicester to walk Chasteauneuf to the Council Chamber, to meet with her councillors.

Elizabeth had played her own trick on Chasteauneuf. He had prob-ably expected to be badly received but the opposite had occured; she had instead showed her willingness to turn a blind eye to his actions if he would do the same for her—and presumably she hoped this would allow her to continue fortifying her alliance with Henry III. Elizabeth and Henry had to find a way to overcome their differences, given the challenges they faced. Spain and the Guises had made an alliance that could threaten both their realms, and neither party could afford to hold grudges, however aggrieved Catherine might feel. It was a simple exchange: Chasteauneuf had to be forgiven for his secret correspondence with Mary and for the possible plot against Elizabeth, and Henry had to forgive Elizabeth for her decision. Furthermore, Elizabeth had more on her mind than French displeasure. With Spain on the rampage, she looked to put all her energy into defending her realm from Philip II and his nephew, the Duke of Parma. Drake's reports had made her realize the danger was more imminent than she had expected. So, on May 14, after receiving his safe-conduct, des Trappes left for Paris and the affair was closed. Elizabeth had made the first step toward reconciliation—hoping that both she and Henry could move on.

For Catherine, however, things were a little different. She was finding it hard not to dwell on Mary's execution, and Elizabeth's role in it. At the news of her former daughter-in-law's death, she could not help but deplore, "No queen has ever had justice over another."[3]

However, as disgusted as she was with Elizabeth's recent actions, Catherine was still a pragmatic woman; she realized that Elizabeth's decision to send back the French ambassador's servant showed that she was desperate to remain in the French rulers' good books. She saw an opportunity to make some demands regarding Elizabeth's assistance to the king of Navarre, and she shared her ideas with her son:

"Tell the queen of England that you will that she and her subjects would not give any assistance to the king of Navarre and those of the new religion, and instead advise them to respect their duties toward you."[4]

For Catherine, putting an end to the English aid to the Huguenots was paramount if they wanted to bring peace to France, and this at least was something Elizabeth could help with. Unfortunately, the situation in France was not improving. The eighth religious civil war was becoming bloodier by the day and, in May 1587, a group of influential courtiers, councillors, and members of the Parlement de Paris sought out the French king at Le Louvre to complain about the state of the realm.

"I know too well and ever better than you do what my people need me to do, and the state of my finances and realm," he told the assembled men.[5] But he was powerless, his finances ravaged by the war, and he could offer no remedies. Meanwhile, the king of Navarre was gaining territory in the region of Poitou. The Guises, leading the Catholic League, were still determined to crush all reformers, and continued to blame any and all Protestants for the untimely death of their cousin. They had also now secured the support of Spain, who had a similarly strong stance and had vowed to murder all heretics in Europe. Henry III and Catherine struggled to see what their next move could be, with crises at home and abroad.

The French were also becoming anxious about the naval forces Philip II was building—they began to suspect that this might was not just aimed at England but could also be used against France, and that perhaps Philip had decided to focus his attention on helping the Guises overthrow Henry. These fears had flared up when a surprising rumor of a new English–Spanish alliance reached the French court.

"I had forgotten to write you a thing worth laughing at, of news that is here that a great many did believe of a treaty of peace with Spain and her Majesty, the queen of England,"[6] Stafford reported to the English court.

These rumors—though obviously untrue given the great animosity that existed between Elizabeth and Philip—were stoked by Catherine's particular enmity with Elizabeth following Mary's death. She was now fully prepared to believe that Elizabeth was an enemy of the French crown in every respect. She now complained relentlessly to Chasteauneuf of the threat that Elizabeth posed to them. He needed, she insisted, to convince her to stop supporting the Huguenots. Until she did so, there would be no safety, and certainly no reconciliation between the realms.

> You will remind her that it goes against the treaties of alliance signed by our two countries. You will insist that she revokes all her help and support in their favour and will keep an eye on her to ensure that she does.[7]

Catherine's complaints were in vain. Elizabeth knew that one way to undermine Spain's growing strength was by continuing to support Protestants all over Europe, including those in the Netherlands and in France. It was a long game, certainly, but one that she very much intended to win. She wanted to be known as the savior of all Protestants in Europe.

"It is clear now that the queen of England will never abandon the king of Navarre and his cause," Catherine said, when she had received the latest reports of Elizabeth's actions. "When he is in distress, she will aim to help him up and rescue him by all possible means. You will have to remind her, Monsieur de Chasteauneuf, however, that the prosperity and tranquillity of our realm depends on the safety and conservation of hers."[8]

However, Catherine's personal feelings were starting to put her at odds with her son. Henry had begun to doubt that Elizabeth was the enemy of the crown that his mother liked to depict, and felt that there might be an opportunity for them to work together.

On February 24, 1588, Stafford was invited to a private audience with the French king; in the middle of the night, an unknown man arrived at the English ambassador's house to take him to Henry. When Stafford arrived at his destination, he realized that the king had ordered his servants to leave the two of them alone—in a private chamber.

"I need this audience to remain private," Henry whispered. "No one from this court can know that we met. I would also like you to report this audience only to your mistress, the queen of England, and no one else."[9]

Stafford nodded, though he was completely puzzled by such secrecy.

Henry went on to explain that he had had time to think about the situation he was in and that he now believed that Elizabeth was not his enemy.

"It is the queen mother and my council who are certain that her Majesty, the queen of England, should not meddle between me and my subjects," he told Stafford. He paused for a moment and then, in a serious tone, he continued, "I beseech your queen with all my heart to do me this favour and to persuade the king of Navarre to find a compromise with me, in such sort as the League might have no more pretence to ruin both France and myself."

Stafford now understood the purpose of this meeting, as well as the new conciliatory approach being taken by the French king. "I am afraid that the queen cannot interfere regarding the king of Navarre's religion," he said quietly.

Henry was upset, and explained that he was committed to the Roman Catholic religion, but also so saddened to see France ravaged by blood and fire.

Stafford listened but remained firm on Elizabeth's stance. He had received clear instructions: she would not convince the king of Navarre to convert, but she was at least willing to help promote peace talks between the two parties. After all, she also wished France to be at peace again.

Firmly, Henry spoke to the English ambassador of a possible truce: "I know that my enemies are hers."[10]

The king begged Stafford to appeal to Elizabeth, and to broker a secret alliance between them; the massacres in France were simply unbearable, and could not continue.

Stafford nodded. An important shift in Anglo-French relations, one of which Catherine was totally unaware, had just occurred.

★

Over a month later, and it seemed that the plea to Elizabeth had worked. Elizabeth sent a letter written in her own hand, and ordered it to be given directly to Henry by her ambassador. Along with this were several other messages regarding a potential alliance between the two monarchs.

Henry was so delighted with her letter, coming just when he needed it most, that he exclaimed, "Holy God! What a woman she is! I wish that God had broken one of my fingers if it had made me as wise as her Majesty!"[11]

The situation in France had worsened yet further in the weeks he had been waiting for Elizabeth's response, and now the Guises were open in their hostility toward Henry. This time, he decided to go against his mother's advice and make a proper alliance with his brother-in-law, the Huguenot leader, Henry of Navarre.

"I wish you had let me counsel you as I would have done it with your best interest at heart,"[12] Catherine lamented, once she discovered the news. For the queen mother, any sign of tolerance—especially at this stage of the war—was a sign of weakness. Furthermore, though Catherine was still very much involved in domestic affairs, overseeing the strategies of different cities in collaboration with their governors, and ensuring their provisions—she could not ignore the fact that her influence over her son had been diminishing for some time. In her view, by turning his back on the Guises and the League, Henry was making a terrible mistake that could have dramatic consequences. She was not wrong.

The Guises, who already suspected Henry III of France of making an alliance with the Huguenots, felt they had only one option: to take Paris with their army and force the French king to flee. So, in early May 1588, they besieged the city. It was a horrendous scene, and culminated in Henry's rushed departure from the capital.

"The king suddenly departed with six or seven of the chief of his council, some without boots, some without spurs, some upon foot cloths," Stafford reported. Their destination was Chartres. "His mother is marvellously amazed at it for he had sent her to the Duke of Guise to find a compromise. The queen, his wife, melancholy, keeps weeping and lamenting." Stafford also revealed that the king had commanded his mother "not to follow him, that he would within a day or two send her his will."[13]

Upon hearing the news, Elizabeth secretly sent a messenger, Thomas Bodley, to give Henry another handwritten letter.

"My very dear brother," she wrote, "how I wish that you had listened to all my necessary and affectionate warning, advice, and recommendation, so that you were not suffering the situation you are in today." Throughout the last few years, during Stafford's audiences and in private letters, Elizabeth had warned Henry about the Guises. The Huguenots, she had said, were not the ones who were trying to overthrow him. Instead, it had always been the Leaguers and the Guises. As she continued her letter, she showed some compassion for his precarious situation. "Nevertheless, I cannot not send you this gentleman to tell you how utterly heartbroken I am at the news that your state and own safety are now in danger."

She went on to advise him, "For the name of God, cut off the ears of those who tell you to be scared of shadows, and step into the sunlight where everyone can see you. You cannot truly believe that I am on any other side but yours."[14]

It was not in her interest for him to be overthrown. If the Guises came to power in France, they would almost certainly make an alliance with Spain—threatening England with an even greater potential invasion. But she also seemed to feel genuine concern; she knew all too well what it was like to have one's life endangered, and on this account she had some genuine sympathy for Henry.

Meanwhile, Catherine had been left behind in Paris. She had been overwhelmed by recent events and, with Henry gone, she also had to act as the public face of the monarchy, and persuade the court that her son's departure to Chartres was not a sign that he had abandoned his loyal servants and subjects. Catherine was once again the face of her son's authority in the capital.

"I will subdue Paris and ensure it stays fully obedient and under your authority,"[15] she promised him.

She took over important government responsibilities, as well as ordering the defense of towns around the capital: Mantes, Meulan, Pont-de-l'Arche, Vernon, Corbeil, Compiègne, Meaux, and Melun. She also wrote to the finance chamber (the *Chambre des comptes*) to raise funds for her son's army. Just as when she was briefly in charge of the realm during her husband's reign, Catherine showed her control, resilience, and royal expertise. Unfortunately, despite her Herculean efforts, the royal armies faced humiliating defeats, especially at Coutras. She desperately needed Henry III to step in and reassure his people that he was still the king of France.

Henry eventually did so, giving a speech in front of the Paris *cour de parlement* in Chartres, in which he vouched for reconciliation and peace. The text of the speech was then printed and circulated all over France.

"I am your natural and legitimate king," he said, "and I want to receive and kiss those who entered Paris as my predecessors did, like a good father to his children and a good king to his subjects. When they will be ready to confess their faults and testify, therefore, their regrets, I will receive them and kiss them like my subjects. I want them to recognise me as their king and master."

He swore, "I am no usurper, I am a legitimate king through succession—as you all know—and from a race which has always ruled gently, but patience can turn into fury, and you know how an offended king can react. I will use all my power, and will not neglect any means to avenge myself. Although I do not have a vindictive mind, I want my people to know that I have a heart and stomach of a king as big as any of my predecessors'."[16]

It may have been a powerful speech, but words alone could not put an end to the chaos. The Parisian people were feeling the effects of the war that had now reached their city and, though he had given a rousing speech, there was frustration that the king still stayed away from the capital. It took over a month for the king and the Leaguers to find a compromise, which involved allowing the Guises more control to preserve their religion. It was, however, very clear to the French king that such a compromise was also a threat, giving the Guises an opportunity to take control of the city; yet again, he had to play the game until he could once more gain the upper hand. He feigned, therefore, to have forgiven his mortal enemies' siege of Paris and, on August 26, he declared the Duke of Guise his Lieutenant General of the Realm. It was a decision highly approved of by Catherine, and may even have been suggested by her.

★

Across the Channel, Elizabeth was facing the Spanish Armada sent to invade her realm. It was a formidable fleet, called "by the arrogant name of Invincible" and "consisted of 130 ships: in which were 19,290 soldiers, 8,350 mariners, 2,080 galley-slaves."[17] By July, the fleet had made its way to the English coast. All-out war was the result.

For weeks, great battles took place at sea, and every English sailor, including Drake, was called to the front line. Elizabeth's more man-euvrable ships meant that they were less vulnerable to strong winds than the Spanish fleet and, when a violent storm hit the coast, the

English vessels finally managed to take the advantage over their Spanish enemies.

On August 4, James VI of Scotland, who had been following the events as they unfolded, promised Elizabeth his unwavering support.

> I offer unto you my forces, my person, and all that I may command, to be employed against these strangers in whatsoever fashion and by whatsoever means as may best serve for the defence of your country. Wherein I promise to behave myself not as a stranger and foreign prince but as your natural son and compatriot of your country in all respects.[18]

During this time, Elizabeth needed all the allies she could get. James happily obliged and sent financial support to his English counterpart.

On August 8, Elizabeth left St. James's Palace to go to Tilbury camp in Essex, where 18,000 footmen and 2,000 horsemen were readying themselves for battle. She was told that the Spanish fleet had been dispersed, many of their ships having been caught in tumultuous sea currents. The Duke of Parma's army was still a threat, however, and could still potentially land in England. She wanted to show her support for her troops, and steel them for any further conflict.

Upon her arrival, Elizabeth was received by loud shots launched from forts on each side of the river, and the next day she addressed her troops with a speech that would go on to resonate for centuries to come. It would cement her reputation as a powerful ruler, and also influenced how she would be remembered in posterity.

> My loving people, I have been persuaded by some that are careful of my safety to take heed how I commit myself to armed multitudes, for fear of treachery. But I tell you that I would not desire to live to distrust my faithful and loving people. Let tyrants fear: I have so behaved myself that under God I have placed my chiefest strength and safeguard in the loyal hearts and goodwill of my subjects.

Wherefore I am come among you at this time but for my recreation and pleasure, being resolved in the midst and heat of the battle to live and die amongst you all, to lay down for my God and for my kingdom and for my people mine honour and my blood even in the dust. I know I have the body but of a weak and feeble woman, but I have the heart and stomach of a king and of a king of England too—and take foul scorn that Parma or any prince of Europe should dare to invade the borders of my realm.[19]

The soldiers were inspired, finding themselves in awe of such a demonstration of courage and faith in God. Elizabeth departed for Greenwich, so that she might be safer should the conflict reach the shore, and after a few days the news reached the mainland: the Armada had been defeated, in a humiliating loss for the Spanish, who had seemed so close to victory. The English had done what had seemed unthinkable when the Armada first loomed: Elizabeth's army had defeated the most powerful king of Europe, Philip II of Spain.

News of the victory quickly reached the rest of Europe and beyond. Abu Faris 'Abd al-'Aziz al-Fishtali, scribe at the Moroccan court of Sultan Ahmad al-Mansur, wrote admiringly of the outcome:

The enemy of religion, the infidel, the tyrant of Castile who is today against Islam and who is the pillar of polytheism and the one against whom both sword and destruction should, by religious duty, be wielded: he met his kind in the Sultana of the lands of England whom God had turned, from among his own kind, into an enemy to preoccupy him.

He added that England had been blessed by God to win over Spain:

God sent a sharp wind against the fleets of the tyrant that broke up their forces and pushed them onto the enemy's land, bringing down their flags and banners. England saw an opportunity and seized it: the English fleet attacked that strong fleet and brought upon it defeat.[20]

And yet the ruler was not God, but a woman. And Elizabeth's greatness was now acclaimed throughout the world.

However, in France, the perspective on events was somewhat different. Bernardino de Mendoza, the Spanish ambassador, first attempted to spread rumors in Henry's court that Spain had in fact triumphed against England. He had his reasons: he wanted to stir fears that Spain would next target France, in order to ensure that Catholicism would be triumphant and that the king of Navarre would once and for all be annihilated. Stafford, who had finally heard from England that this was not the case, hastily set the record straight.

"To have the revenge of the Spanish ambassador, who set out lies," Stafford explained, "I have ordered the printing of a pamphlet telling everyone the truth about what happened at sea." This pamphlet was shared among courtiers and finally reached Henry III, who invited him for an audience.

"The king, as soon as ever he saw it, would have laid a wager it was my doing and laughed at it heartily."

Mendoza, who had not yet heard of Stafford's actions, came to find the king. "My master, the king of Spain, earnestly entreats you not to succour her Majesty, the queen of England, being an heretic, and support this great enterprise of my master, which is for the amplification of the Catholic religion."

Henry chuckled. "The queen's Majesty did not need to demand succour as she does not seem to need it."[21]

While Henry was relieved that Spain was no longer the ultimate power of Europe, the news was downplayed by the French people, suspicious of the English queen, with pamphlets and discourses asserting that it was God, rather than Elizabeth, who had prevailed:

This great and frightful Spanish navy was threatening to horribly reduce England to nothing and was also a potential threat to France, which had been keeping an eye on it for some time, that God decided to put an end to its fate and miraculously it was ruined, defeated, and reduced to nothing thanks to the wind that God commanded and not because of the English fleet's power (though some wrongly attribute this victory to them).[22]

The majority of the French refused to give credit where it was due, and even Catherine—somewhat surprisingly—kept her feelings about the news to herself. She might even have wished that the Spanish would teach Elizabeth a lesson for committing the unthinkable, ordering the execution of another anointed queen. The queen mother did, however, find an opportunity to show her rival that she was not impressed by recent events.

Lady Douglas Sheffield, wife of Edward Stafford—who had been in France since her husband had been appointed resident ambassador to the French court in 1583—had decided to return to England after the English victory. Over the years, she had formed a warm friendship with Catherine, and the two women were occasionally to be found in each other's company, laughing and talking. Lady Sheffield was also a former mistress and lover of Elizabeth's dearest favorite, Robert Dudley, Earl of Leicester. One can easily imagine, therefore, that there must have been some hard feelings between the two women. On August 23, 1588, when there was no longer any doubt that England had been victorious, Catherine saw her friend's departure as an opportunity to write her very last letter to the Tudor queen.

"You must find it strange that I write to you after such a long silence but I could not let Madam Sheffield come back to you without writing to you. I would like to testify for the great affectionate servant that you have in this lady, who has behaved with prudence and affection and ensured that good relations between our two crowns were pursued. In particular, she has always showed me great affection," Catherine wrote, before adding in a sarcastic aside, "a token I am sure of your own affection for myself."[23]

Every single word of their correspondence had always been carefully considered, and this was no different. The fact that the queen mother had chosen to write a letter to Elizabeth at her pinnacle of glory, without mentioning her victory and instead praising a rival in Dudley's affections, was an audacious move, and a sign of her personal disrespect. It was also a way of downplaying the importance of Elizabeth's victory, though both of them knew that a shift of power in Europe had just occurred. Finally, Elizabeth had her long-awaited revenge over the loss of Calais, which had dogged the early days of her reign.

★

Despite Henry's efforts at reconciliation with the Guises, the eighth religious war continued to ravage France. The Huguenots were gaining strength and territory with every month that passed and, with the defeat of the Armada, the Guises' grand plan to have Spain conquer France after successfully conquering England came to nothing. Their own ships and armaments had also been destroyed in the fierce storm and they needed to regroup in Spain before even beginning to consider how they could help their fellow Catholic Leaguers in France.

In October 1588, a gathering of the Estates General of France took place in Blois, and there Henry faced protest and remonstrations. Nevertheless, as he gave his speech, Henry promised again to preserve the Roman Catholic religion, and to protect his people. On this occasion, he also spoke of his mother, paying tribute to Catherine's devotion to France.

"She is not only the cause through the grace of God, that I am in this world to be your king," he began,

> but through her constant and holy deeds, laudable actions and virtuous examples, she has so much engraved in my soul a right intention to promote God's honour, to propagate the Holy Catholic, Apostolic and Roman Church, and to reform of my state, that I have vowed before you to strive for all the good things which, I am more certain than ever, come from her, who has never complained about her hard work, discomfort and inconvenience, in spite of her age, where she acknowledged that she could serve this state. She has so many times preserved it, that she not only has to have the name of Mother of your King, but also Mother of the State and of the Realm.[24]

Despite their recent differences, Henry had always recognized Catherine's influence over his politics and kingship. She had shaped his reign—and recent French history—in countless ways, and he wanted to acknowledge that. Maybe it was also a way for him to become reconciled with his mother, who was in the audience when he delivered the speech. However, Catherine did not show any emotion—at least not any that could have been reported by witnesses— and did not comment on his words. Knowing the deep love she had for her son, as she did for all her children, it is hard to believe that she was holding any grudges against him. In truth, by October 1588 she was much weakened, suffering from a bad lung infection, so it is possible that what might have come across as disinterest could, in fact, have been exhaustion.

The Leaguers who attended the speech protested against Henry's promises to put an end to the so-called heresy, suspecting it would mean another edict of pacification, forcing them to accept Henry of Navarre as the rightful heir to the crown. But the king was determined to forge ahead and, he added pointedly, this would also help put an end to the corruption in France that threatened the stability of his rule. These barbed words were directed at the Leaguers, who had challenged his royal authority so openly.

"Some great nobles of my kingdom have formed leagues and associations, but, as evidence of my habitual kindness, I am prepared in this regard to forget the past,"[25] Henry told them. It was a thinly veiled attack on the Guises, and they were outraged at its implications, demanding that the printed version of the speech excised these words.

Catherine, whose illness perhaps meant that she sought stability more than usual, begged Henry to accept their demand and he did so, but it was clear that peace in France was far from a foregone conclusion.

*

By December, Catherine was confined to her bed, her lung condition having deteriorated. Meanwhile, the Guises had of course resumed their plots against her son. Henry had been concerned about such things: with the defeat of the Spanish Armada, he had felt that the Guises' power was surely about to come to an end, even if he had never truly forgiven them for forcing him to leave Paris and flee to Chartres. It had been such a massive humiliation for him. So, when new rumors that the Guises were planning to overthrow him reached his ear, he decided that this time he would indeed retaliate. And so it was that Henry ordered the assassination of the Duke of Guise, which was planned for December 23.

The duke's supporters suspected such a plan, and warned him of the French king's intentions. Some councillors tried to talk Catherine into reasoning with Henry, but the queen mother was too ill to do what she had done so well for so many years: protect and preserve the Valois dynasty. In Henry's mind, ordering the assassination of his mortal enemy was now the only way to maintain his royal authority, and he ignored the possible consequences of such a reckless act and how it would be perceived by his people, as well as by the rest of Europe. Two days before the planned execution, the Duke of Guise confronted Henry in a heated exchange.

"I want to offer my resignation as Lieutenant General of the Realm,"[26] said the duke. For Henry, it was a sign of trouble ahead: surely the duke would only do this if he sought more power, perhaps even the role of Constable of France—and maybe even the *king* of France.

It confirmed his course of action. Henry knew now what he needed to do, and that the duke was, in many ways, his own Mary Stuart; he believed that if he were to protect his position, only one of them could live.

On a dark and gloomy December 23, the Duke of Guise arrived at a council meeting. The atmosphere of the meeting was electric, the tension palpable. The duke was invited by a servant to go into an antechamber. He did so, realizing far too late what was happening. The assassins were waiting, and drew their daggers, stabbing him multiple times. He died soon after at the foot of the king's bed.

Henry had been watching nearby as the murder took place, and as the duke expired he came closer. He leaned forward and, looking him in the eyes one last time, said, "Look at him, the king of Paris. Not so big now!" It was a vengeful statement for someone who had seemed, early in his reign, to be a mild ruler.

When Catherine heard the news on her sick bed, despair overcame her. She knew what such an assassination could lead to. "He is headed towards ruin and I fear he will lose his body, his soul and his kingdom!"[27]

Her own power was now ebbing away. She no longer had the influence over Henry that she had once exercised, and no longer had power over the course of French politics. Her favorite son had committed what she believed was an unforgivable crime, and her health took a turn for the worse. Perhaps she had now very little reason to keep fighting the disease that was ravaging her body.

*

On the morning of January 5, 1589, Catherine was having great difficulty breathing, so she asked her secretary to bring her some paper and ink; she sensed that the end was near, and she wanted to write her final will.

The woman who had been so resilient for decades knew what was coming. She had achieved a great deal, securing the Valois dynasty by giving four sons to France and steering their reigns, but the successes were tinged with sadness: she had witnessed three of her boys die, and one of them betray her. It wasn't just her life force that was leaving her; her faith and hope in the dynasty were also slipping away.

She had, she felt, failed to bring peace or stability to France.

After receiving the Sacrament, Catherine passed away at half past one in the afternoon, in the comfort of her own bed in the castle of Blois. She was sixty-nine. Henry remained by her side until she drew her last breath—suggesting that in the end there must have been some sort of reconciliation between them. Ultimately, Catherine surely wanted to forgive her favorite son.

When the news reached Paris, she was mourned, but the epitaphs reminded the people of her many contradictions:

> The queen who lies here was a devil and an angel,
> Full of blame and full of praise:
> She upheld the state and brought it low;
> She made accords and no fewer debates:
> She bore three kings and five civil wars,
> Had chateaux built and towns destroyed,
> Made many good laws and bad edicts.
> Salute her passing, heaven and hell.[28]

Her legacy was a complex one, interwoven with so much trauma from years of conflict that it was easy for her detractors to diminish her character and her reign.

*

When Elizabeth received the news of Catherine's death, she sent a letter to Henry III.

In this note, Elizabeth had crossed out many lines, perhaps an indication of just how moved she was by the news, and how complex her relationship with this strong woman had been. Perhaps she didn't quite know how to express her feelings. Elizabeth paid tribute to Catherine and recognized her as a true counterpart in the politics of European rule:

> My very dear and very loved brother and cousin, I know how incredibly touched and hurt you must be regarding the death of the princess, our very dear and very loved good sister and cousin, the very high and very excellent queen, your very honoured mother, whom we had seen all our life as a stalwart that we could rely on. We share this same sharp feeling and send you our natural compassion as we share your pain. We honoured and loved your mother, the queen, as we were bound to her in a strong and sincere friendship.[29]

This letter was full of affection for another rival queen of Europe, quite surprising given that in the last few years of Catherine's life, the two queens barely shared any direct correspondence. Instead, they had seemed to become enemies. And yet despite their differences and rivalry, at Catherine's death, Elizabeth showed the respect she ultimately had for the queen with whom she had had such an enduring relationship, who had come so close to becoming a family member. After all, she had remained a political player to the very end, even as her strength diminished. During the last year of Catherine's life, it seemed that Elizabeth had the upper hand in their long rivalry, especially with her victory over the Armada. And in many ways, Catherine's death, and Mary's too, marked the start of a new chapter in Elizabeth's reign, one where the English queen would have no female rivals. It would be the Elizabethan Golden Age.

Catherine's death marked a turning point for France, and the year that followed was an extremely dark one in the nation's history, culminating on August 2, in the murder of her son, Henry III himself. Without Catherine to guide it, the Valois dynasty had come abruptly to an end.

With the death of Henry III later in 1589, Elizabeth's ally, Henry of Navarre, finally became the new king of France. His kingship was still contested and the eighth French religious civil war continued to rage, and Elizabeth was ready to further assume her role as defender of Protestantism in Europe. She was now feared by her enemies—the Spanish and the Leaguers—and she would continue to send financial and military support to both the Netherlands and the Huguenots.

Elizabeth had survived both her rival queens, and she was now a king among kings.

Epilogue

Queen of Hearts & Queen of Spades: The Women Behind the Legends

On November 30, 1597, André Hurault, Sieur de Maisse, landed at Dover.

He was a special envoy sent by Henry IV, king of France, to the English court, and he had a tricky mission: to find out if Elizabeth was willing to join peace talks with Spain to put an end to the war between the three countries, and if so, what her conditions were.

The years that followed 1589 were not peaceful. The rivalry between England and Spain continued to rage as the eighth religious civil war continued to ravage France. England's power grew immensely on the European political scene, so much so that it now rivaled even Spain as the dominant nation on the continent. In 1593 Henry IV was forced to convert to Catholicism—trying to bring peace to his bleeding country—but it wasn't enough. The Leaguers continued to contest his authority.

Meanwhile, in 1596, England, France, and the United Netherlands had formed the Triple Alliance, which stipulated that none of them could unilaterally conclude peace with Spain without the agreement of the other parties. The continued bloodshed in France had taken its toll and Henry IV was now contemplating a possible truce. All he had to do was convince Elizabeth. Of course, the victory over the Armada in 1588 did not mean that Elizabeth had won the war against Spain with any finality, but it had meant that England, for now at least, was the stronger state within the alliance.

Hurault sought an audience with the queen as soon as possible at her convenience, and on December 8, she granted his wish: he was invited to Whitehall Palace on the banks of the Thames. He arrived through a small entrance by the riverside, which was very narrow, dark, and lugubrious, and awaited his meeting with trepidation.

The portraits of Elizabeth that had been commissioned in the 1590s revealed a woman who had never aged, and whose glory continued to inspire the following generations. The reality, however, was somewhat different. By 1597 Elizabeth was sixty-four. Her teeth had rotted by sugar, which she had enjoyed consuming throughout her life, and her skin showed the inevitable signs of aging. She was no longer the best match in Europe—the fairest of them all—yet she was still the glorious Elizabeth I of England, who continued to successfully defend Protestant Europe.

After making his way through several corridors and taking many stairs, Hurault finally arrived in Elizabeth's privy chamber, where he found the queen sitting in a low chair, by herself. Her lords and ladies were, unusually, assembled silently some distance from her.

Hurault bowed to her as she stood and walked toward him. He kissed the fringe of her robe and she embraced him with both hands.

"I am so sorry I could not give you an audience at an earlier date," she said kindly, "but I have been quite unwell."

He nodded.

"I am also sorry that I receive you in this apparel," she continued, looking down at her nightgown. This was not the first time she had received visitors in such clothes, but on this occasion it seemed to embarrass her.

"Your Majesty, please," Hurault stated, "there is no need to make excuses on my account, for I have come to service and honour you, not to be an inconvenience to you."

"I am happy to see you, ambassador," she said, smiling.

He kissed her hands, telling her it was Henry IV's command that he should do so.

Elizabeth smiled again as she returned to her chair, then she ordered a stool to be brought over so that Hurault could sit next to her.

Elizabeth's nightgown was nevertheless fine apparel, made of silver cloth with white and crimson, with slashed sleeves of red taffeta. Hurault could not help but notice, however, that "the front of her dress was open, and one could see the whole of her bosom, and passing low, and often she would open the front of this robe with her hands as if she was too hot." She seemed very warm, in spite of the weather, and one might speculate it may have been the menopause giving her such hot flushes.

She was still a grand presence, even in her nightgown. There were beautiful necklaces hanging at her neck and chest, made of rubies and pearls, and a garland with the same stones adorning her reddish-colored wig. On her forehead there hung a few pearls, and on either side of her ears, two great curls of hair spiraled down to her shoulders.

Nevertheless, Hurault noted the passing of time. He found her bosom "somewhat wrinkled," and her face was drawn, "long and thin, her teeth very yellow, unequal compared with what they were formerly, so they say, and on the left side less than on the right. Many of them are missing so that one cannot understand her easily when she speaks quickly." But, he said, she was in some ways still very imposing: "fair and tall and graceful in whatever she does, so far as maybe she keeps her dignity, yet humbly and graciously withal."[1]

Hurault was there to discuss relations with Spain and France, but his report back to his country was fixated on Elizabeth's appearance, offering a portrait of the woman herself, the person behind the legend. An older and perhaps more frail woman who was still ruling her country with verve, but one who was also tired of protocol and false pretenses. After losing the rivals in her life, from Mary to Catherine, perhaps she had also lost some of her drive.

As for England, the country remained at war with Spain until 1604—after Elizabeth's death on March 24, 1603—when the Treaty of London, finally establishing formal peace between the two realms, was eventually signed.

★

Elizabeth and Catherine had many things in common: their talent for politics, their intellectual capabilities, and their devotion to their respective countries. They were, of course, divided by religion, with the twists and turns of European geopolitics constantly setting them against each other as a result.

Yet, in the end, they were the most powerful women in sixteenth-century Europe—or, as Sir Francis Bacon put it: "They two were the only pair of female princes, from whom, for experience and arts of government, there was no less expected than from the greatest kings."[2]

Catherine has been recognized, alongside Mary Stuart and Queen Victoria, as one of the grandmothers of modern Europe, yet she was cursed by the Valois dynasty's inability to reproduce. Ironically, though she bore so many kings and queens herself, they had been unable to secure the line with their own heirs. Later, Catherine's reputation became stained by the numerous religious civil wars that ravaged France in her lifetime, as well as the St. Bartholomew's Day massacre. Nevertheless, the alternative to a clearly delineated hereditary line (which itself was no absolute guarantee of civil peace) was civil strife, and she negotiated her way through the tumult skillfully, through both the logic and the insanity of the wars of religion, attempting to safeguard her dynasty as she did so. Of course, she never achieved her ultimate goal, which had been to bring Elizabeth into her extended family through marriage, and secure the final triumph of her dynasty. Even so, their fates and their lives remained intricately intertwined, and Catherine's influence over Elizabeth in the wider political landscape was as strong as—perhaps stronger than—that exerted by the other two queens in her life, her sister Mary I and her cousin Mary Stuart. In fact, in many ways it was her relationship with Catherine de Medici that ultimately shaped the course of sixteenth-century European politics.

These women were very different in significant ways: a young queen and an older, more experienced one. One supposedly a Protestant savior and the other a Catholic champion. A bastard and an orphan. A queen regnant and a queen mother. But in the end they were simply two women facing countless dangers in a masculine political landscape, seeking out positions of strength for both themselves and their nations.

They would also inspire future generations of queens. From Christina of Sweden, who embraced her singlehood before renouncing her throne to Marie de Medici, who tried to succeed where Catherine had failed in terms of securing the dynasty, to Anne Stuart, who endeavored to combine both Elizabeth's and Catherine's dual strengths of motherhood and kingship, their legacies would live on.

Author's Note

As one of my favorite nonfiction authors, Erik Larson, explains when telling the stories of notable figures from history (in the case of this book, people who lived over four hundred years ago), it is sometimes challenging to bring these individuals "back to life" in a captivating, compelling way.

This is a book about the two most powerful queens of the second half of the sixteenth century. They exchanged dozens of letters with each other and used their diplomats and ambassadors as their own mouthpieces through which to discuss with one another, yet the two queens never actually met.

Translating and transcribing sixteenth-century French and English sources into modern English presents its own challenges. With this in mind, I beg readers to forgive me for having taken some liberties to make the story more compelling. To reconstruct conversations and dialogues, I have used multiple references from diverse sources (all are listed in the bibliography, with the main sources in the notes). I have also taken some liberties in using a more modern English to make the story flow more smoothly. However, readers can be assured that this book remains a work of nonfiction and all dialogues and conversations created are based on thorough research and primary evidence of what took place all those years ago.

In the end, it is a story that—even though it happened over four hundred years ago—shaped our perceptions of queens and female rulership, with one queen being glorified and the other being vilified for centuries to come.

I hope that I have succeeded in bringing their passion, resilience, and determination back to life. Their relationship had a huge influence on Anglo-French relations; they also deserve to be remembered for that.

Estelle Paranque, Colchester, 2021

Endnotes

Prologue: The Art of Making Peace

1 Sir Nicholas Throckmorton to Elizabeth I, 29 April 1564, State Papers (*henceforth* SP) 70/70, f. 110.
2 Sir Thomas Smith to Throckmorton, 13 September 1563, SP 70/62, f. 179v.
3 *Lettres de Catherine de Medicis* (*henceforth* LCM), Vol. 2, xxiii.
4 Ibid, xxiii–xxiv.
5 Smith to Elizabeth, 18 August 1563, SP 70/62, f. 154.
6 Throckmorton to Smith, 25 August 1563, SP 70/62, f. 178.
7 Throckmorton to Smith, 2 October 1563, SP 70/63, f. 82.
8 Throckmorton to Elizabeth, 10 November 1563, SP 70/65, f. 32.
9 Ibid.
10 Throckmorton to Elizabeth, 29 February 1564, SP 70/68, f. 86.
11 Throckmorton to Elizabeth, 8 April 1564, SP 70/70, f. 18.
12 Ibid, f. 19.
13 Ibid, f. 20.
14 Smith and Throckmorton to Elizabeth, 14 April 1564, SP 70/70, f. 67.
15 Throckmorton to Elizabeth, 26 April 1564, SP 70/70, f. 102.

1: Love and Scandals, 1533–1536

1 *Letters and Papers*, Vol. 6, 264.
2 Ibid, 277.
3 Chapuys to Charles V, 28 June 1533, *Letters and Papers*, Vol. 6, 317.
4 Chapuys to Charles V, 13 August 1533, *Letters and Papers*, Vol. 6, 420–1.
5 *Letters and Papers*, Vol. 6, 464.
6 Chapuys to Charles V, 10 September 1533, *Letters and Papers*, Vol. 6, 465.
7 Ibid, 469.
8 Francis I to Jean de Dinteville, Bailly of Troyes, 17 September 1533, *Letters and Papers*, Vol. 6, 475.
9 De Reumont, *La jeunesse de Catherine de Médicis*, 37.
10 Ibid, 42.
11 Lanz, *Correspondance de L'Empereur Charles-Quint*, 507.
12 Frieda, *Catherine de Medici*, 47.
13 Ibid, 49.

14 *LCM*, Vol. 1, xxv.

15 Chapuys to Charles V, 2 May 1536, *Letters and Papers*, Vol. 10, 330.

16 Alexander Ales to Elizabeth, 1 September 1559, SP 70/7, f. 3.

17 Ibid, f. 4.

18 Ibid.

19 *Original Letters*, ed. Henry Ellis, Vol. 2, 65.

20 Alexander Ales to Elizabeth, 1 September 1559, SP 70/7, f. 6.

2: In the Shadows of the Royal Courts, 1537–1546

1 Brantôme, *Vies des dames illustres*, 44.

2 *LCM*, Vol. 1, xxxv.

3 Ibid, xxxvi.

4 Ibid.

5 Frieda, *Catherine de Medici*, 63.

6 *LCM*, Vol. 1, 181.

7 Orieux, *Catherine de Médicis*, 155.

8 Catherine de Medici to Montmorency, June 1543, *LCM*, 6.

9 *LCM*, Vol. 1, xxxvi.

10 Catherine to Cosimo, Duke of Florence, 5 May 1545, *LCM*, 10.

11 Lady Bryan to Thomas Cromwell, August 1536, BL Cotton Otho C/X, f. 226.

12 *Original Letters*, ed. Henry Ellis, 2nd series, Vol. 2, 78–83.

13 Williams, *Elizabeth I of England*, 7.

14 Charles de Marillac to Francis I of France, 12 August 1541, *Letters and Papers*, Vol. 16, 519.

15 *Letters and Papers*, Vol. 19, Part 1, 477.

16 Princess Elizabeth to Queen Katherine, 31 July 1544, *Elizabeth I: Collected Works* (henceforth *ECW*), 5. Also see BL Cotton Otho C/X, f. 235r.

17 The Regency, 7 July 1544, SP 1/189, f. 184.

18 25 July 1544, SP 1/190, f. 160.

19 *Letters and Papers*, Vol. 19, Part 1, 632.

20 10 September 1544, *Letters and Papers*, Vol. 19, Part 2, 113 and 18 September 1544, *Letters and Papers*, Vol. 19, Part 2, 127.

21 *ECW*, 6.

22 Ibid, 10.

23 Ibid, 9–10.

3: Courts of Wolves and She-Wolves, 1547–1553

1 Hayward, *The Life and Reign of Edward the Sixth*, 4–5.

2 *Calendar of the Patent Rolls: Edward VI*, Vol. 2, 20 and Thomas Rymer, *Rymer's Foedera*, volume 15 (London: Apud Joannem Neulme, 1760), 116.

3 Haynes, *A Collection of State Papers*, 96.

4 Ibid, 99.

5 Ibid.

6 *Katherine Parr: Complete Works and Correspondence*, 169.

7 Haynes, *A Collection of State Papers*, 96.

8 Elizabeth to Dowager Queen Katherine, c. June 1548, SP 10/2, f. 84c.

9 Elizabeth to the Duke of Somerset, September 1548, SP 10/5, f. 8a.

10 The Duke of Somerset to Lord Seymour, 1 September 1548, SP 10/2, f. 3.

11 Haynes, *A Collection of State Papers*, 69.

12 Ibid, 97.

13 Ibid, 95.
14 Ibid, 70, 95, 71.
15 *ECW*, 24.
16 Ibid, 36.
17 Baschet, *La Diplomatie Vénitienne*, 431.
18 *LCM*, Vol. 1, xvviv.
19 Ibid, xi.
20 Baschet, *La Diplomatie Vénitienne*, 439.
21 *Lettres inédites de Diane de Poitiers*, 47.
22 Ibid.
23 *Lettres inédites de Diane de Poitiers*, 83.
24 *LCM*, Vol. 1, 20 and 23.
25 *Lettres de Marie Stuart*, Vol. 1, 32 and 11.
26 *LCM*, Vol. 1, xiv.

4: *Struggle to Power, 1553–1558*

1 *The Chronicle of Queen Jane, and of two years of Queen Mary*, 2.
2 Agnes Strickland, *Lives of the Queens of England, From the Norman Conquest: With Anecdotes of Their Courts* (London: H. Colburn, 1840–1848), Vol. 4, 186.
3 Ibid, 10.
4 *The Diary of Henry Machyn*, 37.
5 *Tudor Royal Proclamations*, Vol. 2, 5–8.
6 Strickland, *Lives of the Queens of England*, Vol. 4, 227.
7 *The Diary of Henry Machyn*, 53.
8 *The Chronicle of Queen Jane, and of two years of Queen Mary*, 55–8.
9 Elizabeth to Mary, 16 March 1554, *ECW*, 41–2.
10 Elizabeth to Mary, 2 August 1556, *ECW*, 44.
11 *LCM*, Vol. 1, li–lii.
12 Baschet, *La Diplomatie Vénitienne*, 482.
13 *LCM*, Vol. 1, lii.
14 Baschet, *La Diplomatie Vénitienne*, 483.

5: *When Death Brings Glory, 1558–1559*

1 Rodrigues-Salgado and Adams, "Feria's Despatch," 329–34.
2 Ibid, 331.
3 Bayne, "Coronation of Queen Elizabeth," 667.
4 Ibid, 668.
5 Ibid, 670.
6 Henry II of France to Elizabeth, 30 December 1558, BL Cotton Caligula E/V, f. 53.
7 Elizabeth to Henry II of France, 8 January 1559, SP 70/2, f. 25.
8 Elizabeth's instructions to the commissioners in France, January 1559, *Calendar of State Papers Foreign*, Vol. 1: 1558–1559, 109.
9 Elizabeth to Throckmorton, 9 January 1559, *Calendar of the Manuscripts of the Most Hon. The Marquis of Salisbury (henceforth CMMH)*, Vol. 1: 1306–1571, 165.
10 De Ruble, *Le Traité de Cateau-Cambrésis*, 19–20.
11 Ibid, 21.
12 Ibid, 23.
13 Ibid, 25.
14 Henry II of France to Elizabeth, 21 April 1559, SP 70/3, f. 156.

15 Mary Stuart to Elizabeth, 21 April 1559, *Lettres de Marie Stuart*, Vol. 1, 62–3.
16 Richerand, *Ambroisé Paré, le Plutarque français*, 2.
17 Orieux, *Catherine de Médicis*, 234–5.
18 Ibid, 236. Also see MS Fr 23330.
19 Catherine to Joanna, Princess of Portugal, 8 August 1559, *LCM*, Vol. 1, 121.
20 Gilles de Noailles to the Constable of France, 10 July 1559, AE MD Angleterre, Register IV, f. 272. Cited in Paranque, *Elizabeth I of England Through Valois Eyes*, 24.
21 Elizabeth to Francis II, 23 July 1559, SP 70/5, f. 163.
22 Catherine to Elizabeth, 11 September 1559, *LCM*, Vol. 1, 125.

6: Fight for Peace, 1559–1560

1 Elizabeth to Francis II, 19 July 1559, SP 70/5, f. 147.
2 Throckmorton to Elizabeth, 24 September 1559, SP 70/7, f. 80.
3 Throckmorton to Elizabeth, 27 February 1560, SP 70/11, ff. 86–7.
4 Ibid, 88.
5 Ibid, 89.
6 Catherine to Elizabeth, March 1560, *LCM*, Vol. 1, 132.
7 Orieux, *Catherine de Médicis*, 258.
8 Throckmorton to Elizabeth, 12 April 1560, SP 70/13, f. 78.
9 Mary Stuart to Marie de Guise, Spring 1560, *Lettres de Marie Stuart*, Vol. 1, 71.
10 Ibid.
11 Throckmorton to Elizabeth, 24 June 1560, SP 70/15, f. 77.
12 Ibid, f. 78.
13 Elizabeth to Philip II of Spain, 24 July 1560, SP 70/16, f. 62.
14 Cited in Guy, *My Heart is My Own*, 115.
15 Catherine to the Duchess of Savoy, late November 1560, *LCM*, Vol. 1, 154.
16 Catherine to Elisabeth, Queen of Spain, mid-December 1560, *LCM*, Vol. 1, 158.

7: The King in All But Name, the Virgin, the "Gouvernante," and the Widow, 1561

1 Frieda, *Catherine de Medici*, 166.
2 Baschet, *La Diplomatie Vénitienne*, 508.
3 Ibid, 509.
4 Roeder, *Catherine de Medici and the Lost Revolution*, 259.
5 Catherine to Elisabeth, Queen of Spain, 10 November 1560, *LCM*, Vol. 1, 152–3.
6 Catherine to the Bishop of Limoges, 21 April 1561, *LCM*, Vol. 1, 188–90.
7 Catherine to Elizabeth, 20 February 1561, *LCM*, Vol. 1, 170.
8 Elizabeth to Throckmorton, 29 March 1561, SP 70/24, f. 62.
9 Throckmorton to Elizabeth, 29 April 1561, SP 70/25, ff. 113–14.
10 Throckmorton to Elizabeth, 10 January 1561, SP 70/22, f. 39.
11 Throckmorton to Elizabeth, 29 April 1561, SP 70/25, ff. 116–17.
12 Elizabeth to Throckmorton, 6 May 1561, SP 70/26, f. 49.
13 Chéruel, *Marie Stuart et Catherine de Médicis*, 17.
14 Throckmorton to Elizabeth, 23 June 1561, SP 70/27, f. 47–8.
15 Elizabeth to Randolph, 1 July 1561, SP 52/6, f. 100.
16 Elizabeth to Throckmorton, 13 July 1561, SP 70/28, f. 25.
17 Elizabeth to Charles and Catherine, 14 July 1561, SP 70/28, f. 44.
18 Mary to Elizabeth, 2 August 1561, SP 52/6, f. 126.
19 Ibid, f. 124.

20 Throckmorton to Elizabeth, 20 September 1561, SP 70/30, ff. 54–5.
21 Elizabeth to Throckmorton, 2 October 1561, S 70/31, f. 3.
22 Catherine to Throckmorton for Elizabeth, 8 October 1561, *LCM*, Vol. 1, 237.
23 Throckmorton to Elizabeth, 8 October 1561, SP 70/31, f. 11.

8: The Lying Game, 1562–1564

1 Elizabeth to Throckmorton, 30 April 1564, SP 70/70, f. 114.
2 Throckmorton to Elizabeth, 6 April 1562, SP 70/35, f. 78.
3 Ibid, f. 79.
4 Elizabeth to Throckmorton, March 1562, SP 70/35, f. 86.
5 Catherine to the Prince of Condé, 16 March 1562, BNF, Cinq cents Colbert, n° 390, f. 129–31.
6 Throckmorton to Elizabeth, 23 July 1562, SP 70/39, f. 125.
7 Ibid, f. 130.
8 Elizabeth to Throckmorton, 28 July 1562, SP 70/39, f. 178.
9 Lady Throckmorton to Throckmorton, 20 September 1562, SP 70/41, f. 177.
10 Frieda, *Catherine de Medici*, 191.
11 Elizabeth to Philip II, 22 September 1562, SP 70/41, f. 239.
12 Elizabeth to Edward Ormsby, 30 September 1562, SP 70/41, f. 298.
13 Catherine to Throckmorton, 5 September 1562, *LCM*, Vol. 1, 395–6.
14 Throckmorton to Elizabeth, 9 September 1562, SP 70/41, ff. 68–9.
15 Catherine to Throckmorton, 17 September 1562, *LCM*, Vol. 1, 400–2.
16 Throckmorton to Catherine, 15 October 1562, SP 70/43, f. 31.
17 Throckmorton to Elizabeth, 20 November 1562, SP 70/45, ff. 46–7.
18 Catherine to Anne d'Este, Duchess of Guise, end of February, *LCM*, Vol. 1, 519.
19 Frieda, *Catherine de Medici*, 196.
20 Catherine to Elizabeth, 25 January 1563, *LCM*, Vol. 1, 486–7.
21 Elizabeth to Catherine, 7 February 1563, SP 70/50, f. 112.
22 Elizabeth to Smith, 20 April 1563, SP 70/55, f. 32.
23 Catherine to Paul de Foix, 17 May 1563, *LCM*, Vol. 2, 39–41.
24 Frieda, *Catherine de Medici*, 198.
25 Catherine to the Maréchal de Brissac, 10–15 June 1563, *LCM*, Vol. 2, 55–6.
26 Catherine to Smith, 26 July 1563, *LCM*, Vol. 2, 74.

9: Charles, the Boy King, 1564–1569

1 Gilles de Noailles to Monsieur de Gondran, Garde des Sceaux de Dijon, 15 June 1559, AE MD Angleterre, Register IV, f. 251. Op. cit. in Paranque, *Elizabeth I of England Through Valois Eyes*, 32.
2 *ECW*, 72.
3 Paul de Foix to Catherine, 3 March 1564, BNF MS Fr 6613, f. 13.
4 Catherine to Paul de Foix, 24 January 1565, BNF MS Fr 15888, f. 234.
5 Paul de Foix to Catherine, 14 February 1565, BNF MS Fr 15888, f. 235.
6 Ibid.
7 Paul de Foix to Catherine, 4 June 1565, BNF MS Fr 15888, f. 32r–v.
8 Catherine to Paul de Foix, 31 July 1565, *LCM*, Vol. 2, 307.
9 Elizabeth to Smith, 21 August 1565, SP 70/79, f. 172.
10 Catherine to Paul de Foix, 14 August 1565, *LCM*, Vol. 2, 311.
11 James Stuart, Earl of Moray, to Elizabeth, 10 September 1565, SP 52/11, f. 75.
12 Cited in Guy, *My Heart is My Own*, 217.

13 *ECW*, 95–6.
14 Ibid, 105–8.
15 Randolph to Cecil, 25 December 1565, SP 52/11, f. 231.
16 Guy, *My Heart is My Own*, 249.
17 Ibid.
18 Ibid, 118.
19 Elizabeth to Mary, 24 February 1567, *ECW*, 116.
20 Guy, *My Heart is My Own*, 327.
21 Elizabeth to Mary, 23 June 1567, *ECW*, 118.
22 Cited from *LCM*, Vol. 3, 37.
23 Catherine to Elizabeth, 16 July 1567, *LCM*, Vol. 3, 46.
24 Mary to Elizabeth, 17 May 1568, *Letters of Mary, Queen of Scots, and documents connected with her personal history*, 43–4.
25 Catherine to Elizabeth, 26 May 1568, BL Cotton Caligula, C.1, Plut XX D, f. 74.
26 Catherine to Elizabeth, July 1568, *LCM*, Vol. 3, 153.
27 La Mothe Fénélon to Charles IX, 27 July 1569, 117–27.

10: *Henry, Overshadowed, 1570–1571*

1 La Mothe Fénélon to Charles IX of France, 5 September 1570, *Correspondance diplomatique de Bertrand de Salignac de la Mothe Fénélon, ambassadeur de France en Angleterre, de 1568 à 1575 (henceforth CD)*, Vol. 3, Années 1570 et 1571, 289.
2 Ibid, 290.
3 Ibid.
4 For more information on hunting in the early modern period, see Griffin, *Blood Sport*.
5 Turbervile, *Booke of Hunting*, 133.
6 Nichols, *The Progresses and Public Processions of Queen Elizabeth*, 17.
7 La Mothe Fénélon to Catherine de Medici, 29 December 1570, *CD*, Vol. 3, 419.
8 Catherine to La Mothe Fénélon, 26 September 1570, *LCM*, Vol. 4, 4.
9 Cardinal of Châtillon to Catherine, 4 March 1568, BNF MS Fr 6611, f. 8.
10 Catherine to La Mothe Fénélon, 20 October 1570, *LCM*, Vol. 4, 7.
11 Ibid, 9.
12 Ibid, 10.
13 La Mothe Fénélon to Catherine, 29 November 1570, *CD*, Vol. 3, 418–19.
14 La Mothe Fénélon to Catherine, 18 January 1571, *CD*, Vol. 3, 440.
15 Zim, "Dialogue and Discretion," 287–310.
16 Elizabeth to Francis Walsingham, 12 May 1571, BL Harley 260, f. 97.
17 Elizabeth to Catherine, 6 June 1571, SP 70/118, f. 77.
18 Catherine to Elizabeth, 1 August 1571, *LCM*, Vol. 4, 61–2.
19 Elizabeth to Francis Walsingham, 2 September 1571, SP 70/120, f. 9.
20 Larchant to Catherine, 5 September 1571, cited in *LCM*, Vol. 4, 61.
21 La Mothe Fénélon to Charles IX, 18 August 1570, *CD*, Vol. 3, 276.
22 La Mothe Fénélon to Charles IX, 23 January 1571, *CD*, Vol. 3, 443.
23 Mason, *The Royal Exchange*, 11.
24 La Mothe Fénélon to Charles IX, 31 January 1571, *CD*, Vol. 3, 450.
25 La Mothe Fénélon to Catherine, 31 January 1571, *CD*, Vol. 3, 454.

11: *Tears and Fury: Francis, Elizabeth's "Frog," 1572–1578*

1 Smith and Walsingham to Elizabeth, 3 April 1572, Cotton Caligula C/III, ff. 462–4.
2 Catherine to Elizabeth, 22 April 1572, *LCM*, Vol. 4, 97–8.

3 *LCM*, Vol. 4, xli–xlii.
4 Ibid, xlii.
5 Ibid.
6 Ibid, xliv.
7 Catherine to Elizabeth, 5 June 1572, *LCM*, Vol. 4, 104.
8 Catherine to Elizabeth, 21 June 1572, *LCM*, Vol. 4, 105.
9 Elizabeth to Walsingham, 20 July 1572, SP 70/124, f. 77.
10 Elizabeth to Walsingham, 23 July 1572, SP 70/124, f. 88.
11 Elizabeth to Walsingham, 25 July 1572, BL Harley 260, f. 275.
12 Catherine to La Mothe Fénélon, 21 August 1572, *LCM*, Vol. 4, 111.
13 Frieda, *Catherine de Medici*, 296.
14 Carroll, *Martyrs and Murderers*, 193.
15 Noguères, *La Saint-Barthélemy, 24 août 1572*, 134.
16 Walsingham to Smith, 27 August 1572, BL Harley 260, f. 292.
17 Digges, *The Compleat Ambassador*, 298.
18 La Mothe Fénélon to Charles IX, 14 September 1572, *CD*, Vol. 5, 122. Also cited in Paranque, *Elizabeth I of England Through Valois Eyes*, 98.
19 La Mothe Fénélon to Charles IX, 14 September 1572, *CD*, Vol. 5, 124–6.
20 La Mothe Fénélon to Charles IX, 4 November 1572, *CD*, Vol. 5, 195.
21 Charles IX to Elizabeth and Elisabeth of Austria to Elizabeth, 19 November 1572, *CD*, Vol. 7, 399–400.
22 La Mothe Fénélon to Charles IX, 23 November 1572, *CD*, Vol. 5, 205.
23 Catherine to La Mothe Fénélon, 30 March 1573, *LCM*, Vol. 4, 190.
24 Catherine to Elizabeth, 26 April 1573, SP 70/127, f. 55.
25 Elizabeth to Catherine, 21 May 1573, SP 70/127, f. 106.
26 Frieda, *Catherine de Medici*, 350.
27 Catherine to Elizabeth, 10 July 1574, SP 70/131, f. 141.
28 Catherine to Henry III, 26 September 1575, *LCM*, Vol. 5, 140.
29 La Mothe Fénélon to Henry III, 26 May 1575, *CD*, Vol. 6, 431.
30 La Mothe Fénélon to Henry III, 13 July 1575, *CD*, Vol. 6, 465–71.
31 La Mothe Fénélon to Henry III, 20 September 1575, *CD*, Vol. 6, 502.
32 Catherine to Mauvissière, 3 August 1577, *LCM*, Vol. 5, 271.

12: Last Chance at Marriage and a Lost Mother, 1579–1584

1 Catherine to Elizabeth, 3 June 1572, *LCM*, Vol. 4, 104.
2 Francis to Elizabeth, 4 January 1579, SP 78/3, f. 1.
3 Simier to the Queen, 9 January 1579, *CMMH*, Vol. 2, 304.
4 Bernardino de Mendoza to Philip II of Spain, 15 January 1579, *Calendar of State Papers Spain (henceforth CSPS)*, Vol. 2, 542.
5 Elizabeth to Catherine, 9 March 1579, SP 78/3, f. 4.
6 Mendoza to Philip II, 12 April 1579, *CSPS*, Vol. 2, 667.
7 Simier to des Pruneaux, 12 April 1579, SP 78/3, f. 20.
8 Mendoza to Philip II, 14 May 1579, *CSPS*, Vol. 2, 674–5.
9 Mendoza to Philip II, 24 June 1579, *CSPS*, Vol. 2, 679.
10 Elizabeth to Anjou, 1579, *CMMH*, Vol. 2, 298.
11 Stubbs, *The discoverie of a gaping gulf*, 12.
12 Venetian Ambassador to the Senate, 30 August 1579, *Calendar of State Papers Relating to English Affairs in the Archives of Venice*, Vol. 7, 611.
13 *CSPS*, Vol. 2, 694.
14 *Calendar of State Papers Relating to English Affairs in the Archives of Venice*, Vol. 7, 614.
15 Anjou to Elizabeth, 29 August 1579, *CMMH*, Vol. 2, 265.

16 Mendoza to Philip, 13 September 1579, *CSPS*, Vol. 2, 695.
17 Mendoza to Philip, 28 November 1579, *CSPS*, Vol. 2, 705.
18 Elizabeth to Francis, 17 January 1580, *CMMH*, 305; Elizabeth to Francis, 17 March 1580, *CMMH*, Vol. 2, 380.
19 Catherine to Elizabeth, 8 February 1580, BNF MS Fr 3307, f. 6 v.
20 Cobham to the Secretaries, 21 February 1580, SP 78/4A.
21 Mendoza to Philip, 28 February 1580, *CSPS*, Vol. 3, 14.
22 Ibid, 15.
23 Catherine to Elizabeth, 15 August 1580, BNF MS Fr 3307, f. 18 r.
24 Dee, *Rehearsal*, 18.
25 Catherine to Elizabeth, 11 December 1580, *LCM*, Vol. 7, 299.
26 BL Lansdowne 33/70.
27 Mendoza to Philip, 7 May 1581, *CSPS*, Vol. 3, 113.
28 Henry III to Elizabeth, 5 May 1581, SP 78/5, f. 66.
29 Mendoza to Philip, 11 November 1581, *CSPS*, Vol. 3, 208.
30 Mendoza to Philip, 24 November 1581, *CSPS*, Vol. 3, 226.
31 Mendoza to Philip, 25 December 1581, *CSPS*, Vol. 3, 242–4.
32 Catherine to Elizabeth, 20 December 1583, SP 78/100, f. 100.
33 Elizabeth to Catherine, July 1584, *ECW*, 263.

13: *A Protestant Champion and a Catholic Hammer, 1585*

1 Declaration of Cardinal de Bourbon, 31 March 1585, *Mémoires de la Ligue*, Vol. 1, 56.
2 Lake and Questier, *All Hail to the Archpriest*, 37.
3 BL Additional 48027, ff. 244–5, cited in Cooper, *The Queen's Agent*, 198–9.
4 *Holinshed's Chronicles*, Vol. 4, 567–8.
5 Elizabeth to Henry III, 12 February 1585, SP 78/13, f. 24.
6 Henry III to Mauvissière, 17 February 1585, BNF Cinq cent Colbert n° 470, ff. 113–15.
7 De L'Estoile, *Première-partie du tome premier, Registre-Journal de Henri III*, 181.
8 Derby and Stafford to Walsingham, 3 March 1585, SP 78/13, ff. 43–4
9 Ibid, ff. 45–6.
10 Elizabeth to Henry III, 10 March 1585, SP 78/13, f. 55.
11 Elizabeth to Catherine, 10 March 1585, SP 78/13, f. 56.
12 De L'Estoile, *Première-partie du tome premier, Registre-Journal de Henri III*, 186.
13 Ibid, 187.
14 Elizabeth to the States General, 3 September 1585, SP 84/3, f. 6.
15 Henry III to Elizabeth, 21 December 1585, BNF MS Fr 3309, f. 95v°.
16 Stafford to Elizabeth, 29 December 1585, SP 78/14, f. 117.

14: *The Rose and the Thistle, 1586*

1 Henry III to Chasteauneuf, 13 March 1586, BNF MS Fr 3305, f. 20v°.
2 Catherine to Philip II of Spain, 9 April 1586, *LCM*, Vol. 9, 11–12.
3 Henry III to Elizabeth, April 1586, SP 78/15, f. 89 and Henry III to Elizabeth, May 1586, SP 78/15, f. 91.
4 Henry III to Chasteauneuf, 7 April 1586, BNF MS Fr 3305, f. 26v°.
5 Henry III to Chasteauneuf, 29 June 1586, BNF MS Fr 3305, f. 25r°.
6 Elizabeth to Sir Amias Paulet, June 1586, SP 53/18, f. 55.
7 Bernardino de Mendoza to Philip II, 30 March 1586, *CSPS*, Vol. 3, 573.
8 Elizabeth to James VI of Scotland, 26 April 1586, *CMMH*, Vol. 13, 293. Elizabeth wrote: "The most expert seamen make vaunt of their best ships when they pass the highest

billows without yielding, and brook amidst the roughest storms. The like proof I supposed may best be made and surest boast of friends when greatest persuasions and mightiest enemies oppose themselves for parties. If then a constant irremovable goodwill appear, there is best trial made; for that I know there is no worse orator for truth than malice nor shrewder inveigher than envy, and that I am sure you have wanted neither to assail your mind to win it from our friendship."

9 James VI of Scotland to Elizabeth, 10 May 1586, SP 52/39, f. 71.
10 Babington to Mary Stuart, 6 July 1586, *A Complete Collection of State Trials*, Vol. 1, 1174–6.
11 Bernardino de Mendoza to Philip II, 24 June 1586, *CSPS*, Vol. 3, 588.
12 Bernardino de Mendoza to Philip II, 19 July 1586, *CSPS*, Vol. 3, 592.
13 Mary Stuart to Babington, 17 July 1586, *Lettres de Marie Stuart*, Vol. 6, 386–94.
14 Walsingham to Leicester, 9 July 1586, BL Cotton Galba, C/IX, f. 290.
15 John Savage's Trial, 13 September 1586, *A Complete Collection of State Trials*, Vol. 1, 1131–8.
16 Elizabeth to the Commoners of London, 18 August 1586, *ECW*, 285.
17 Elizabeth to Sir Amias Paulet, August 1586, SP 53/19, f. 55.
18 *Letters of Mary Stuart Queen of Scotland*, 356.
19 Davison to Burghley, 8 October 1586, BL Harley 290, f. 180.
20 Elizabeth to Mary, 6 October 1586, SP 53/20, f. 6.
21 *A Complete Collection of State Trials*, Vol. 1, 1171.
22 Lewis, *The Trial of Mary Queen of Scots*, 95.
23 Ibid, 95–6.
24 Ibid, 98.
25 Ibid, 101–2.
26 Ibid, 105–6.
27 Ibid, 106–7.
28 *LCM*, Vol. 9, 113–14.

15: A Queen Must Die, November 1586–March 1587

1 *The Proceedings in the Parliaments of Elizabeth I (henceforth PPE)*, Vol. 2, 1584–1589, 215–7.
2 Ibid, 217–18.
3 Ibid, 246.
4 *ECW*, 188.
5 Ibid, 189.
6 *PPE*, Vol. 2, 247.
7 Ibid, 262.
8 *ECW*, 197.
9 Ibid, 198–9.
10 Catherine to Villeroy, 20 December 1586, *LCM*, Vol. 9, 125.
11 Catherine to Courcelles, 20 December 1586, *LCM*, Vol. 9, 125.
12 BL Cotton Caligula B/VIII, f. 170.
13 Ibid, f. 171–2.
14 Ibid, f. 173–5.
15 Mary to Elizabeth, 19 December 1586, Lewis, *The Trial of Mary Queen of Scots*, 85.
16 Catherine to Bellièvre, January 1587, *LCM*, Vol. 9, 135.
17 De L'Estoile, *Première-partie du tome premier, Registre-Journal de Henri III*, 208–9.
18 Catherine to Bellièvre, January 1587, *LCM*, Vol. 9, 135.
19 SP 12/197, f. 10.
20 Ibid, f. 15.
21 Elizabeth to Henry III, January 1587, SP 78/17, f. 7.
22 Waad to Walsingham and Davison, 30 January 1587, SP 78/17, ff. 26–7.

23 Ibid, f. 130.
24 Harris Nicolas, *Life of William Davison*, 237.
25 Ibid, 258.
26 Ibid, 276.
27 Catherine to Henry III, 7 February 1587, *LCM*, Vol. 9, 155.
28 Mary to Elisabeth, Queen of Spain, 24 September 1568, *Letters of Mary, Queen of Scots, and documents connected with her personal history*, 86–7.
29 Lewis, *The Trial of Mary Queen of Scots*, 115.
30 Ibid, 116–17.
31 Ibid, 118–19.
32 Catherine to Henry III, 15 February 1587, *LCM*, Vol. 9, 169–70.
33 Catherine to Bellièvre, 14 February 1587, *LCM*, Vol. 9, 166.
34 Stafford to Burghley, 6 March 1587, SP 78/17, f. 69.
35 Catherine to Bellièvre, 8 March 1587, *LCM*, Vol. 9, 191.
36 Catherine to Villeroy, 14 March 1587, *LCM*, Vol. 9, 194.

16: *Endgame, April 1587–August 1589*

1   Corbett, *Sir Francis Drake*, 109–11.
2   Teulet, *Relations Politiques de la France et de l'Espagne avec l'Ecosse au XVIe siècle*, Vol. 4, 194–202.
3   Catherine to Bellièvre, 14 February 1587, *LCM*, Vol. 9, 166.
4   Catherine to Henry III, 23 May 1587, *LCM*, Vol. 9, 213.
5   De L'Estoile, *Première-partie du tome premier, Registre-Journal de Henri III*, 225.
6   Stafford to Walsingham, 1 October 1587, SP 78/17, f. 270.
7   Catherine to Chasteauneuf, 5 January 1588, *LCM*, Vol. 9, 323.
8   Catherine to Chasteauneuf, 2 February 1588, *LCM*, Vol. 9, 326.
9   Stafford to Elizabeth, 25 February 1588, SP 78/18, f. 52.
10 Ibid, f. 55.
11 Stafford to Elizabeth, 5 April 1588, SP 78/18, f. 119. The expression about the broken finger is an old saying emphasising sincerity when declaring something incredible. Praising a woman like this, even a queen, especially at that time, was very unusual and frowned upon.
12 Stafford to Elizabeth, 29 April 1588, SP 78/18, f. 164.
13 Stafford to Walsingham, 5 May 1588, SP 78/18, f. 175.
14 Elizabeth to Henry III, 11 May 1588, SP 78/18, f. 178.
15 Catherine to Henry III, 20 May 1588, *LCM*, Vol. 9, 344.
16 "Propos que le roi a tenu à Chartres aux Députés de la cour de parlement, imprimé à Paris, chez Lhuillier," May 1588, *Mémoires de la Ligue*, Vol. 2, 362–4.
17 Camden, *The History of the most renowned and victorious Princess Elizabeth, late queen of England*, 319.
18 James VI to Elizabeth, 4 August 1588, *CMMH*, Vol. 13, 380.
19 *ECW*, 325–6.
20 Matar, *Europe Through Arab Eyes*, 144–5.
21 Stafford to Walsingham, 9 August 1588, SP 78/18, f. 302.
22 De L'Estoile, *Première-partie du tome premier, Registre-Journal de Henri III*, 262.
23 Catherine to Elizabeth, 23 August 1588, *LCM*, Vol. 9, 381.
24 BNF MS Fr 314539, f. 4.
25 Frieda, *Catherine de Medici*, 436.
26 Ibid, 437.
27 Ibid, 441–2.

28 De L'Estoile, *Première-partie du tome premier, Registre-Journal de Henri III*, 279.
29 Elizabeth to Henry III, 4 February 1589, SP 78/19, f. 76.

Epilogue: Queen of Hearts & Queen of Spades

1 De Maisse, *A Journal of All that was Accomplished by Monsieur de Maisse*, 24–6.
2 Dutton, *Sir Francis Bacon's Journal: The Rarest of Princes*, 296.

Bibliography

Manuscript sources

Archives Étrangères (AE)

AE MD Angleterre, Register IV

Bibliothèque Nationale de France (BNF)

Cinq cent Colbert, n° 390
Cinq cent Colbert, n° 470
MS Français (Fr)
MS Fr 3305
MS Fr 3307
MS Fr 3309
MS Fr 6611
MS Fr 6613
MS Fr 15888
MS Fr 23330

The British Library (BL)

Additional 48027
Caligula
Galba
Otho
Harley 260
Harley 290
Lansdowne 33/70

The National Archives

State Papers (SP)
SP 1/189
SP 1/190

SP 10/2
SP 10/5
SP 12/197
SP 52/6
SP 52/11
SP 52/39
SP 53/18
SP 53/19
SP 53/20
SP 70/2
SP 70/3
SP 70/5
SP 70/7
SP 70/11
SP 70/13
SP 70/15
SP 70/16
SP 70/22
SP 70/24
SP 70/25
SP 70/26
SP 70/27
SP 70/28
SP 70/30
SP 70/31
SP 70/35
SP 70/39
SP 70/41
SP 70/43
SP 70/45
SP 70/50
SP 70/55
SP 70/62
SP 70/63
SP 70/65
SP 70/68
SP 70/70
SP 70/79
SP 70/118
SP 70/120
SP 70/124
SP 70/127
SP 70/131
SP 78/3
SP 78/4A
SP 78/5
SP 78/13
SP 78/14
SP 78/15
SP 78/17
SP 78/18
SP 78/19

SP 78/100
SP 84/3

Printed primary sources

Abbreviations

CD: *Correspondance diplomatique de Bertrand de Salignac de la Mothe Fénélon, ambassadeur de France en Angleterre, de 1568 à 1575*
CMMH: *Calendar of the Manuscripts of the Most Honourable The Marquis of Salisbury*
CSPS: *Calendar of State Papers Spain*
ECW: *Elizabeth I: Collected Works*
LCM: *Lettres de Catherine de Medicis*
PPE: *The Proceedings in the Parliaments of Elizabeth I*

Sources

Baschet, Armand. *La Diplomatie Vénitienne* (Paris: Henri Plon, 1862).

Brantôme, Pierre de Bourdeille. *Vies des dames illustres françaises et étrangères* (Paris: Garnier Frères, 1868).

Calendar of the Patent Rolls preserved in the Public Record Office: Edward VI, Vol. 2 (Nendeln, Liechtenstein: Kraus Reprint, 1970).

Calendar of State Papers Foreign: Elizabeth, edited by Joseph Stevenson, Vol. 1 (London: Her Majesty's Stationery Office, 1863).

Calendar of State Papers Relating to English Affairs in the Archives of Venice, edited by Rawdon Brown and G. Cavendish Bentinck, Vol. 7 (London: Her Majesty's Stationery Office, 1890).

Calendar of State Papers Spain, edited by G. A. Bergenroth, Vol. 2 (London: Her Majesty's Stationery Office, 1866).

Calendar of State Papers Spain, edited by Pascual de Gayangos, Vol. 3 (London: Her Majesty's Stationery Office, 1877).

Calendar of the Manuscripts of the Most Honourable The Marquis of Salisbury, Vol. 1 (London: Her Majesty's Stationery Office, 1883).

Calendar of the Manuscripts of the Most Honourable The Marquis of Salisbury, Vol. 2 (London: Her Majesty's Stationery Office, 1888).

Calendar of the Manuscripts of the Most Honourable The Marquis of Salisbury, Vol. 13 (London: Her Majesty's Stationery Office, 1915).

Camden, William. *The History of the most renowned and victorious Princess Elizabeth, late queen of England*, edited by Wallace T. MacCaffrey (Chicago: University of Chicago Press, 1970).

The Chronicle of Queen Jane, and of two years of Queen Mary, edited by John Gough Nichols (London: Camden Society, 1850).

A Complete Collection of State Trials, compiled by T. B. Howell, Vol. 1 (London: T. C. Hansard, 1816).

Correspondence diplomatique de Bertrand de Salignac de la Mothe Fénélon, ambassadeur de France en Angleterre, de 1568 à 1575 (referred to as *CD*), Vol. 3 (Paris and London: Archives du Royaume, 1840).

Correspondence diplomatique de Bertrand de Salignac de la Mothe Fénélon, ambassadeur de France en Angleterre, de 1568 à 1575 (referred to as *CD*), Vol. 5 (Paris and London: Archives du Royaume, 1840).

Correspondence diplomatique de Bertrand de Salignac de la Mothe Fénélon, ambassadeur de France en Angleterre, de 1568 à 1575 (referred to as CD), Vol. 6 (Paris and London: Archives du Royaume, 1840).

Dee, John. *The Compendious Rehearsal of John Dee His Dutifull Declaration, and Proofe of the Course and Race of His Studious Life . . . and of the Very Great Injuries, Damages, and Indignities, which for These Last Nine Years He Hath in England Sustained* (London, 1727).

De L'Estoile, Pierre. *Première Partie du Tome Premier, Registre-Journal de Henry III 1574–1589*, edited by MM. Champollion-Figeac and Aimé Champollion fils (Paris: Edouard Proux et Compagnie, 1837).

De Maisse, André. *A Journal of All that was Accomplished by Monsieur de Maisse, Ambassador in England from King Henri IV to Queen Elizabeth* (London: The Nonesuch Press, 1931).

De Ruble, Alphonse. *Le Traité de Cateau-Cambrésis* (Paris: Labitte, 1889).

The Diary of Henry Machyn, edited by John Gough Nichols (London: Camden Society, 1848).

Digges, Dudley. *The Compleat Ambassador: Or Two Treaties of the intended marriage of Qu. Elizabeth of Glorious Memory: Comprised in Letters of Negotiation of Sir Francis Walsingham, her Resident in France Together with the Answers of the Lord Burleigh, the Earl of Leicester, Sir Tho: Smith, and others Wherein, as in a dear Mirror, may be seen the Faces of the two Courts of England and France, as they then stood; with many remarkable passed of State, not at all mentioned in any History* (London: Thomas Newcomb, 1655).

Elizabeth I: Collected Works, edited by Leah Marcus, Janel Mueller, and Mary Beth Rose (Chicago and London: University of Chicago Press, 2000).

Harris Nicolas, Nicholas. *Life of William Davison* (London: Society of Antiquaries, 1823).

Haynes, Samuel. *A Collection of State Papers relating to affairs in the reigns of King Henry VIII, Edward VI, Queen Mary, and Queen Elizabeth* (Bowyer, 1740).

Hayward, John. *The Life and Reign of Edward the Sixth* (London: John Partridge, 1630).

Holinshed, Raphael. *Holinshed's Chronicles of England, Scotland, and Ireland: In Six Volumes*, Vol. 4 (London: Johnson and Rivington et al: 1809).

Katherine Parr: Complete Works and Correspondence, edited by Janel M. Mueller (Chicago: Chicago University Press, 2014).

Lanz, Karl. *Correspondance de L'Empereur Charles-Quint* (Leipzig: Brockhaus, 1844, French translation and edition, 2016).

Letters and Papers, Foreign and Domestic, of the Reign of Henry VIII, edited by James Gairdner, Vol. 6 (London: Her Majesty's Stationery Office, 1882).

Letters and Papers, Foreign and Domestic, of the Reign of Henry VIII, edited by James Gairdner, Vol. 10 (London: Her Majesty's Stationery Office, 1887).

Letters and Papers, Foreign and Domestic, of the Reign of Henry VIII, edited by James Gairdner, Vol. 16 (London: Her Majesty's Stationery Office, 1898).

Letters and Papers, Foreign and Domestic, of the Reign of Henry VIII, edited by James Gairdner and R. H. Brodie, Vol. 19 Part 1 (London: Her Majesty's Stationery Office, 1903).

Letters and Papers, Foreign and Domestic, of the Reign of Henry VIII, edited by James Gairdner and R. H. Brodie, Vol. 19 Part 2 (London: Her Majesty's Stationery Office, 1905).

Letters of Mary, Queen of Scots, and documents connected with her personal history, edited by Agnes Strickland, Vol. 1 (London: Henry Colburn Publisher, 1842).

Letters of Mary Stuart Queen of Scotland, edited by William Turnbull (London: Charles Dolman, 1845).

Lettres de Catherine de Médicis, published by M. Le Cte Hector de la Ferrière, Vol. 1 (Paris: Imprimerie Nationale, 1883).

Lettres de Catherine de Médicis, published by M. Le Cte Hector de la Ferrière, Vol. 2 (Paris: Imprimerie Nationale, 1885).

Lettres de Catherine de Médicis, published by M. Le Cte Hector de la Ferrière, Vol. 3 (Paris: Imprimerie Nationale, 1887).

Lettres de Catherine de Médicis, published by M. Le Cte Hector de la Ferrière, Vol. 4 (Paris: Imprimerie Nationale, 1889).

Lettres de Catherine de Médicis, published by M. Le Cte Hector de la Ferrière, Vol. 5 (Paris: Imprimerie Nationale, 1892).

Lettres de Catherine de Médicis, published by M. Le Cte Baguenault de Puchesse, Vol. 6 (Paris: Imprimerie Nationale, 1895).

Lettres de Catherine de Médicis, published by M. Le Cte Baguenault de Puchesse, Vol. 9 (Paris: Imprimerie Nationale, 1905).

Lettres de Catherine de Médicis, published by M. Le Cte Baguenault de Puchesse, Vol. 10 (Paris: Imprimerie Nationale, 1909).

Lettres de Marie Stuart, edited by Alexander Labanoff, Vol. 1 (Paris: Hovyn de Tranchère, 1886).

Lettres de Marie Stuart, edited by Alexander Labanoff, Vol. 6 (Paris: Hovyn de Tranchère, 1895).

Lettres inédites de Diane de Poitiers (Paris: Jules Renouard, 1866).

Lewis, Jayne E. *The Trial of Mary Queen of Scots: A Brief History with Documents* (New York: Palgrave Macmillan, 1999).

Mémoires de la Ligue, Vol. 1 (Amsterdam: Arkstée & Merkus, 1758).

Mémoires de la Ligue, Vol. 2 (Amsterdam: Arkstée & Merkus, 1758).

Nichols, John. *The Progresses and Public Processions of Queen Elizabeth*, Vol. 1 (London: Society of Antiquaries, 1823).

Original Letters, edited by Henry Ellis, Vol. 2 (London: Harding and Lepart, 1827).

The Proceedings in the Parliaments of Elizabeth I, edited by Terence Hartley, Vol. 2 (Leicester: Leicester University Press, 1995).

Rodrigues-Salgado, M. J., and Adams, Simon, *The Count of Feria's Dispatch to Philip II of Spain* Camden Fourth Series, Vol. 29 (London: Offices of the Royal Historical Society, University College London, 1984).

Stubbs, John. *The discoverie of a gaping gulf whereinto England is like to be swallowed by another French marriage, if the Lord forbid not the banes, by letting her maiestie see the sin and punishment thereof* (London: H. Singleton for W. Page, 1579).

Teulet, Alexandre. *Relations Politiques de la France et de l'Espagne avec l'Ecosse au XVIe siècle*, Vol. 4 (Paris: Jules Renouard, 1860).

Tudor Royal Proclamations, edited by Paul L. Hughes and James F. Larkin (New Haven and London: Yale University Press, 1969).

Turbervile, George. *Booke of Hunting* (London, 1576).

Secondary Works

Barraclough Pullman, Michael. *The Elizabethan privy council in the fifteen-seventies* (Berkeley and Los Angeles: University of California Press, 1971).

Barrett-Graves, Debra. "'Highly touched in honour': Elizabeth I and the Alençon Controversy," in Carole Levin, Jo Eldridge Carney, and Debra Barrett-Graves, eds. *Elizabeth I: Always her own free woman* (Aldershot: Ashgate, 2003).

Bayne, C. G. "Coronation of Queen Elizabeth," *The English Historical Review*, 25:99 (1910), 650–73.

Beem, Charles, ed. *The Foreign Relations of Elizabeth I* (New York: Palgrave MacMillan, 2011).

Bell, Ilona. *Elizabeth I: The Voice of a Monarch* (New York: Palgrave MacMillan, 2010).

Bossy, John. *Giordano Bruno and the Embassy Affair* (New Haven and London: Yale Nota Bene and Yale University Press, 2002, first published 1991).

Bossy, John. *Under The Molehill: An Elizabethan Spy Story* (New Haven and London: Yale University Press, 2001).

Boucher, Jacqueline. *La cour de Henry III* (Rennes: Ouest France, 1986).

Bourgeon, Jean-Louis. *Charles IX devant la Saint Barthélémy* (Geneva: Droz, 1995).

Brigg, Robin. *Early Modern France 1560–1715* (Oxford, London, New York: Oxford University Press, 1977).

Carroll, Stuart. *Martyrs & Murderers: The Guise Family and the Making of Europe* (Oxford: Oxford University Press, 2009).

Chéruel, Adolphe. *Marie Stuart et Catherine de Médicis, étude historique* (Paris: Hachette, 1858).

Cooper, John. *The Queen's Agent: Francis Walsingham at the Court of Elizabeth I* (London: Faber & Faber, 2011).

Corbett, Julian. *Sir Francis Drake* (London: Macmillan, 1922).

Cosandey, Fanny. *La Reine de France. Symbole et Pouvoir, XVe et XVIIIe siècle* (Paris: Gallimard, 2000).

De Reumont, A. *La jeunesse de Catherine de Médicis* (Paris: Henri Plon, 1866).

Doran, Susan. *Monarchy and Matrimony, the Courtships of Elizabeth I* (London and New York: Routledge, 1996).

Dutton, Elaine Mary. *Sir Francis Bacon's Journal: The Rarest of Princes* (Bloomington: iUniverse, 2007).

Frieda, Leonie. *Catherine de Medici* (London: W&N, 2005).

Griffin, Emma. *Blood Sport: Hunting in Britain since 1066* (New York: Yale University Press, 2007).

Guy, John. *"My Heart is My Own": The Life of Mary Queen of Scots* (London: Fourth Estate, 2004).

Lake, Peter. *Bad Queen Bess? Libels, Secret Histories, and the Politics of Publicity in the Reign of Queen Elizabeth I* (Oxford: Oxford University Press, 2016).

Lake, Peter, and Questier, Michael. *All Hail to the Archpriest: Confessional Conflict, Toleration, and the Politics of Publicity in Post-Reformation England* (Oxford: Oxford University Press, 2019).

Le Person, Xavier. *"Practiques et Practiqueurs," La vie politique à la fin du règne de Henry III (1584–1589)* (Geneva: Droz, 2002).

Levin, Carole. *"The heart and stomach of a King": Elizabeth I and the politics of sex and power* (Philadelphia: University of Pennsylvania Press, 2013, first published in 1994).

Mason, Alfred E. W. *The Royal Exchange: a note on the occasion of the bicentenary of the Royal Exchange Assurance* (London: Royal Exchange, 1920).

Matar, Nabil. *Europe Through Arab Eyes, 1578–1727* (New York: Columbia University Press, 2008).

Noguères, Henri. *La Saint-Barthélémy, 24 août 1572* (Paris: R. Laffont, 1959).

Orieux, Jean. *Catherine de Médicis* (Paris: Flammarion, 1992).

Paranque, Estelle. *Elizabeth I of England Through Valois Eyes: Power, Representation, Diplomacy in the Reign of the Queen, 1558–1588* (New York: Palgrave Macmillan, 2019).

Richerand, Anthelme. *Ambroise Paré, le Plutarque français* (Paris: Béchet jeune, 1815).

Roeder, Ralph. *Catherine de Medici and the Lost Revolution* (New York: Garden City, 1939).

Sharpe, Kevin. *Selling the Tudor Monarchy: Authority and Image in Sixteenth Century England* (New Haven: Yale University Press, 2009).

Williams, Neville. *Elizabeth I of England* (London: W&N, 1992).

Zim, Rivkha. "Dialogue and Discretion: Thomas Sackville, Catherine de Medici and the Anjou Marriage Proposal, 1571," *The Historical Journal*, 40:2 (1997), 287–310.

Acknowledgments

People say "it takes a village to write a book" and they could not be more right.

For a book to exist, an idea needs to be pursued, nurtured, and believed in. This is not an easy thing to do in a world where instant gratification via social media is what people crave and value. From ideas to research to more ideas and to several drafts and edits, it takes years to share a book with an audience and it takes great support from friends and family to be able to do so.

The first two people I'd like to thank are—weirdly, or perhaps not when you think about it—the two protagonists of this book: Elizabeth I of England and Catherine de Medici. I'm incredibly grateful for the life lessons they have shared through their stories and the letters they wrote when alive. Over the years, they have inspired me and I hope that this book not only does justice to them individually for their remarkable resilience and intelligence, but also reveals their incredible and complex relationship.

This book would have never existed without my wonderful agent, Rachel Conway, who took a leap of faith meeting me over three years ago in her office in Central London, listening to me and my passion for queens. Since then, she has been a true supporter of my dreams and I could not have hoped for a better agent than her.

It has been a real pleasure to be working alongside my wonderful editor, Carrie Napolitano, who shared a true passion and love for these two queens. I also would like to thank everyone at Hachette Books for being so supportive of my work.

Friends are the ones you can share your trouble and joy with. Writing a book during the pandemic was not easy but I knew I could rely on my dear friends who have offered constant support and encouragement. I will not name them all, they know who they are, but I must make a special mention to people who have read part of this book and supported me throughout: Michael Questier, Lindsey Fitzharris (my true blue friend), Olivette Otele, and Gareth Russell. I would also like to thank Carole Levin, Eilish Gregory, Renee Langlois, Mike Peacey, Owen Emmerson, Lauren Mackay, Leighan Renaud, Joanne Paul, Justine Brun, Laetitia Calabrese, Marie Armilano, and Lizzy V. Merchant, for supporting me, distracting me with other life matters, and for just being there for me when I needed it the most.

My family, in its broader sense as it has kept growing in the past few years, also deserves its round of applause, particularly my parents, Bernard and Joëlle Paranque, who have always supported my dreams and believed in me, merci du fond du cœur. My sister, Sandrine Doré, and her children. My cousin, Nicolas Paranque, who always offers great advice. I would also like to thank my in-laws for the meals they cooked when I was busy, for the walks we took when I needed a stroll, and for their constant interest in my work: Sally Jean Gill, Michael J. Green, David Gill and his family, and Danielle Graham and her family.

A special mention to my son Zachary Aurélien Gill. You have given me the strength and the determination to keep on writing even when I thought I couldn't. You truly are a blessing.

On an even more personal note, I have to admit that this book would not have been possible without the constant and unwavering support of my one and only, Nick St. John Gill. This is why it is dedicated to him. "Je t'aime le plus."

Index